D1209067

A Cricket in the Thorn Tree

Helen Suzman and the
Progressive Party of South Africa

JOANNA STRANGWAYES-BOOTH

Indiana University Press
Bloomington & London

First published in the United States by Indiana University Press
Copyright © 1976 by Joanna Strangwayes-Booth

All rights reserved

No part of this book may be reproduced or utilized in any form
or by any means, electronic or mechanical, including photocopying
and recording, or by any information storage and retrieval system,
without permission in writing from the publisher. The Association
of American University Presses' Resolution on Permissions constitutes
the only exception to this prohibition.

Manufactured in Great Britain

ISBN 0–253–31483–6

Library of Congress Catalog Card No. 76–486

329.968
S891c
180907

*To Dermot, Venetia, Alexandra and Emma
and, of course, not forgetting Joan.*

I have little to recommend my opinions. They come from one who has been no tool of power, no flatterer of greatness; and who in his last acts does not wish to belye the tenour of his life. They come from one, almost the whole of whose public exertion has been a struggle for the liberty of others; from one in whose breast no anger durable or vehement has ever been kindled, but by what he considered as tyranny; and who snatches from his share in the endeavours which are used by good men to discredit opulent oppressions, the hours he has employed on your affairs; and who in so doing persuades himself he has not departed from his usual office: they come from one who desires honours, distinctions, and emoluments but little; and who expects them not at all; who has no contempt for fame and no fear of obloquy. . . .

EDMUND BURKE *Reflections on the Revolution in France*

CONTENTS

LIST OF ILLUSTRATIONS

ACKNOWLEDGEMENTS

My particular thanks go to Helen Suzman herself who gave up so much of her precious time and devoted so much energy and thought to answering my questions and helping me in my research for this book.

I would also like to thank Sigma Xi, the Scientific Research Society of North America, for its Grant-in-Aid of Research; Mr H. F. Oppenheimer, Mr R. Raphaely and Davis, Borkum, Hare and Co Inc. for their generous grants which enabled me to write this book. I would like to thank Thelma Henderson for her advice, Miss M. Farmer of the Gubbins Library, Mrs E. Williamson of the Reference and Government Publications Library at the University of the Witwatersrand and Jan Edwards, the Librarian of the South African Institute of Race Relations, for their assistance; the Jewish Board of Deputies for permission to use their Press Digests; the South African Associated Newspapers Group for permission to use their press-cutting library; Sybil and Connell Maggs, who lent me their guest cottage while I was researching in Cape Town, Ingrid and Charles Maggs and Stella and John Cavill, who gave me the run of their houses while I was researching in London; Betty Suzman, who lent me a spare room around which I strewed my documents and papers while researching, and Kobus du Plessis for his help in translating those Afrikaans phrases with which my *Laer Taalbond* could not cope; the Progressive Party of South Africa for giving me access to its archives and its telex; the United Party for access to minute books; Mr P. Gotz for two years of patience and understanding; all those people who allowed me to use their documents and letters and their personal recollections without which it would have been impossible to write this book; my husband, Dermot, and my mother, Joan, for their advice on cutting and shaping, Diana King for her help in typing the manuscript, and finally Rosina Setshogoe and Wilson Mabaso for making me endless cups of coffee and looking after my children while I worked.

AUTHOR'S NOTE

In describing South Africa's different non-White race groups I have in the earlier part of the book used the terms 'Native' and 'non-European' which were in common popular usage from the turn of the century until the 1950s when Dr Verwoerd introduced the collective noun 'Bantu', which is still in official use today, to describe South Africa's African population. In the later stages, however, I have preferred the now current term 'Black' collectively to describe those of South Africa's race groups who are not White and where I refer to members of a particular Black race group, I describe them specifically as Africans, Indians or Coloureds.

INTRODUCTION

To write Helen Suzman's story is to write the history of the Progressive Party of South Africa, and, conversely, the Party's history cannot be written without becoming to a large extent the personal saga of the woman who for thirteen years, from 1961 to 1974, was its sole representative in the South African Parliament. One of the favourite taunts of the Progressives' opponents during those years was that, without the member for Houghton, the Party would have ceased to exist: there is more than a kernel of truth in this allegation. Splinter parties in South Africa, with very few exceptions, have been, if not still-born, sickly infants which have scarcely survived their deliveries: the only two exceptions still represented in Parliament are the ruling National Party, which in 1934 split from its parent party at the time of fusion between the National and South African parties, to form the Herenigde Nasionale Party, and which has governed the country since 1948; and the Progressive Party, which broke away from the United Party in 1959. The Nationalists owe their success to grass-roots Afrikaner nationalism which brought their party to power only fourteen years after its formation: the Progressive cause, by contrast, relying as it does on an appeal to reason, to principle and traditional Western liberal values in what must be one of the most reactionary electorates in the world, has for most of its existence been on the verge of extinction, and only its successes in the 1974 general election have finally ensured its survival.

During those years, however, the Progressive Party's voice was heard persistently in the Assembly through the hundreds of speeches and questions of the remarkable parliamentarian who represented it there and who, in the process, became a household word and a heroine to many millions of South Africa's unenfranchised citizens. Helen Suzman's political career is far from over, and her full story will not, I hope, be written for many years.

But in this book I have tried to describe a unique episode in the history of Western parliamentary democracy; in which one woman, virtually unaided, saved from otherwise almost certain political destruction a political movement which many believe offers one of the few hopes for a peaceful solution to the gigantic racial problems of South Africa. I have, in addition, attempted to outline the qualities which have enabled Mrs Suzman to maintain her position in the face of such fearful odds: her courage, her persistence, her tireless energy, her uncompromising integrity, but above all, her deep-rooted concern for her country's disenfranchised millions persecuted and oppressed by the myriad injustices of the society in which she and they live.

Johannesburg
1972–4

Chapter One Propolitical

April 24, 1974, saw a general election in South Africa to elect the fourth Parliament of the Republic. After the polls closed the night, at the high altitude of the Witwatersrand, was cold, and, later, the chill would turn to icy rain: but at about eleven o'clock a wildly cheering throng of several hundred people was tightly jammed about the doors of the Rosebank Primary School in the northern suburbs of Johannesburg, to hear the electoral officer, his voice almost inaudible above the crowd's triumphant roar, announce, with the election of Gordon Waddell as member of Parliament and Peter Nixon as provincial councillor for the constituency of Johannesburg North, the first of six victories for the Progressive Party.

To an outsider, the reaction of the Progressive voters, as they sang, wept and embraced each other in the damp suburban streets, littered with torn election posters, might have seemed both excessive and unrealistic, for the ruling National Party was sweeping back to power all over the country with increased majorities. But for the Progressives, who for thirteen years had watched their party's sole representative in Parliament, Helen Suzman, battle – in the face of derision and abuse from the Government and the official opposition – to strip (as she had said in 1962) 'the shabby façade of democracy behind which this Government is hiding' and to keep alive a flicker of liberal demo-cratic thought in South Africa against the growing forces of reaction and oppression, the five Progressive victories ushered in what they believed would be a new era. And later, as they gathered in Helen's own constituency of Houghton in the sodden, grey autumn dawn of the following day to cheer their new MPs and MPCs and to await the final result – the victory of the Party's leader, Colin Eglin, in the Cape Town seat of Sea Point, which set the seal on their triumph – many in that damp and exhausted gathering, drunk with relief, euphoria, fatigue and red wine, could be heard repeating to each other, over and over again, like a chant of victory: 'Helen's not alone any more!'

Helen Gavronsky was born on 7 November 1917 in Princes Street, Germiston, a town ten miles south-east of Johannesburg, the centre of the world's largest gold-mining industry. She was the second daughter of Samuel Gavronsky, a handsome, thickset, Lithuanian Jew who had immigrated to South Africa in 1904, and Frieda David, a member of another Lithuanian immigrant family who grew up in Kimberley. Her mother, remembered by the Gavronsky family as 'the beautiful, gentle Frieda', died two weeks after Helen was born, victim of a combination of inefficient post-natal care and of the Spanish influenza which, in the year that followed, claimed more than 139 000 South African lives. Inconsolable, Sam moved himself, his elder daughter Gertrude, aged four, and the infant Helen to the nearby rambling house belonging to Oscar Gavronsky, his brother and his partner in his wholesale and retail butchery and hides and skins businesses. Oscar had married Frieda's elder sister, Hansa, a nordically beautiful woman, the possessor of a temperament as cold as the northern winters, and childless. Gertrude recalls that from the moment their small family took up residence under her aunt's roof, all warmth went out of *her* life. But the two-week-old Helen brought out Hansa's repressed maternal instincts. For the next ten years she lavished all the affection of which she was capable on her younger niece, becoming emotionally involved with her to an almost obsessive degree.

As Sam and Oscar's chain of shops expanded, they began to find the confines of provincial Germiston too small for their growing aspirations. In 1921 the whole Gavronsky ménage, now swollen by the addition of two more nieces, the daughters of Hansa's eldest sister, moved to Johannesburg, to a house in Alexandra Street, Berea. Today, Berea is a rather dilapidated area, full of seedy, rent-controlled flats and broken-down boarding houses, but in 1921 it housed the respectable petty bourgeoisie of Johannesburg: the English and Jewish immigrants who had come to the city in the wake of the gold rush to found and develop its secondary industries. The Gavronskys had moved a step up in the social world.

Helen's childhood was not unhappy. When she was four she became a pupil at St George's School close to the house in Alexandra Street. Here she remained till she was ten when the nuns of the Parktown Convent were given charge of her education. Her sister and cousins always called her 'Auntie's pet', and, believing that she was on 'Auntie's side' and so on the side of all grown-ups, used to exclude her from their games and secrets on the afternoons when school was over and Hansa, invariably, as was her curious wont, lay down with a self-exculpatory migraine and left the child alone. Her exclusion by the other children seemed to make no impression on Helen, but it must have been at this point in time that that protective shell which was to prove so useful an armour in her Parliamentary life began to form itself about her. Her burgeoning self-reliance, later to be both staff and weapon, was also attributable in some part to her father, who adored her, not only because she was so pretty – she had inherited her mother's face – but because her quick and lively mind matched his own. Till she was ten the family atmosphere in which she grew up was a typically Jewish one, close-knit and secure, a self-enclosed unit that was scarcely, if at all, affected by the political events of that particular period of South African history.

Though Union had been achieved in South Africa in 1910, the memory of the Anglo-Boer War, concluded only eight years previously, still possessed the minds of the majority of English- and Afrikaans-speaking Whites. By agreement, the first cabinet of the Union was representative of both white population groups, but it was headed by an Afrikaner, General Louis Botha, who had included amongst his ministers two notable Boer generals, J. C. Smuts and J. B. Hertzog. Botha and Smuts shared a political philosophy which envisaged that the only way to construct a truly South African state was to pursue a policy of conciliation between the two white population groups. 'We must work away from racialism,' said Smuts, meaning by this not black–white racialism (which for several years was to be pushed far into the background of South African politics) but English–Afrikaans racialism. Hertzog, however, was bent on a policy that would force English- and Afrikaans-speaking South Africans to develop along parallel paths, each according to its own beliefs and traditions. The climax of his 'twin-stream' philosophy would be achieved and a true South African nationalism attained when Afrikaner nationalism finally emerged to dominate and absorb the English-speaking group. In support of this ultimate aim, he postulated the proposition that South Africa could never be truly independent until it was once again a republic, free from any British taint. The intransigence and strength of his views, conflicting so directly with those held by Botha and Smuts, brought about, in 1912, Hertzog's expulsion from the ruling South African National Party* and led to the formation by him of an exclusively Afrikaner National Party. The policy of conciliation had not only failed to reconcile the two opposed groups: it had actually succeeded in further alienating the extremist nationalist Afrikaners and by its close association with the dominant plutocracy (created by Botha's ready appreciation of the value of the mining industry in South Africa's developing economy), had also managed to estrange the English-speaking radicals of the Labour Party.[1]

World War I, in which the Union played an active part, served to increase the continuing tensions between the National Party and the Government, although, for the duration of the war, the Labour Party lent its support to the ruling party. Hertzog had opposed South Africa's entry into the war and remained aloof from the war effort. Many Afrikaners, too, were overtly hostile to what they called 'Britain's war' and an abortive rebellion, quickly suppressed, broke out in 1914. Though Botha, in general, followed a policy of magnanimity towards the rebels, some, notably commissioned officers of the Defence Force who had participated in the uprising, were court-martialled and shot, becoming new martyrs for the Afrikaner nationalist cause.

In 1915, when the first general election after Union was held, the South African Party, mainly due to the dubious good graces of the predominantly English-speaking and unashamedly imperialist Unionist Party, succeeded in remaining in office, but the

---

*Before Union, Botha's and Smuts' party was known as *Het Volk* (The People) but was renamed shortly before Union. When Hertzog formed his National Party in 1914, Botha dropped National from his party's name and it was henceforward known as the South African Party (or SAP).

National Party polled nearly one-third of the total votes cast, or half the total Afrikaner vote.[2]

In 1919 Botha died and Smuts became South Africa's second Prime Minister. He had earned international repute by his work in the Imperial War Cabinet, his participation in drafting the Charter of the League of Nations and his efforts at the Paris Peace Conference. But he was less highly regarded at home than abroad, his enemies claiming, with a modicum of truth, that he was an imperialist who found his own country too small for him.[3] His party also had the unenviable task of attempting to combat the spiralling cost of living in the years just after the war, and when the next general election was held in 1920, Labour swept the towns at the expense of the Unionists; the Nationalists were returned as the largest single party; and the South African Party, the Unionists and the Independents allied only gave Smuts a slender majority of four.[4] Eleven months later, however, the Unionists merged with the South African Party in what Smuts called 'a great step forward on the path of racial unity and nationhood',[5] enabling him to feel strong enough to call a snap election. The South African Party was returned with an absolute majority of twenty-four, but to many Afrikaners the merger emphasized its growing anglicization.

In 1922 Smuts' victory was brought to an early end by a domestic crisis involving the country's most vital industry. For some years, production costs in the mines had been rising steadily while, almost as steadily, the gold price had been declining. The Chamber of Mines, which traditionally operated two separate labour markets, one white and one black (the wages of one white miner at that time being almost double the wages of eight Blacks), gave notice that it intended terminating its traditional *status quo* agreement, guaranteeing Whites employment on the mines and preventing Blacks from doing skilled and semi-skilled jobs. The white gold miners now came out on strike to be followed almost immediately by their fellows in the collieries. Smuts attempted to mediate between the strikers and the Chamber of Mines and succeeded in forcing the Chamber to make several concessions, one of which was the retention of the *status quo* agreement on the higher grade mines. But the strikers refused to be satisfied with anything less than total capitulation by the employers. Militant strike commandos were formed and, inflamed by a handful of local Communists who had coined the curious slogan 'Workers of the World unite for a White South Africa', launched an armed revolt. For several days most of the Witwatersrand was in their hands. The rebellion was finally suppressed by the militia of the Active Citizen Force, but more Whites lost their lives in the uprising than in the whole of the campaign in German South-West Africa during the war.

The political repercussions of the Miners' Strike were far-reaching. Smuts' popularity declined still further and the National and Labour parties announced that they would work together against Smuts and Capital. When Parliament met in 1924, the Government was attacked on two fronts. The Labour Party pressed for tariff protection against external competition, while the National Party campaigned for what it called the right of the white man to live a *civilized** existence in South Africa – an odd phrase employed by Hertzog to mean that a line should be drawn between civilized (white) labour and uncivilized (black) labour. Indians were included in the 'uncivilized' category, but the then enfranchised Cape Coloureds, whose votes the Nationalists found useful, were not.

Support for the Labour–National Pact was greatly enhanced by a drought which ravaged the country for three successive years. Bankrupt farmers and *bywoners*† were flocking to the cities seeking work at a time when there was none. Since a 'civilized' labour policy and industrial protection meant that jobs would be created for these Whites at the expense of the Blacks, the electorate, in 1924, voted the Pact (as it was known)[6] into power with Hertzog as Prime Minister.

The Pact government pursued its 'civilized' labour policy with great vigour. It introduced the Industrial Conciliation Act which provided for the registration and regulation of trades unions. Most black men (but not women) were excluded from the definition of 'employee', which, in effect, meant that they could not be members of registered trade unions and that black unions were not

*Civilized labour was defined in a government report 'as the standard generally recognized as tolerable from the usual European standpoint'.

†Tenant farmers or squatters, who formed the nucleus of South Africa's poor white problem.

officially recognized. Under the Masters and Servants Act and
the Native Labour Regulation Act,[7] strikes by Blacks could be
held to be criminal offences, an irrationality that was followed
by the introduction of a 'civilized' labour policy into the civil
service and by the bitterly fought Mines and Works Amendment
Act of 1926, which limited the granting of certificates of compe-
tency (essential for the achievement of 'skilled' status) to Whites
and Cape Coloureds – a white monopoly on skilled and semi-
skilled jobs which was extended into the newly developing
Government-sponsored Iron and Steel Corporation (ISCOR).

The Pact government also ensured the enforcement of Hertzog's 'twin-stream' philosophy. Bilingualism was encouraged, a
Union Flag was designed (but not without a bitter and strenuous
opposition) to fly alongside the Union Jack, and 'Die Stem van
Suid-Afrika' became the second national anthem, having equal
status with 'God Save the King'. As a sop to his English-speaking
colleagues, Hertzog shelved his republican aspirations, and once
the Balfour Declaration of 1926 asserted the equality of the
Dominions with Great Britain, pronounced himself satisfied that
South Africa was truly independent for the first time since Union.

The first Pact government's rule lasted for five years, a beneficial time for Hertzog, coinciding as it did with a brief period of
world prosperity. For the first time since Union, a government
was able to withdraw its attention from the English–Afrikaans
racial struggle and focus it on what came to be known as the
'Native Problem'.

The 1913 Native Land and Trust Act had laid down the principle of segregation in land and ownership as between Africans and
other races; Hertzog's Government now enunciated an extension
of this policy. Africans would have separate 'assignments of land
and labour, two social pyramids instead of one, with freedom for
every man to rise to the top of his own pyramid'.[8] Pursuing this
policy Hertzog, in 1926, introduced four interdependent segregation measures to Parliament and invited Smuts' co-operation
in passing them. Of the four Bills, the Representation of Natives
Bill was designed to deprive Cape Africans of the franchise, and the
Union Native Council Bill proposed the establishment of a Native
Council, to be controlled by the Government, which would pass
legislation binding on Africans alone. The Native Land Bill was

designed to fulfil the promise made by Botha to provide more land for the Africans, and the Coloured Persons' Rights Bill, which left the Indians untouched, ensured, among other clauses, the retention of the Cape and Natal Coloured franchise. Hertzog did not get as much support for the Bills from his own supporters as he had expected and, rejecting Smuts' suggestion that the whole scheme be put to a National Convention, referred the Bills to a select committee which reported in 1929. In the end, only two of the four Bills, now re-drafted on even less liberal lines, were introduced by the Government, and when at a Joint Sitting[9] of both House of Parliament the re-titled Natives' Parliamentary Representation Bill failed to achieve the necessary two-thirds majority for the Government, it and its sister Bill, the Coloured Persons' Rights Bill, were withdrawn.

To political observers it was now plain that the next and all successive elections would be fought on the issue of the preservation of the white races in the face of encroaching *swart gevaar*.* Those Blacks displaced by the Pact's 'civilized' labour policy had already begun banding together in illegal trade unions or were joining the African National Congress, formed in 1912, or the South African Indian Congress, and a confrontation between Whites and a united black front appeared for the first time to be a real possibility.

While these political events were shaping South Africa's political destiny, a major change had taken place in Helen Gavronsky's personal life. In 1927 her father re-married. The marriage came as a great blow to Hansa, unable with her peculiar temperament to resist feeling that 'her child' had been torn from her and given into the keeping of another woman: but for both Gertrude and Helen the re-marriage was the beginning of a new life that was to lead them once again out of a background that their father had outgrown.

In the mining camp that in the short space of forty years had become the city of Johannesburg, wealth set the pattern that defined the bounds of the new society. The mining magnates – Sir J. B. Robinson, Sir Lionel Phillips, Sir George Albu, the

*Black peril.

Oppenheimers and Herman Eckstein – had chosen Parktown, with its uninterrupted view across the open veld towards Pretoria and the distant Magaliesberg mountains, as the suburb in which to lead their insulated and luxurious lives. Sam Gavronsky, although himself entirely devoid of social ambition, now moved with his new wife, Debby, and his daughters to 13 Eton Road, Parktown, a large sprawling house in spacious grounds, where he lived until his death in 1965.

Growing up in Parktown, Helen, like so many thousands of young white South Africans, was sheltered from the concept of poverty. The Depression, which drove Afrikaner *bywoners* in ever-increasing numbers from the land to look for work in the cities, thereby creating the poor white problem which was to hang around South Africa's neck for so many years and to have such massive political repercussions, hardly touched the fringes of her sheltered life. Now a pupil at Parktown Convent, she moved in an exclusively Anglo-Jewish English-speaking society in which the Afrikaner, and his aspirations for himself and his language, played no part at all. Her only contact with Blacks was on a master–servant basis, although at this time it was customary among people of the Gavronskys' financial standing to employ white chauffeurs and children's nurses. Johannesburg was a predominantly white city: a permanent black population was to come later.

Helen's school reports show that her teachers thought of her as a well above average pupil who excelled both in class-work and at games, notably swimming. One of her fellow-pupils, now Sister Maria Bindon, remembers that Helen was immensely popular. 'Highly attractive, with blue, blue eyes and wildly curling hair, she exercised', says Sister Maria, 'a charismatic effect on all of us. She had an instinctive ability to command respect, not only because she was so good-looking and intelligent but because she had the gift of appearing to be interested in the least of us.' But some of her contemporaries felt diminished by her: possibly, they say, because she had everything. She never entered a room or arrived at a tennis party without becoming the immediate centre of attraction.

Helen's precocity of intellect, which persuaded the nuns to push her into matriculating too early, is thought by her now to have been a drawback. In 1933, at the age of sixteen, she left school with a second-class matriculation pass and a good result in book-keeping that decided her to enrol for a Bachelor of Commerce degree at the University of the Witwatersrand. Had she matriculated later or entered the University at the usual age of eighteen with the probable first class that two further years of schooling would have given her, her university career might have taken a very different course, leading her to a law degree. Her choice of a commercial course soon proved to have been a great mistake. She did quite well in her first year of study but subsequently seems to have undergone a form of collapse. At the end of 1935 she went on a students' tour to Europe and from London wrote to her father begging to be allowed to enrol at the London School of Economics. Her plea was refused, her father possibly thinking her too young, and reluctantly she returned to South Africa and her second year at the University, where she unenthusiastically continued with her courses. She did not obtain enough credits to graduate in 1936.

During that year, at a Johannesburg riding school, she met Moses Meyer Suzman, who, at the age of thirty-three, was already beginning to be singled out as a brilliant specialist physician.

'Mosie' Suzman (whose eminence in his own field almost matches, in medical eyes, that of his wife's in politics) was the second youngest son of a well-known South African Jewish family, the father and founder of whom was Lewis Suzman, who had emigrated to South Africa from Russia in 1889 and opened in the gold-rush city of Johannesburg a small tobacconist's shop that was to grow into South Africa's largest tobacco wholesale company. The Suzmans, Lewis and his wife, Rebecca, had eight children, five sons and three daughters, and were one of the country's most respected Jewish families, eminent in law, medicine, the arts and academic life as well as in commerce. But Helen was less than awed by the aura then attaching to the name. 'Mosie', she says, 'had a horse I coveted. To get it, I had to marry him!' And so she did, aged nineteen, in Johannesburg's Great Synagogue on 13 August 1937. Some months later, returning from a European honeymoon, they moved into a newly built house in Northcliff, a growing suburb, built over a large *koppie* on the north-western side of the city.

In the two years that preceded the outbreak of World War II, the young Suzmans lived an unremarkable social life of dinner parties, golf, tennis and riding. Between their remote privileged white South African world and threatened Europe lay a distance of 6000 miles. Only a small minority of politically aware South Africans realized that their country's ultimate involvement in the second Armageddon of the century was inevitable. The professional politicians had for ten years been fighting battles of so introverted a nature that the rise of the extremist movements and of the dictators of Europe had had little interest for them except in so far as their own abstract racial theories might be affected.

The 1929 election had, predictably in view of the deteriorating racial situation in the labour field, been fought on the issue of black peril. Hertzog's attempt to force through the two revised colour bills (the Natives' Parliamentary Representation Bill and the Coloured Persons' Rights Bill) had been a calculated political tactic intended to place the colour issue squarely before the South African electorate. Smuts' South African Party had fought both Bills clause by clause but had suggested no alternative policy. The only positive recommendation made by Smuts was the vague one of 'patient consultation' with Blacks, with a further suggestion that a National Convention or Commission should be convened whose mandate of debate would be an attempt to remove 'Native policy' into a non-controversial cloud-cuckoo land outside party politics. Smuts also admitted that his party was not irrevocably bound to retain the entrenched Cape African franchise.[10] But for Hertzog this matter admitted of no 'perhaps'. He saw the handful of enfranchised Cape Africans only as a danger to the Whites, since (he argued) they would, one day, force the white voters into granting them equal rights. To avoid so unthinkable a possibility, the entrenched clauses of the 1909 Constitution would have to be altered.

When Parliament rose at the end of February 1929, Smuts, for a short space of time, felt confident of winning the election. He believed that the split which had taken place in 1928 in the Labour Party, forcing Hertzog to resign and reform his cabinet without several of his former Labour supporters, could only benefit the South African Party. Hertzog soon destroyed Smuts'

confidence. In a speech in the Transvaal *platteland** town of
Ermelo, Smuts was reported to have said: 'Let us cultivate
feelings of friendship over this African continent, so that one day
we will have a British confederation of African states . . . a great
African Domination stretching unbroken throughout Africa . . .
That is the cardinal point of my policy.'[11] Hertzog seized upon the
words 'African Domination' as indisputable proof that Smuts
stood for integration. To vote for Smuts and the South African
Party was to vote black; to vote for Hertzog and his Nationalists
was to vote white. This distorted propaganda paid off. The
predominantly white electorate returned the National Party to
power with an absolute majority of eight over all the other parties,
and Hertzog knew that, in addition, his working majority would
be increased with the support of the diminished but still not
unimportant Labour Party.[12]

What Hertzog, concentrating his whole election campaign on
the colour issue, failed to realize was that South Africa was about
to follow the rest of the world into a period of economic recession.
His party's previous period of office had been distinguished by
four years of prosperity, and, as the backwash of depression hit
South Africa, his Finance Minister, N. C. Havenga, attempted to
remain economically independent of Great Britain by keeping the
country on the Gold Standard, and, to this end, assumed dicta-
torial powers to regulate currency and exchange. He imposed
dumping duties on goods from countries which had gone off gold,
and subsidized exports, imposing, in order to finance these
subsidies, a primage duty on imports.[13] Havenga's financial policy,
for a country with only three significant exports (gold, diamonds
and wool) and dependent on imports for almost all its manufactured goods, proved disastrous. At the end of 1932, after a year of
economic turmoil exacerbated by one of South Africa's periodic
droughts which had devastated the country for three years, the
Government's losing hand was forced. Tielman Roos, a former
Nationalist Minister of Justice, now an Appeal Court judge,
left the Bench, and, making a bid for political power, began a
behind-the-scenes attempt to arrange talks between Smuts and
Hertzog with a view to the formation of a coalition government
committed to the abandonment of the Gold Standard. Roos'

*Country or rural districts.

influence within the National Party was such that although his efforts were abortive, Havenga turned his policy about and took the country off gold and into the sterling area. Although the economy benefited almost instantly from the change, the political area, from Hertzog's point of view, did not, and fluidity set in to what had been a stable situation. Roos attempted to combine with Smuts in a new party, but Smuts, who distrusted him, managed to convince his caucus that for the sake of national unity it should throw in its lot with Hertzog to form a National government. After several weeks of negotiation he and Hertzog managed to reach an agreement enabling them to establish a coalition, and in a general election held in May 1933 the allied National and South African parties swept to victory with an overall majority of 144 against a tiny opposition of 6. In the new Government Hertzog remained Prime Minister and Smuts self-effacingly accepted the post of Minister of Justice.

In the year that followed, the majority of white South Africans fervently hoped for a total fusion between the two hitherto disparate parties, convinced that the differences between the two leaders had ceased to be irreconcilable. Both, after all, stood firmly for South Africa's sovereign equality in the community of nations and both had a vision of a South Africa based on equality between the two white races. The hopes of the electorate seemed to be realized in the June of that promising year when the two parties fused to form the United South African National Party, whose guiding principle was to be 'a predominant sense of South African national unity, based on the equality of the Afrikaans- and English-speaking sections of the community . . .'[14]

Euphoria now set in among most Whites, and for the first time since the Boer War a belief began to emerge that the different attitudes and values of the two white population groups might find a working basis which would lead to co-operation, co-existence and a united nation. But a large section of Afrikanerdom remained aloof. Dr Daniel François Malan, once one of Hertzog's staunchest supporters and in 1914 a founder member of the National Party, now deserted Hertzog to form, with a large number of sympathizers, the *Gesuiwerde Nasionale Party**, in the sincere belief that

*Purified National Party.

Hertzog was betraying the Afrikaner nation by his attempts to unite with the English.

Hertzog could see no betrayal. Since 1926, he had believed that total independence for South Africa had been achieved through the Balfour Declaration, a conviction that had been reinforced by the passing, in 1931, of the Statute of Westminster, which gave full legal sovereignty to the Dominion Parliaments, and, in 1934, of the Status of the Union Act, giving the Union Parliament sole executive authority in foreign as well as in domestic affairs. On the formation of the United South African National Party (or 'United Party', as it soon became known), Smuts and Hertzog had drawn up a series of principles which they hoped might satisfy the widely divergent political views of their supporters. Well aware of the dangers of what they were doing but believing that the end they had in mind – a harmonious merging of so many shades of political opinion now gathered, willy-nilly, in one umbrella party – justified the casuistic means, they deliberately couched two of the Party's most important guiding principles so ambiguously that they could be interpreted at will.

The first, intended to appeal to the republican convictions held by the greater number of ex-Nationalists, declared 'that while the Party stands for the maintenance of the present constitutional position, no one will be denied the right to express his individual opinion or advocate his honest convictions in connection with any change of our form of government'.[15] It led to the defection of Colonel C. F. Stallard and six other Natalian English-speaking members to form the Dominion Party.

The second, and most important, principle, which stated that 'a solution of the political aspect of . . . [Native Policy] on the basis of separate representation of Europeans and Natives . . . being fundamental in character, and not hitherto . . . a matter of party division, should be left to the free exercise of the discretion of the individual members representing the party in Parliament',[16] could only be seen as a victory for Hertzog. The Prime Minister was still determined to remove the Cape Africans, who had been enfranchised since 1853 and who made up no more than 1.1 per cent of the Union's electorate, from the common roll. This ambition was achieved in 1936 when, at a Joint Sitting of both Houses, the first of the entrenched clauses in the South Africa

Act was abolished and the enfranchised Cape Africans were placed on a separate communal roll entitled to elect three white representatives in the House of Assembly and two Whites to the Cape Provincial Council. Africans throughout the country could elect four white Senators, and an advisory but effectively impotent body called the Natives' Representative Council was created, under the chairmanship of the Secretary for Native Affairs, with five white official members, four nominated Africans and twelve elected African members.[17] Provision was also made in the Native Trust and Land Act of 1936 for the purchase of 15 million acres of land to be added to the existing 22 million acres which had been set aside for Native Reserves by the 1913 Native Trust and Land Act. Smuts genuinely believed that the additional land would be considered a satisfactory *quid pro quo* for the loss of the franchise, but those Africans who constituted the more informed part of their section of the population were very far from satisfied, fully realizing that, effectively, both Acts would make the practice of segregation both more easily justifiable and more easily implemented.[18]

The 'Native Question' seemingly disposed of and satisfactorily out of the way, Smuts and Hertzog were content, failing to recognize the existence of another rock on which one or other might founder. This was the question of South Africa's neutrality in the event of a European war. The two leaders never discussed such a possibility, except in the most general terms: they must have known the rift it would create. Each placed a different interpretation upon the fact that the Union Parliament possessed sole legislative authority and the Government sole executive authority in foreign as well as in domestic affairs, and that South Africa's participation in any future war would depend upon the Government's command of majority support in Parliament. Smuts, fully aware of the true nature of Hitler's nationalist aspirations, believed that Western democracy must be defended at all costs and declared his unshakable conviction that in a world war South Africa would take her stand alongside Britain and the Commonwealth. Hertzog, always more isolationist in his thinking, failed completely to understand Hitler's political and territorial ambitions. His judgement, possibly, was clouded by his sympathy with Germany over the treatment she had received in the Treaty of

Versailles in 1919. Like so many others in Europe, whose views only subsequent events were to change, he saw Germany as a bulwark against an expansionist Bolshevik Russia. On the third side of the political triangle, Malan and his Purified Nationalists knew, without doubt or hesitation, precisely what *their* attitude would be should war be declared. They stood for one thing and one thing only – a neutral Afrikaner Republic. This determined ambition was regarded by most English-speaking South Africans and many Afrikaners as no more than a bad joke; all its critics were totally unaware of the growing influence of this fanatical band of nationalists. This was probably because the small Purified Nationalist Party was, in reality, no more than a political front for a large number of Afrikaner social, cultural and religious organizations of which the *Broederbond** was the most powerful and influential. A self-perpetuating secret society, it had been founded in 1918 to determine the nature of Afrikaner patriotism and to attempt to ensure that only duly approved patriots be appointed to such public positions as were open to them. It also co-ordinated other wings of the Afrikaner nationalist movement, the cultural organizations, the *Reddingsdaadbond*† and the churches. During the 1930s the spirit of Afrikaner nationalism had been growing ever stronger, fanned firstly by the sufferings of the Afrikaners during the Depression years – proportionately greater, it seemed to them, than those of the other white groups – and secondly by the success of National Socialism in Germany. In 1938 further fuel was provided for the growing fire by the Great Trek Centenary celebrations, which, in an extraordinary pilgrimage, brought Afrikaners from all parts of South Africa together to dedicate the monolithic granite Voortrekker Monument on the heights overlooking Pretoria.

Besides these groups, several militant offshoots of the Nationalist movement had arisen in the late 1930s of which two, the Greyshirts and the *Ossewabrandwag*,‡ closely paralleled similar groups in Europe. The concentrated propaganda of so many

*Band of Brothers.
†Economic Assistance Organization. Its function was to establish a separate Afrikaner economic and business structure within an economy almost exclusively controlled by English-speakers.
‡Ox Wagon Guard.

organizations led an increasing number of voters into support for the Party's doctrines of racial division and white Afrikaner exclusivity. At this time, J. H. Hofmeyr, the United Party's liberal-minded future deputy Prime Minister, prophetically wrote to a friend: 'Your hundred-percent Afrikaner is out to create new inequalities . . . His idea of a South African nation is an Afrikaner bloc which may perhaps graciously absorb a few English-speaking South Africans, leaving the rest as an unassimilable minority group.'[19]

But liberal South Africans, deeply preoccupied with the events taking place in Europe, continued to be sublimely unaware of the threat posed to Western democratic ideals by Malan and his supporters, and were not alarmed by the remarkable increase in the Nationalist vote in the general election of 1938.[20]

Fortuitously, the outbreak of war found the Union Parliament assembled for a special session intended to prolong the life of the Senate (originally due to expire on 5 September) for a few extra weeks. The whole neutrality problem which Hertzog and Smuts had for so long so carefully avoided discussing immediately took precedence. Seven members of the Cabinet voted for Smuts and war, and six for Hertzog and neutrality. On 4 September 1939 Smuts and Hertzog took their differences to the House of Assembly. Had Hertzog contented himself with recommending qualified neutrality he might perhaps have carried the day. But he argued too strongly in favour of Hitler, and, although he won the support of more than one-third of his own party and the whole of the Purified National Party, he was defeated by eighty votes to sixty-seven, giving Smuts a slender majority of thirteen.[21] Hertzog resigned as Prime Minister and the Governor-General, Sir Patrick Duncan, called upon Smuts to form a coalition government which would include the leaders of the minority Dominion and Labour Parties. On 5 September 1939 South Africa followed Great Britain into the war against Germany.

War found Helen still living in Northcliff, where her elder daughter, Frances, had been born a few weeks previously. South Africa's participation in the war came as a great emotional relief to English and Jewish South Africans, who for months had feared that Hertzog would force a policy of neutrality upon the country. The 93 000-odd Jews, by virtue of being white, were unique in world Jewry in that they were members of a ruling élite. South African anti-semitism was, and still is, socio-economic rather than political (outside the National Party, with its unashamed bias in favour of Afrikaners). Jews could not go to certain schools, nor join certain clubs; certain financial groups (notably mining houses) would not employ them and their upward mobility in government departments was restricted. But in spite of Malan's success, as a member of the Pact cabinet of 1930, in forcing through the Immigration Quota Act restricting the entry of immigrants from Eastern Europe who were almost entirely Jews, and of its successor, the Aliens Act of 1937, which disastrously curtailed the entry of German-Jewish refugees from the Nazi persecution, there was no legislative discrimination against them. The white power élite, already seriously split between English and Afrikaner, could not afford any further splinter groups which might weaken its structure.

Many older, more orthodox South African Jews were relieved to be able to identify themselves with the *status quo*. With their memories of pogroms and race persecution in Central and Eastern Europe, they felt a deep gratitude to the Union for offering them shelter, and were content to play little or no part in its politics. But many of their children and grandchildren, who had had the advantages of a more liberal education and who moved in a wider white society, were experiencing certain twinges of guilt. South Africa's political and social structure, based as it was (and is) on race oppression, grated against certain fundamentals of their Jewish *ethos*. This guilt manifested itself in several forms: either channelled into non-political involvement with black charities and self-help organizations; or into more controversial but still apolitical organizations like the South African Institute of Race Relations; and lastly into active involvement in politics. Many of these intellectual young South African Jews left (and still leave) for Europe or America, thus permanently shrugging off any responsibility for the system. Like so many of her generation, Helen was aware of racial oppression, but the insulated environment in which she had grown up makes it probable that her awareness was of a sub-conscious nature, now brought to the surface by the rise of Nazism in Germany and its ripple effect in South Africa.

Having observed the early activities of the Austrian Nazi Party on her honeymoon in Vienna shortly before the *Anschluss*, Helen was in the forefront of many young married women whose husbands on the outbreak of war volunteered for the armed forces, and who themselves were in a fever to involve themselves in the Allied cause. Her first move was to go and see her friend and former lecturer, Hansi Pollak, then second-in-command of the Women's Army Auxiliary Services. Hansi was astounded.

'Haven't you just had a baby?' she asked.

'Yes,' replied Helen.

'Well then, you'd better go home and look after it.'

This abrupt rejection enraged the eager recruit. Motherhood appeared to have ruined her war. Longing to be in uniform, she was forced to find a temporary outlet for her energy working for the Governor-General's War Fund, a charitable organization which helped the mothers and wives of servicemen. The monotonous clerical work of handing out small cash sums to soldiers' dependants soon palled. She asked herself why she had not completed her degree, and at the beginning of 1941 she returned to the University of the Witwatersrand. By the end of that year she completed her unfinished courses, obtaining first-class passes in both her major subjects, economics and economic history. Her then Professor of Economics, Herbert Frankel, writes:

The examination papers, and especially the essays she wrote, were a joy to read! . . . What distinguished all her work was the originality it displayed. She was always adept at applying what she studied to some pressing practical problem of the day. She was very quick to see the main point of the argument, its strength and weakness, and to state and examine it fearlessly. It was a pleasure to have her in one's classes. Helen . . . was [one of] the best students I had in South Africa.[22]

Having graduated, she begun looking around for satisfactory war work where she could use her degree. Help came from an unexpected quarter. Professor Herbert Greenwood, her Professor of Accountancy in her early university days, invited her to join his staff at the War Supplies Board, as a collator of statistics on war profiteering, and here, on a part-time basis, she remained until the beginning of 1944. In 1943 her second daughter, Patricia, was born.

In the following year a tutorship in economic history fell vacant and Professor Frankel asked Helen to fill the post. 'Asked', says Helen, 'is perhaps an understatement. He grabbed me one day as I was walking past him and said "You'll do!" ' She 'did' until she resigned in 1953 to go to Parliament, having become a temporary lecturer in the interim.

Helen, deeply involved in her war and university work and with her husband serving in a military hospital in Egypt, was at this time, like so many other South Africans, little concerned with the country's internal politics. Despite the alarming activities of the *Stormjaers** of the *Ossewabrandwag*, the Greyshirts and a newly formed, frankly Nazi party, the New Order, who were now beginning an organized campaign of industrial sabotage, coupled with physical assaults on men in uniform and on known civilian supporters of the war, she relied on Smuts' being in power and likely to remain so. The Government, while harassed by the extremist movements, had graver cause for concern in the catastrophic defeats being suffered by the Allies in Europe, Russia and North Africa, while the Nationalists, on the other hand, saw, in the seeming invincibility of Hitler's armies, the ultimate victory for their own ideologies. Hertzog, who had voted with Malan's Purified Nationalists against South Africa's entering the war, had with his dissident United Party members formed his own party (*Die Volksparty*), but in January 1940 the two organizations merged in a *herinering* (or reunion) into a new party called *Die Herenigde Nasionale of Volksparty*.† This uneasy alliance between Malan and Hertzog lasted only eleven months. In December 1940, at the new party's congress, a Nazi-inspired constitution was drafted, which, while promising English-speaking Whites language and cultural equality, made no mention of any political equality for them with Afrikaners. Hertzog and Havenga rejected the extremism of Malan's Nationalists and left to form yet another group called the *Afrikaner Party*, adhering to a more moderate philosophy of Afrikaner nationalism. Shortly afterwards, politically

*Storm troopers.

†The Reunited National or People's Party, henceforward called the National Party.

destroyed and broken-hearted, Hertzog died and the leadership of the new party passed to Havenga. But the initiative of Afrikaner nationalism, as Hertzog had realized, now lay irrevocably with Malan.

At the beginning of 1944, when an Allied victory had begun to appear inevitable, Malan, who for a brief period during 1943, under pressure from the more extreme elements in his party, had assumed the title of *Volksleier*,* now began to play down his alliance with the *Ossewabrandwag* and the New Order and to woo English and Afrikaans supporters of the war to his cause. But in the 'khaki' election of 1943 the Smuts coalition Government supported by the votes of thousands of soldiers in North Africa swept to victory with 107 seats to the National Party's 43. The New Order, which had made the error of fielding some candidates, was heavily defeated, as were the representatives of the Afrikaner Party.[23] The Nationalists, however, polled 343 180 votes to the Coalition's 530 478 and Smuts was warned that the ratio of Afrikaners supporting what he called 'racial co-operation parties' had fallen from the 1938 figure of 184 : 100 to 160 : 100 in 1943. A large percentage of the new voters appeared to have voted for Malan's party and although, on the surface, the electorate seemed to have endorsed the pursuance of the war policy, Professor J. L. Grey, in a contemporary article, sounded a note of warning to the United Party: 'The underlying political complexion of white South Africa has hardly changed at all as a result of the war. The war, in fact, is a side issue . . . The position is deteriorating. It can only be retrieved by extremely vigilant and efficient government in the next five critical years.'[24] This warning Smuts and his party seem to have ignored completely. For four years, impervious to the storm signals, the United Party policy-makers had been feeding its supporters, Helen amongst them, a strong diet of propaganda, continually emphasizing the essential permanence of liberal-democratic traditions. Smuts had promised them that once Nazism was defeated he would implement the Atlantic Charter with its revolutionary views on race relations and its promises to obliterate social inequality and poverty. Already black and white South Africans were fighting together in the desert against a common enemy; it seemed that once the war was

*People's leader.

over they would inevitably continue to co-operate in the building
of a happier South Africa. As more and more Africans poured into
the cities to work in the factories, Smuts declared: 'Segregation
tried to stop it [the urbanward movement]. It has, however, not
stopped it in the least. The process has been accelerated. You
might as well try to sweep the ocean back with a broom.'[25] The
war ended and the young generation flooded back from the
battlefields of Europe. The post-war University of the Witwatersrand mirrored their mood, and the majority of its students were
ex-servicemen with very definite and radical political views.
Unlike the University of the 1930s, it was now racially 'open',
and there were several black students on the campus. For the
first time English-speaking students were made personally
conscious of traditional segregation policies and of the maze of
restrictive laws which inhibited the upward mobility of Blacks.
Helen, through her intensive research into the economic history
of South Africa, was one of the very first of the University's
lecturers at that time to speak on this theme. Lack of source books
forced her to turn to government publications on migratory labour
and on labour laws, and these early factual studies gave her a
depth of understanding of the socio-economic problems of South
Africa which was to prove invaluable in her parliamentary career.
Students who flocked to her lectures because she was young,
attractive and had a gift of mimicry and a biting wit which could
keep a class roaring with laughter, soon discovered that under-
neath these exterior qualities lay a solid core of realistic thinking.
Her lectures on the irrationality of South Africa's economic
structure and her arguments for social and economic change, so
in advance of general white South African thought, soon brought
her to the attention of the executive of the South African Institute
of Race Relations, who not only invited her to join their organization but asked her to be their representative at a conference on
Human Rights in London in June 1947.

Returning to South Africa after the conference, Helen said in
a newspaper interview[26] that she had had great difficulty in
stating South Africa's case since the delegates from fifteen
different countries, who opposed South Africa's discriminatory
laws and regarded them as a classical example of the infringement
of human rights, did not 'realize the South African rural Native's

extreme primitiveness, both in his mentality and his living conditions, and the difficulty at this juncture of allowing him to vote and the responsibility that went with it, without previously subjecting him to some kind of literacy test to determine his capability of voting'. She went on to qualify this statement by declaring that she thought 'South Africans were equally unaware of the rights and needs of the urban Native, who had progressed far beyond the rural Native mentally, and did not have sufficient provision for his mental and physical status'.

Shortly after her visit to London, she was asked by the Institute to help prepare evidence to be submitted to the Native Laws Commission under the chairmanship of Judge Henry Fagan, an invitation which provided her with the final incentive to make politics her career.

At this time (1947) the United Party Government was greatly concerned with the plight of those Africans, who, attracted by increased job opportunities created by the war, had in recent years been flocking to the cities in search of work.[27] It was the nature of white South African thinking to regard African urban workers as temporary sojourners, who, once the Whites no longer required their labour, would return to the tribal reserves: in these distant and supposedly idyllic pastures, it was assumed, they would happily survive by the practice of subsistence agriculture. Indeed the Stallard Commission, which had reported to the Smuts administration of 1923, had recommended that this philosophy be accepted as official government policy. But over the years the pattern of migratory labour had changed. Instead of returning to the reserves as was expected of them, more and more Africans were bringing their families to the towns to join them. The local urban authorities, not anticipating this influx, failed to provide adequate housing. By the end of the war slums and shanty-towns were springing up in large numbers on the outskirts of all South Africa's major cities. The task of the Fagan Commission (as the Native Laws Commission soon became known) was to advise the government how best it could reclaim '. . . the poor Native, now floating like flotsam and jetsam to . . . our great cities'.[28] Although more formally phrased, Helen's task was similar. She was to investigate 'the employment in Mines and other Industries of migratory labour, the economic and social effects upon the lives of the people concerned; and the future policy to be followed in regard thereto'.[29]

It took the young economist five months to prepare her evidence for the Fagan Commission. With the typical thoroughness that still characterizes all her work, she spent long weeks researching evidence submitted to previous commissions. Her discoveries appalled her. She had always believed that she understood the significance of the innumerable pinpricks affecting African existence in South Africa. She now realized that there were vast gaps in her knowledge. For the first time in her life she became fully aware of the real disabilities under which Africans suffered in a determinedly white-dominated society, of their low wages, their lack of mobility and, above all, of the misery and disruption that the migratory system brought to their family life.

The evidence finally submitted by her to the Commission was voiced in uncompromising terms. She pointed out that, at the rate at which the process of African urbanization was accelerating, it was imperative that the Government should regard Africans as an integral part of South African cities. The migratory labour system should be gradually phased out. Wages should be increased and some form of negotiating machinery set up through which African workers could voice their grievances. She advocated the removal of restrictions, both legislative and customary, '. . . which prevent the adequate training and most beneficial employment opportunities which will enable unskilled workers to acquire and utilize the maximum skills'.[30] Though her recommendations ran counter to accepted South African socio-economic practices she had high hopes that the United Party, by the very act of appointing the Commission, was on the verge of a radical political change.

While the Fagan Commission was deliberating its findings, another Commission was also preparing a report on the same problem. This was the Sauer Commission of the newly-formed Afrikaner-Nationalist dominated *Suid-Afrikaanse Buro vir Rasse Aangeleenthede** (SABRA), which had been formed as a conscious counterpart to the SAIRR. Now, for the first time, the theory of apartheid, a justification of the National Party's segregation policy, was clearly laid down. The Sauer Commission unequivocally stated that, while Blacks had legitimate claims to civil and political

*South African Bureau of Racial Affairs.

equality, unless this took place separately from white development, the Whites of South Africa would, as they put it, 'seal their doom'. Total territorial separation was essential. A member of SABRA, Professor Willi Eiselen, said: 'By separation . . . I mean the separating of the heterogeneous groups . . . into separate socio-economic units, inhabiting different parts of the country, and each enjoying in its own area full citizenship rights.'[31]

The report of the Sauer Commission underlined the widening gap between National and United Party thinking. When the results of the Fagan Commission's deliberations were made public in March 1948, they appeared far too liberal to the Nationalists, while to the more enlightened members of the United Party they were pusillanimous and inadequate. The Commission, though admitting the permanency of African urban dwellers, remained in favour of retaining the restrictive pass laws because 'racial differences necessitate the regulation of contacts between Black and White'. However, it recommended that Africans born in urban areas be allowed to have their wives and families living with them, and suggested that better housing be provided and that 'legislation and administration [be turned] in a direction which will make the worker feel that in a town in which he works, he can find a home, not merely a temporary dormitory from which he may in the near future be expelled'.[32] Optimistically, the Commission saw South Africa as a dynamic society in which the law must allow for growth, change and experiment.

Smuts adopted the Fagan Commission's recommendations as part of the official United Party policy and promised that they would be implemented after the general election due to take place in May 1948. The Institute of Race Relations, though considering both the recommendations of the Commission and the promises of the Prime Minister insufficiently far-reaching, decided to adopt a wait-and-see attitude. Helen herself was profoundly dissatisfied with the Fagan Commission's timorous proposals. By now, it had become increasingly clear to her that no real change would ever be effected in South Africa through indirect pressure groups like the Institute. She came to a final conclusion. Laws could only be changed through direct political action. Her mind finally made up, she joined the United Party and immediately plunged herself into pre-election politics.

Chapter Two 1948-53

The United Party, fourteen years after Fusion, remained the same unwieldy amalgam of varying political views. The one umbrella still sheltered a heterogeneous membership ranging from *platteland* Afrikaners through a large conservative business-orientated centre to a small but vociferous left led by Smuts' heir-designate, Jan Hofmeyr. Neither the Dominion Party's obsession with the rights of English-speaking Natalians, nor the Labour Party's goal of an 'ultimate achievement of a democratic and socialist commonwealth', attracted Helen. For her and most liberally-minded white South Africans the appeal of the United Party lay in Hofmeyr, a man of formidable intellect and a convinced but not a courageous liberal, who, they hoped, would ultimately influence the Party's thinking and its policy. Foremost of those parliamentarians who kept up a continuous onslaught on the Nationalists, Hofmeyr, as far back as 1936, had been one of only eleven members who opposed the disenfranchisement of the Cape Africans. Attacking this retrogressive piece of legislation, he said at the time: '. . . there is . . . a rising tide of liberalism in South Africa. It is notably the younger people who are in the forefront of the tide. It is they who are the custodians of the future.'[1] Before the 1948 election he had postulated a new concept in United Party thinking – white *leierskap*,* a policy of participation of all races on merit under a benevolent and paternal white government contrasting with the traditional policy of *baasskap*† – and urged all South African liberals to join the United Party to contain the advance of Afrikaner Nationalism.

What Helen and the other followers of Hofmeyr failed at that stage to realize was that a large section of the United Party, notably the *platteland* and Natal members, were implacably

*Leadership.
†Domination.

opposed to any change whatsoever in party policy and that against this united intransigence Hofmeyr's philosophy must break. She was not to recognize this until some time after she joined the Party caucus five years later.

Once an Allied victory in Europe was assured, it became obvious that more than ever before post-war South African politics would be dominated by race relations. The 'Indian problem' provided the country with its first foretaste of future white attitudes. Between 1860 and 1872 the sugar planters of Natal had imported large numbers of indentured coolie labourers from India to work their plantations. Once their indentures ended most of the coolies, in spite of financial inducements and the increasingly repressive laws of the Natal legislative council, refused repatriation, preferring to stay in Natal and work as petty artisans, small shop-keepers and domestic servants. They were much hated by the white Natalians. In 1927, by which time the Indian population in Natal had risen to 174000,[2] the Indian and South African governments had signed a voluntary repatriation agreement, but few South African Indians availed themselves of it. As the Indian population continued to grow in size, particularly in Natal, white Natalians exerted continuous pressure upon the Government to enforce upon it residential segregation and other restrictive measures. In 1943 the Smuts administration passed the Trading and Occupation of Land (Transvaal and Natal) Restriction Act which pegged the Indians' occupation of land and the issue to them of trading licences in the two provinces for three years. In 1946, despite growing opposition from the Indians, the Government bowed to white pressure and introduced the Asiatic Land Tenure and Indian Representation Act. Under the Act, apart from certain exempted areas, no Indian could acquire fixed property from a White in the Transvaal or Natal except under permit.[3] Provision was made in the Second Chapter of the Act for Transvaal and Natal male Indians, possessing certain educational and financial qualifications, to be given communal representation by three Whites in Parliament and by two Whites or Indian members in the Natal Provincial Council, with additional representation in the Senate of two white Senators, one elected and one nominated. As might have been expected, the Act satisfied no one. The Indians refused to accept any form of political representation which was not based on full franchise rights: the Whites believed that Smuts, influenced by Hofmeyr, was throwing the country open to further 'coolie' infiltration. Only the Nationalists benefited from the tension arising out of the Asiatic legislation, skilfully capitalizing on the anti-Indian feeling in Natal and the Transvaal to strengthen their party's position.[4] So this small minority section of the population[5] became a shuttlecock in an election whose result was to deprive them even of those inadequate rights Smuts had offered them.

Before the war had ended, the National Party leaders, realizing that an Allied victory was inevitable, clearly saw that a temporary change in tactics would be to their future advantage and started to play Afrikaner 'exclusivity' on a very low key. They declared that '. . . the party could no longer afford to slam its door in the face of the English and shake its fist at them through the grille',[6] while Malan used every means to his hand to attract the growing dissident English vote on the right wing of the United Party. Using a statement made by Hofmeyr at a by-election in 1947 in Hottentots-Holland in the Cape Province, in which the Deputy Prime Minister had said that although the United Party advocated a policy of white leadership, it was necessary to give every race group in South Africa the chance to develop freely in terms of its potential, Malan accused Hofmeyr (and the United Party) of condemning South Africa to becoming the home of a 'coffee-coloured race'. He emphasized that the National Party would never allow integration and would 'preserve the rule, the purity and the civilization of the white race' by implementing its new apartheid policy. The four racial groups of South Africa, he assured the electorate, would be permanently segregated and each group would have the opportunity of developing along its own lines in its own designated area. '*Kaffer op sy plek en koelie uit die land*'* was not the National Party's only election cry. As a parallel ploy Malan was also cleverly hammering 'bread-and-butter' issues. The United Party Government, in common with most post-war governments, was battling with reconstruction problems. While

---

*Kaffir in his place and coolie out of the country (i.e. back to India).

the war was being fought, it had promised to ensure work for all returned ex-servicemen; to rectify the serious housing shortages; and to abandon the stringent food controls which so irritated an electorate unaccustomed to shared national hardship. When the time came for their implementation, the United Party found itself unable to fulfil these wartime pledges. Malan now promised that should his party be returned to power, it would lift food controls, grant tax relief for the white middle- and lower-income groups and give priority to constructing cheap houses for white urban workers; in short that all promises made to ex-servicemen but not kept by the United Party would be carried out by the National Party. By early 1948 it should have been quite apparent to the Government that the white electorate was quite prepared to mortgage its future and vote Nationalist for hypothetical immediate benefits.[7] But the Government chose to ignore the warning signals. O. Oosthuizen, the United Party's General Secretary, blithely assured Smuts that victory was inevitable in spite of the fact that since 1945 the National Party had won four out of eight by-elections, the most notable being the defeat of a rising young protégé of Smuts, Sir de Villiers Graaff, at Hottentots-Holland in January 1947, where a United Party majority of 637 votes was wiped out and turned into a National Party majority of 1228. Even Hofmeyr, addressing the Party's Witwatersrand General Council, declared: '. . . The United Party is well prepared for a General Election and is exceptionally strong financially'.[8] This mood of complacency permeated the Party. Hardly any electioneering was done in the constituencies; Party officials and workers seemed to have assumed that the majority of the electorate would, as a United Party newspaper put it, automatically vote for General Smuts because of his personal prestige and because of the war record of the United Party government.[9] So, while the National Party aggressively pushed its new philosophy of apartheid and attacked Hofmeyr as the man destined to destroy South Africa, Smuts produced no counter-propaganda. Apart from pointing out that the United Party had adopted the Fagan Commission's recommendations as part of its policy, all he could produce in the way of an election battle-cry was 'South Africa must go ahead on the path which has served her so well in the past'. One of the Natives' Representatives, Donald Molteno,

commented bitterly: 'This statement of Smuts' expresses the
essence of the United Party's policy. Their appeal is neither to
the emergencies of the present nor to the necessities of a perilous
future but exclusively to the complacencies of a none too brilliant
past.'[10] But no one, not even Dr Malan (who was planning for a
National Party victory in 1953), expected the United Party to be
defeated. Réné de Villiers, one of South Africa's most astute
political commentators, who was to become a Progressive MP in
1974, wrote: '. . . the National Party, led by Dr Malan, cannot,
unless some miracle happens between now and the end of this
year, expect to win the next general election'.[11] Yet the miracle
happened. On 26 May 1948 the country went to the polls and
the National Party was returned with a slender majority of
five.[12] Its unexpected victory was not only due to the United
Party's lethargic complacency but also to the illogicalities of
the South African electoral laws.[13] Although the United Party
had received almost 60 per cent of the votes cast – a figure which
indicated that all the English-speaking voters and about one-third
of the United Party's *bloedsap** had remained loyal to it, the
15 per cent under- and overloading factor on rural and urban seats
had caused the United Party to build up enormous and useless
majorities in the cities, while on the *platteland* the Nationalists had
won seats with as little as 40 per cent of the total votes cast. The
population shifts which had taken place during and after the war
had brought a large influx of Afrikaner voters from the country
to the cities and had caused many peri-urban seats on the outskirts
of Johannesburg and Cape Town to fall to the National Party.
Smuts had failed to heed warnings in recent years that the curious
delimitation rules of weighting urban and rural votes differently
would adversely affect his party: he refused to alter these rules
and his refusal was a significant factor in his defeat. The old man's
integrity for once overcame his political astuteness. 'The existing
electoral arrangements . . .' he told the officials who suggested
changing the Act, 'had their roots in the pact of good faith which
had created and must still sustain the constitution.'[14]

While the National Party supporters were celebrating their
unexpected victory with torchlight processions, dancing in

*Roughly 'dyed in the wool'. A term applied to rural Afrikaans-speaking
UP voters.

the streets of Pretoria and jubilantly chanting *Die Stem* and
Kyk hoe lyk hy nou!* English-speaking South Africa was totally
stunned. Helen found herself no exception to the rest of her
language group. Shortly before the election she and Major J. D.
Opperman, a returned ex-serviceman, had formed and worked
in the Milner Park Branch of the United Party. The branch's
area centred on the University of the Witwatersrand and included
a large student population. New as she was to politics, her electioneering had been minimal – nothing more, as she now puts it, than
a lot of light-hearted canvassing. Like all her co-workers, she was
so sure of a United Party victory that she had not bothered to
attend the polling booths on the evening of election day, but had
gone to a performance of Sartre's *The Flies* which was being given
in the Great Hall of the University. Several members of the
audience had brought portable wirelesses with them to listen to
the election results. When the news was broadcast that Smuts
had lost his own seat, Standerton, the Transvaal *platteland*
constituency he had represented for twenty-four years, the play
came to an abrupt halt. The audience streamed out of the Hall
and most of them drove to the centre of Johannesburg to join
the crowd gathered round the *Rand Daily Mail*'s election baro-
meter. One by one the 'safe' United Party seats in the urban centres
fell to the Nationalists and by midnight, with only the *platteland*
results outstanding, the United Party defeat was in no doubt.
People stood in the streets with tears streaming down their faces.
It was, Helen remembers feeling, as if the world had come to an
end. Certainly South Africa would never be the same again.
Smuts had said, in a moment of depression in 1944: '. . . victory
will never come to me any more. It seems as if night will overcome
me and my works.'[15] Now indeed that night had fallen, sooner
than Smuts or his party had imagined, and he, the United Party,
and South Africa itself were to enter into darkness. In spite of
the fact that the country's franchise was a limited one and that
blatant economic and social discrimination existed, certain basic
Western values had until now always been adhered to. The
freedom of speech, of assembly, of the Press were now to be
threatened or destroyed. The processes of law were no longer to

---

**Die Stem van Suid-Afrika* (The Voice of South Africa) is the National
Anthem. *Kyk hoe lyk hy nou* = look at him now.

be inviolate. The Afrikaners had achieved their freedom: but they could only maintain it at the expense of the freedom of their compatriots.

Malan spent the next eighteen months consolidating his party's position in Parliament and in the country. To ensure a working majority he formed a loose alliance with the Afrikaner Party and made its leader, N. C. Havenga, his Minister of Finance. Apart from repealing the unpopular Indian Representation Act,[16] the racial legislation introduced by the new Government only served to bolster existing tacit segregation measures. Apartheid signs were erected in post offices and railway stations and separate railway carriages for different race groups were introduced. Some minor election promises were implemented – training schools for black artisans were closed down and black housing schemes were abandoned in favour of white ones. The Government's actions during those eighteen months were cunningly calculated to allay the fears of the English-speaking Whites. But that the National Party had not changed its intention of striking at the Constitution soon became obvious. In reply to a question by Smuts in the House, Malan replied that he intended honouring his party's election pledge to remove Coloured voters from the Common Roll. He was only awaiting legal opinion to see whether the National Party could alter the relative entrenched clause in the South Africa Act by a simple majority vote.

While the National Party was thus establishing a firm base from which to attack the Constitution, the United Party was struggling to revitalize itself. Unlike the National Party – an ideologically highly motivated, disciplined and well-organized body – the United Party with its loose federal structure, flexible policy and pragmatic approach was only held together by Smuts' ability to inspire unquestioning obedience in his followers. In power this ability was a strength but in defeat a terrible weakness. In its election post-mortem the Party's Central Executive discovered that one of the causes of the Party's defeat lay in its lack of internal organization, exemplified by the loss of Vereeniging, one of its key seats, by only 19 votes simply because one of the party officials had failed to register some 350 postal votes.[17] In a frantic attempt to rectify the defects in the moribund party structure and to modernize its organizational methods, Party officials were sent post-haste to England to study British political party organization. There resulted a massive administrative transformation of the United Party over the ensuing five years.[18] A whole series of internal reforms were instituted, divisions for propaganda, fund raising, research and youth were established at a national level while at both provincial and local level the Party which since its election defeat had been flooded with offers to help was reinvigorated by an influx of new, often youthful, workers burning, in the words of the Johannesburg *Sunday Times*, to 'rally and consolidate the forces of democratic majority in South Africa'.[19] One of these was Helen.

Shortly after the election defeat she was invited to a house meeting in Johannesburg North to hear Jan Hofmeyr analyse the causes of the Party's defeat. She emerged from the meeting convinced that she was wasting her time in the Milner Park Branch, which, with its large student population, had too high a membership turnover to make it a satisfactory ground for a young and ambitious politician. She would, she felt, be far better employed working for Hofmeyr in his constituency, Johannesburg North, where in any event she and Mosie now lived, in the new suburb of Hyde Park. One of her friends recalls: 'We were all saying "What can we do, what can we do?" when Helen came forward and said "I'm going to form a committee. We've got to get cracking and get them out".' She bullied, nagged and cajoled her friends until, early in 1949, she formed the Hyde Park Mixed Branch[20] of the United Party, with Edward Joseph, a well-known, popular Johannesburg stockbroker as chairman and herself as secretary. Here she found herself working seriously at the most basic level of political involvement – writing out voters' cards, canvassing, organizing membership drives and selling 'Oom Jannie' (Smuts) Christmas cards for party funds. She had also been elected senior vice-chairman of the Johannesburg North Divisional Committee and as a delegate began attending the Party's monthly Witwatersrand General Council meetings. But it was in the Witwatersrand Women's Council of the Party[21] that her political potential first became apparent.

The Witwatersrand Women's Council had been controlled for fourteen years by the elderly, ultra-conservative Edith Grobbelaar, a Johannesburg City Councillor and also a Transvaal Provincial Councillor. The young women, like Helen, who had become members of the Council after 1948, were unimpressed by the prevailing tea-party atmosphere of its meetings and by the timid approach of its office-bearers to political issues. (A delegate once said in disgust: 'This Council always views anything out of the ordinary suggested to it with fear and perturbation.')[22] The new members optimistically determined on instant reform. But they were too new to the game and their enthusiastic efforts met with no success. At the first Party Provincial Congress attended by Helen, she and a fellow-reformist, Joyce Waring,[23] put forward a resolution from the Women's Council which they hoped would end the rule of Mrs Grobbelaar's Old Guard. In order to render their chairwoman impotent, they proposed that 'no Senator, MP, MPC or City Councillor could hold office on the Witwatersrand and Transvaal Executive'.[24] Harry Rissik, the Witwatersrand General Council Chairman, a pillar of the *bloedsap* establishment, had shrewdly allowed it to go forward to the Congress in spite of intense conservative opposition in the General Council, and it was, as he had anticipated, heavily defeated.

'Blame it on the way we worded it', Helen told her supporters. But a useful purpose had been served: the reformists began fully to appreciate the monolithic conservatism of the United Party establishment. If they were to effect the reforms they so urgently desired, it was clear that they would have to organize themselves into a pressure group and lobby for support to establish their nominees in key posts throughout the Witwatersrand party structure.

Helen began taking a militant line at Women's Council meetings ('I was always', she says, 'jumping up and down making suggestions.') Her aggressive tactics brought her to the other delegates' attention: In early 1951 'Mrs H. *Suzzman*' [*sic*] was elected to the Witwatersrand Executive and even more usefully to the Party's policy-making body, the Action Committee. She had also begun to be much in demand as a speaker at non-political meetings and when in March 1950 the Women's Council appointed her as their Honorary Information Officer, her supporters were elated but not at all surprised.

The duties of this latter post were '. . . to scan Government Gazettes, newspapers, etc. and give a summary of report to the

Council'.[25] To Mosie, who was in America at the time, she wrote: 'That's what you get for becoming a fake expert', but she was in fact delighted. She could at last push for a reformist point of view to a captive, but at the same time appreciative audience. Helen's monthly talks spanned a broad spectrum of political topics. Invariably placing a liberal emphasis on whatever subjects she was dealing with, she was at the same time enlarging her own and her audience's understanding of Nationalist legislation and strategy. But she could have no influence on the grand plan of the Government, which was now inexorably moving towards its fulfilment. The more so, since the very vehicle of opposition, despite all its internal reforms, was faltering.

For while the younger and newer members of the United Party were beginning the struggle to revitalize it, the Party suffered a second grievous blow. In December 1948 Hofmeyr had died suddenly, and now on 11 September 1950 the towering figure of Smuts, the charismatic leader and the Party's unifying force, also disappeared. J. G. N. Strauss, an advocate and former Minister of Agriculture, became leader of the Party. An extremely able, middle-of-the-road conservative, Strauss lacked both the personality and the force of character necessary to hold together the amorphous body he had inherited. His main support lay in the Party's moderate centre, a group headed by Harry Oppenheimer, MP for Kimberley (City) (and son of the mining magnate Sir Ernest Oppenheimer), but at this stage he still had the backing, albeit somewhat grudgingly given, of the conservative mass. Many of these traditionalists, the remnants of the old Hertzog National Party, covertly sympathized with much of the Government's philosophy of apartheid but thought it expedient to adopt a 'wait-and-see' attitude. With its great old leader gone, it was not surprising that the Party, whose outwardly united façade hid so many divergent viewpoints, proved itself incapable of presenting a forceful opposition to the Government's first apartheid onslaught which now broke upon it.

The first four major apartheid measures were passed in 1950. Two – the Immorality Act[26] and the Population Registration Act[27] – served merely to legitimize and to some degree extend traditional segregation policies which had always existed in South Africa, and although the United Party fought the Population Registration

Bill clause by clause (having produced only token opposition to the other and equally contentious piece of legislation), its motivation was tactical rather than humanitarian.

But it was over the Group Areas Bill,[28] described by Dr Malan as the 'kernel of apartheid' and hailed by the Nationalist Press as the first great step in the direction of positive apartheid, that the United Party's schismatic attitudes first emerged into the open. This Bill provided for separate residential areas defined on a race basis. Its implementation meant enforced transfer of whole population groups from one area to another with all the economic and social suffering this entailed. At first the United Party opposed it strenuously. It was, said Strauss, 'a massive, ill-digested Bill with tremendous implications', and should be referred to an impartial Select Commission. When it reached its committee stage, however, much of the United Party's opposition fell away as it became apparent that there were wide areas of agreement between it and the Government on the emotional question of social and residential segregation. While the Natal members of the United Party vied with each other to outdo the National Party in their anti-Indian attitudes, Strauss blandly proclaimed: '. . . the only difference between us is that the United Party stands by the Hertzog [Native] Policy of 1936 while the Government wants to reduce Native rights'.[29] In short, the United Party did not disagree with the Government in principle but in method, and it soon became apparent that what its members most feared was that the Bill would adversely affect the country's economy and their own pockets. At no stage during the debate did Strauss suggest that the United Party, if returned to power, would repeal the Act. Certain features of it might indeed be amended but, for the rest, a United Party government would administer it 'in a spirit of good-will and justice for all'.[30]

During the whole of the 1950 session the United Party put up only one unequivocal fight, against what was to be the first of many 'security' laws, the Suppression of Communism Act,[31] which was forced through the Assembly in thirty hours by ruthless use of the 'guillotine'. The United Party, strongly emphasizing that the Act struck at the fundamental concept of freedom of thought, tabled amendments which would give so-called 'Communists' recourse to the courts, and demanded that limitations be placed on the executive powers the Minister was assuming. Opposition speakers further pleaded for the restriction of the sweeping rights of search, seizure and inquisition which the Bill granted the police. But the Opposition's well-organized attack foundered when Strauss, claiming in so many words to be as anti-Communist as the next white South African, effectively torpedoed it by recommending that Communist activities should be considered high treason carrying the death penalty with the onus of proof resting on the accused. The hilarity upon the Government benches was considerable: the United Party, not for the first time, had spoken with two voices and disastrously discredited itself with liberals and the right wing alike.

By early September 1950 the balance of parties in the Assembly had altered radically, although no further general election had been held, due to the passing in 1949, with Smuts' full co-operation, of legislation to incorporate the League of Nations mandated territory of South West Africa into the Union. The South West Africa Affairs Amendment Act[32] created six new seats in the House of Assembly and four in the Senate, which were all, unsurprisingly in view of the extremely conservative nature of the German and Afrikaner voters of the territory, won by the National Party at a special election in 1950. *Die Vaderland* proclaimed: 'The victory represents an extremely important turning point in our politics.' The precarious balance of power was removed from Havenga's Afrikaner Party and Havenga, who up until this moment had steadfastly refused his agreement to the Nationalists' proposed disenfranchisement of the Coloureds, which he saw as a betrayal of the pledges given by his former leader and friend, General Hertzog, now decided that expediency would stand him in better stead than conscience. Declaring that he was satisfied that the arrangements to disenfranchise the Coloureds would neither diminish the existing political rights of the Coloured population nor conflict with the provisions of the South Africa Act, he announced his party's support for Malan. The right of the Coloureds to vote on the Common Roll was entrenched in the South Africa Act.[33] To remove or alter that clause a statutory two-thirds majority of the members of both Houses of Parliament sitting together at the Third Reading was required. The Government, still not commanding this necessary support, now attempted to validate its proposed action by altering the entrenched clause by a simple majority, on the precedent of a Cape Provincial Supreme Court judgment of 1937.[34] Both Government and Opposition parties prepared themselves for a lengthy battle.

The United Party could not comprehend the disasters that lay ahead for it in the coming efforts of the Government to force coloured disenfranchisement on the country. Under different names and guises the legislation was to be presented eight times over the next five years. Parliament was, in joint and separate sessions, continually occupied with long and bitter debates as the Government made one effort after another to circumvent the obstacles of the entrenched clauses of the Constitution. The courts were assailed. Judgments were handed down which stirred the opposing forces into new engagements. But it was the shattering dissension that the Government's attempts fostered in the Opposition ranks during these years which far outweighed the effects of any other political issues of the time and was the crucial ingredient in the splitting and eventual decline of the United Party. For the time being, however, the Party appeared united in its opposition to the Coloured legislation both in Parliament and outside, where it became a rallying point for the majority of the electorate united in a common anger.

Once the Opposition's attempts to prevent this legislation, known as the Separate Representation of Voters Bill, from being passed, failed (it was passed with a simple majority towards the end of 1951) it was decided to challenge the validity of the Act in the courts.[35] Malan, infuriated by this move, warned the country that, should the courts declare the Act invalid, parliamentary sovereignty would be undermined, since powers belonging exclusively to the legislature would then be shown to have been assumed by the judiciary.[36] Neither he nor his party, he said, could or would tolerate such a situation.

One positive good emerged from this attempt of the Government to tamper with the Constitution. The Opposition electorate, who until the introduction of the Separate Representation of Voters Bill had watched the beginning of the Government's inroads upon its fundamental freedoms with apathetic indifference, were now roused to vigorous and occasionally even to violent protest. To the National Party's claims that behind the 'fig leaves

and the venom [the United Party] was only interested in its loss of
stemvee*', the United Party hotly retorted that its concern was
far less with the loss of voters in several Cape constituencies than
the fact that the matter was one of moral principle affecting the
national prestige and honour of white South Africans who in
1936 had pledged themselves to protect the rights of the Coloured
minority. They did not, however, admit that this moral indignation was tinged with an element of self-interest. Most English-
speaking South Africans well remembered the National Party's
'1940 Constitution' and the subservient role it laid down for them.
If the Coloureds could be disenfranchised by a simple majority
vote, might not the English too be deprived of their 'natural'
rights?

From mass meetings held from May 1951 onwards all over
South Africa to protest against the Government's proposed viola-
tion of the spirit of the Constitution, arose the War Veterans' Action
Committee or Torch Commando, as it later became known from
the flaming 'freedom' torches which were carried by its members
in demonstrations. Led by Louis Kane-Berman, a lawyer, and
A. G. ('Sailor') Malan, an Air Force war hero, it was composed
mainly of ex-servicemen who pledged themselves to defend the
Constitution and to force an immediate general election. The
Torch Commando's great attraction (and ultimately its greatest
weakness) was that it was not, and never attempted to become, a
political party. Attitudes on apartheid might differ widely within
the United Party but common cause had been found in 'saving the
Constitution'. Torchlight rallies were organized, and motorized
'commandos' drove to Cape Town to protest outside Parliament.
The movement clearly had a deep groundswell of support. The
Minister of Justice's somewhat wild claim that the Commando
was a tool of the Communists[37] did not stop voluntary committees
from springing up all over the country, and 'Torch' membership
swelled by mid-1952 to over a quarter of a million.

Helen was brought into the Torch Commando movement in
early 1952 by Guy Nicholson, one of her former students and
secretary to the Johannesburg branch of the Commando. Her
political reputation had been steadily growing. The research

*Voting cattle. The enfranchised Coloureds more often than not supported
United Party candidates.

she was doing for her monthly talks to the Women's Council had enlarged and deepened her political knowledge and she was developing into a first-rate speaker, able to demand attention and to put her points with great force and clarity. 'The monthly reports of the Information Officer', said Mrs I. Turvey, her chairwoman at this time, 'have been most stimulating – they have prevented mental stagnation and have helped keep political thought among the women flamingly alive.'[38] Within the Witwatersrand region of the United Party her influence had been growing steadily. Now, to the idealistic but politically inexperienced Torchers, she seemed an obvious choice as a link with the political opposition. Her decisiveness and her knowledge of legislative procedures would be invaluable in helping them plan their strategy. Even more important, she was an ideal liaison officer between them and the Witwatersrand Executive of the United Party in enlisting the parliamentary support they so urgently needed.

On 20 March 1952 the Appellate Division of the Supreme Court declared the Separate Representation of Voters Act unconstitutional. Malan, incensed by the Court's thwarting of what he called the *volkswil*,* announced that the Government would now take steps to place the legislative sovereignty of Parliament beyond any doubt. 'The court's decision', he stated, 'has created a constitutional position which cannot be accepted . . . No compromise is possible . . . It is a clarion call to battle for the most sacred rights of a nation as it exercises them through Parliament. Our action will be forceful and uncompromising.' The Government immediately introduced what was called the High Court of Parliament Bill,[39] providing that a simple majority of Parliament could confirm, vary or set aside any judgment of the Appellate Division of the Supreme Court which had invalidated any Act of Parliament or refused to give effect to any of its provisions. As soon as the Bill was law and the session ended, the Nationalist members of Parliament, who now, since the Opposition refused to co-operate, constituted the 'High Court' provided for by the new Act, hastily met in Pretoria, and on 27 August 1952 adjudged the Separate Representation of Voters Act valid. Two days later the Cape Division of the Supreme Court invalidated the

*Will of the people.

High Court of Parliament Act, stating that it contravened the entrenched clauses of the Constitution. The Appeal Court subsequently upheld the decision and the Government withdrew. The controversial Act was no longer enforced: the High Court of Parliament was allowed to vanish quietly from the scene.

The Torch Commando, the United Party and the Labour Party now came together to formulate a common scheme to bring about the fall of the Government.[40] At the beginning of April in Cape Town, at a meeting charged with emotion, Strauss announced to a cheering crowd that the three organizations had formed a United Democratic Front:

From now onwards, acting together in the highest good faith, we dedicate ourselves to work in common devotion for the day when all freedom-loving South Africans will once again be united in peace and security under a government pledged to respect the rights and dignity of its citizens, to uphold the Constitution of our Union and to restore South Africa to her rightful place as an honoured member of Western society.[41]

To the public the United Democratic Front gave an illusion of unity. In reality it was an uneasy alliance between three disparate organizations and its unfortunate provision of allowing each of its members to retain its own identity proved its downfall. But for the time being United Party workers were urged to stand behind their Leader and their 'friends the Torch Commando'.[42]

In early June 1952 following an emotional meeting of the local Torch executive, Helen and two of her friends, Marjorie Juta and Ellen Hellmann, retired to what was then Johannesburg's one and only coffee bar, and determined to draw the women of South Africa as a body into the protest movement. 'Our purpose', said Ellen, 'is to make our land fit for our children to live in.'

At the next meeting of the United Party Women's Council, Helen stood up and announced that 'a number of women have got together in order to form a Women's United Front to help this country in its present crisis . . .' She appealed to all the Council members to join Women's Action (as it became known) and to pledge themselves to '. . . a concerted action and sustained effort to unseat the Nationalist government and secure democracy for

South Africa'. A mass protest meeting, she told them, would be held in Pretoria and she urged all the women to attend it. 'Bring your friends. Make them active in this country's affairs.'[43]

The formation of Women's Action – itself no more than a localized organization which mobilized still more workers for the Torch Commando – was the turning point in Helen's political career. She made her public début at its protest meeting in Pretoria. Ellen Hellmann drove her from Johannesburg to the meeting, and recalls: 'Every word of her speech was written out. She kept going through it again and again asking me what I thought of it. She was paralysed with nervousness.'[44] Helen was the third speaker. The speech which had caused her so much anxiety was not one of the most inspired of her career. The *Rand Daily Mail* reported her as saying: 'South Africa is a country of great possibilities. To make it a fine, prosperous and safe country for our children to live in, it needs a sane and stable government which will work towards harmonious relations between the different racial groups.'[45] It must have been the force of her personality which made the 2000 women present at the meeting cheer her as loudly as they did. She was launched as a public figure.

1952 was a decisive year for Helen Suzman. She was seen to be actively involved with the Torch Commando. She established a reputation for herself as an outspoken liberal at the Party's Union Congress, where, as a delegate from the Witwatersrand, she had called for far-reaching reforms in the Party's social welfare, housing and non-European policies. The reformist group, of which she was an acknowledged leader, had succeeded in establishing themselves in key posts on all the Witwatersrand Executive sub-committees and now dominated the Action Committee, the Publicity Committee and the all-powerful Candidates Committee. When nominations for candidates for the 1953 General Election were called for by the Party's Executive, a power struggle, bitterly and acrimoniously fought, ensued between the conservatives and the reformists, the conservatives being determined to retain their existing sitting members. But the reformists in control of the Candidates Committee succeeded in putting forward several of their own nominees, amongst whom were three accredited liberals, Professor I. S. ('Sakkies') Fourie, a former Professor of Economics at the University of the Orange Free State and wartime adviser to General Smuts, John Cope, editor of the liberal journal *The Forum*, and Helen.

It had been known for some time in party circles that Helen was considering becoming a City Councillor, a post which traditionally could lead to the Provincial Council and finally to Parliament. But she was destined to jump these intermediate steps to an Assembly seat. Two branch chairmen within the Houghton Division, Reginald Sidelsky and Fay Lipa, independently of each other now both decided to ask her to contest the Houghton parliamentary nomination in the forthcoming general election. The Houghton constituency – a safe and never contested United Party seat – was an upper-class to upper-middle-class area. Its core was the lavish suburb of Houghton, in whose mansions lived the successors of the Rand millionaires. On the south it was bordered by the expensive flatland of Killarney, and in the north by the prosperous middle-class areas of Waverley and Highlands North. To the east lay a lower-class anomaly, Norwood, whose small houses were at this time largely inhabited by artisans and blue-collar workers, almost all English-speaking and solid United Party supporters.

The sitting member, Eric Bell, whose parents were Rand pioneers, had been a member of the United Party since its inception. In 1940 he became the member of Parliament for Orange Grove, and had moved to Houghton in 1943. Bell was an uninspiring and uninspired member of Parliament. He appeared only occasionally in the Assembly where he limited himself to speaking on financial affairs. Out of session, he rarely visited his constituency so that Reginald Sidelsky, who had been the constituency's Waverley Branch chairman for three years, had never met him. During 1952 Bell was invited by Sidelsky to address his branch, but although he accepted, he failed either to turn up to the meeting or to send an apology. When Helen shortly afterwards was invited to address the branch, Sidelsky, on the spur of the moment, asked her whether she would be interested in standing for nomination in Houghton. Helen, taken completely aback, asked 'Why me?' He explained the general dissatisfaction with the sitting member, and his own view that the constituency needed a young, vital and liberal representative in Parliament. Helen replied that she would have to think about the offer. But before she had time to frame an answer to Sidelsky, the chairwoman of the Highlands North Branch, Fay Lipa, approached her with an identical invitation. Sidelsky and Mrs Lipa calculated that together with the Bramley Branch they could raise eighteen out of thirty-six votes in the constituency's electoral college for Helen and believed that if she, personally, could woo Mrs Sophie Lyons, familiarly known as 'Mama' and chairwoman of the Norwood Branch, into giving a further six votes, they would have the necessary support for their nominee. They calculated that two other, more conservative, divisional branches, Upper and Lower Houghton, were behind Bell, but with twenty-four votes assured, 'it meant', says Sidelsky, 'that at least half the electoral college was thinking along our lines and we decided to go ahead and push Helen's nomination.'

Helen had spent a difficult ten days trying to come to a decision as to how to reconcile a parliamentary career with the needs of her family and her job. The thought of becoming a City Councillor had appealed to her since it would have enabled her to continue her work at the University. Becoming a member of Parliament meant a six-month separation from her family every year while the Assembly sat in Cape Town. Eventually Mosie forced the issue for her.

'You must be crazy. Why don't you do it?' he said.

'The whole proposition is impossible from a family point of view,' Helen replied. 'What about the children – how can I do it? And I like my job.'

'You've been doing an exceptional amount of political work – and there is no reason why you shouldn't fly home every weekend!' urged her husband. Helen, still full of reservations and convinced that she would be defeated in a nomination contest, decided (in her own words) that 'it would be no bad thing to give old Bell a bit of a jolting' and accepted the nomination. By the end of that same day the nomination papers had been sent to the Party offices with more than twenty-five signatures.

The 'safe' Houghton seat now most unexpectedly became the centre of a three-cornered battle. Joyce Waring also put her name forward for nomination. Confident of her popularity as a local City Councillor, she made no effort to lobby for support. Bell, alarmed and insecure, appeared in Houghton for the first time in years and visited all his branch chairmen in a belated

attempt to whip up support. Helen herself did no personal lobbying, preferring to leave vote catching to her sponsors. She did
send a circular letter to members in her constituency.

I am writing to introduce myself to you as a candidate for the Houghton
parliamentary nomination and to set out my qualifications and experience in academic and political activities

she wrote modestly, and having set out her qualifications, went
on to say:

I am not presuming, at this stage, to ask for your support, but I do
hope that I shall have the opportunity of addressing you at one of the
meetings arranged by the Houghton Division next week and of replying
to your questions, so that you will be able to form your own opinion
of my capabilities as a prospective member of Parliament . . .

One of these meetings was attended by 'Mama' Lyons on whom
the necessary six extra votes depended. The doyenne of Norwood
sat in the front row, nodding approvingly. 'We've won her over!'
exulted Helen to Fay Lipa. 'Every time I made a pertinent point
she nodded in agreement.'

'Those nods weren't agreement,' replied Mrs Lipa, ' "Mama"
Lyons has got a tic!' But in this case the nods *had* indicated approval and Norwood's six votes were added to the eighteen.

A week before the nomination contest, Sidelsky, alarmed by the
support Joyce Waring seemed to be gaining, made a surprise
move – only explicable because to him any nominee seemed
preferable to the sitting member – and asked his committee to
give its delegates to the electoral college a directive on how to vote.
It was embarrassing for him as one of Helen's original sponsors
that the branch, in a secret ballot, asked the delegates to vote
for Joyce Waring, Helen and Bell, in that order. Sidelsky still
clung to the hope that after hearing Helen speak at the contest,
and since the committee's directive was not binding, the delegates
would still be swayed into voting for Helen.

The nomination contest was held in a packed, smoke-filled room
at the Oxford Hotel, Rosebank, on 10 December 1952. It had
excited great interest, as it was the first contest of its kind in
Houghton for over ten years, and the atmosphere was tense; the

ranks of the delegates and the branch committees were swelled
by family and friends of the contestants.

Each nominee was allowed to make a fifteen-minute speech.
Bell, as sitting member, spoke first, followed by Joyce Waring.
Helen, the youngest of the candidates, as she rose to her feet
to make the speech which was to decide her future was in the grip
of an attack of influenza and appeared embarrassed and extremely
nervous. In a high-pitched and quivering voice she outlined her
case for nomination. Though she was still riddled with self-doubt
and reservations about the effects of a parliamentary career on
her family and working life, once she had accepted the challenge
it was not in her nature not to exert herself to win. Unlike Bell,
thoroughly demoralized by his unexpected lack of support within
his own constituency, or Joyce Waring, confidently relying on her
popularity, Helen had planned her campaign with painstaking
care. While leaving the lobbying to those committees which
supported her, she had personally written to every constituency
party member and had addressed all five branch nomination
meetings. Once she had assessed the political and economic
climate, she built her final speech around those issues which she
knew would appeal most to her audience. Appreciating that the
bilingual factor, normally essential to an aspirant South African
politician, hardly counted in this predominantly English-speaking
area, she glossed over her inability to speak fluent Afrikaans. She
explained in her very English accent that although she was 'nie
heeltemaal tweetaalig nie . . . ek verstaan Afrikaans sonder te veel
moeite'.* She hardly dealt with the United Party's Native Policy,
or her attitude to it, producing the party's standard bromide
that

. . . there should be better utilization of labour. There should be more
consultation with non-Europeans. The Native Reserves should be
developed to lessen non-European dependence on Europeans. Better
transport, housing and recreational facilities should be provided for
non-Europeans in urban areas.

She went on to attack the Government's increasing inroads into
the personal and economic life of the individual.

*I am not wholly bilingual, but I understand Afrikaans without too much
difficulty.

I deplore the endowing of civil servants and ministers with vast authority. I deplore the government's reluctance to surrender powers which were taken in times of emergency, such war measures as price control and import control which are largely redundant today. I strongly deplore the introduction of further bureaucratic controls over commerce and industry . . . It is my firm conviction that a young and expanding country like South Africa should encourage initiative and free enterprise . . . I pledge myself to work for a policy which implies the minimum amount of State interference in the everyday and business lives of our citizens.

Helen had fairly caught the audience's attention now, and her voice and her delivery gained in confidence and strength.

If I am returned to Parliament as part of the legislative machine that governs this country, it is important that I tell you my views on the actual role of government.

Paraphrasing her favourite economist, Adam Smith, she added:

I believe in the provision of a good defence . . . in the securing of justice between citizens and in the provision of public services such as social welfare, education, the care of the poor, the sick, the old and the indigent.

When assessing the climate in the constituency she had heard that there were objections to her youth, her sex, her political inexperience and to the fact that she was a 'futile academic theorist'. Concluding her speech, she demolished those doubts one by one.

I have served an intensive apprenticeship in political work over the last four years . . . I imagine that anyone of average intelligence can pick up parliamentary procedure in no time. Experience may easily be acquired, knowledge of economics is not so easily gained . . . I hope . . . that my main contribution . . . will be my training and my familiarity with the socio-economic problems which face our country today.

I am glad I am young, for apart from the obvious advantages of youth (which some of you may even remember) I agree with that sage who said 'unless a person has accomplished something in life by the time he is forty, he will never accomplish anything.' I have got just five years to go – one session.

I am a woman. Again agreed. But without any advance of medical science I do not think that my political aspirations need a change of sex . . . I shall not enter the arena as a feminist . . . Just as I would never ask you to vote for me simply because I am a woman, so I hope you will not refuse to vote for me simply because I am a woman. I am here to stand on my merit.[46]

Helen triumphed. When it was announced that she had won with an absolute majority, Joyce Waring left the room in tears, saying, 'What was the use? Helen had those women sewn up.'

Helen's supporters, friends and family were jubilant. Her father, beaming with pride, joked: 'Now you've won, you can resign.' But to Ellen Hellmann, as she left the meeting, Helen said: 'My God. I've got a safe seat in my hot little hands and I don't really want it.' And to a friend she later wrote:

I'm not at all sure I've done the right thing. Mosie said, 'Give it a go', and I did and the darned thing came off! Now I've got to do something to justify the confidence people have placed in me: the burning question is, can I? Even if I have the principles and try to uphold them, there is the all-powerful caucus to keep the new girl quiet. Anyway I shall try.[47]

Chapter Three 1953

By the beginning of January 1953 both the National Party and the United Democratic Front were already openly electioneering, although the election date – 15 April – was not officially announced until 12 February. The UDF, ironically, immediately found itself on the defensive, due to the publication of an announcement by the African National Congress, under the leadership of Albert Luthuli, that from June onwards it proposed to mount a passive resistance campaign against the Pass Laws, the Suppression of Communism Act, the Separate Representation of Voters Act and the Group Areas Act. Despite the assurances of the Congress leaders that their struggle was not directed against any race or national group but against unjust laws,[1] the electorate became uneasy. This uneasiness grew as the Blacks (over 8000 of whom went willingly to gaol for civil disobedience) showed a sense of self-discipline and self-sacrifice which they had never manifested before; and flared into fear when at the end of 1952 race riots in which six Whites were killed erupted in Port Elizabeth, Johannesburg, East London and Kimberley. Dr Malan immediately urged the ANC to co-operate with the Government within the apartheid framework, warned of retaliation if it did not, and set about ordering the arrest or banning of key Congress officials. At the same time, taking advantage of a special short session of Parliament which had been called to pass supplementary financial estimates, the Government rushed through two restrictive measures, the Public Safety Act[2] empowering the Governor-General to declare a State of Emergency to supersede the ordinary law of the land, and the Criminal Laws Amendment Act[3] which created two new classes of offence carrying savage penalties including lashes: that of advocating resistance to any law and that of collecting money to assist the families of resisters. The members of the United Democratic Front differed in their reaction to these Acts.

The Torch Commando Executive denounced them as 'a blank cheque by a bankrupt government . . . an insult to the very Parliament – the *volkswil* which the Nationalists profess to regard as sovereign and supreme'.[4] and called for a nation-wide strike in protest. The Labour Party, too, unequivocally opposed both Acts. But, disastrously, the United Party, the key member of the Front, bowed to pressure from its members in the Eastern Cape (where the rioting had been most severe) and, susceptible as ever to its voters' fear of the *swart gevaar*, refused to oppose the Public Safety Act. When their amendments to this Bill were rejected they meekly voted in favour of the Criminal Laws Amendment Act. Strauss, in an attempt to justify himself, said: '. . . the Defiance Campaign [of the African National Congress] has created a situation of great gravity. In these circumstances it is difficult to see on what possible grounds, the principles of the Bill could be opposed.'[5]

This action threw the United Democratic Front into disarray, and although the majority of Torchers still campaigned for the United Party, they did so with considerably diminished ardour. The liberals within the Party itself were also seriously dismayed by Strauss's action, which forced them to take an ambivalent stance. At a Houghton election meeting Helen described the Bills as '. . . Swart's latest little monsters [which] will require a great deal of plastic surgery to make them acceptable to a democratic country'.[6] The very next day she found herself embarrassingly justifying the Party's support of the Bills to the Women's Council. The Party's decision, she told them, '. . . was taken in [its] best interests as the elections are so near . . .' Strauss had pressed for safeguards which the Government had not granted. As soon as the Party was returned to power, she assured the assembled women: '. . . it would . . . not allow them [the Acts] to remain on the Statute Books any longer'.[7] But the positive stand made by the Labour Party and the Torch Commando against the Government's inroads on fundamental freedoms had been abrogated by the United Party's *niksdoen** approach.

Helen, who had been unopposed at the Nomination Court on 14 March 1953, was now the official United Party Member of

*Do-nothing.

Parliament for Houghton. New to the parliamentary game and assuming that many of her attitudes were in direct conflict with those of her parliamentary colleagues, she took care that her first cautious speeches carefully followed official party policy. Appearing at an election meeting on a platform with Professor I. S. Fourie, who was fighting the marginal seat of Edenvale, she painstakingly stressed the United Party's middle-of-the-road policy, neither of total apartheid nor of total assimilation, but of the interdependence of Black and White. By accepting the recommendations of the Fagan Commission, the United Party had recognized the existence of what she called 'permanently urbanized non-Europeans', and if returned to power, it would set up a commission to explore the possibility of setting aside freehold areas for non-Europeans in the towns, settled family conditions being a vital prerequisite for improved race relations and the combating of Communism. She pointed out that

It is among the best educated and more civilized members of the native population that resentment is greatest . . . The United Party would ensure . . . that the more moderate native leaders are given a reasonable and effective say in matters concerning their own people . . . It is for this reason that Mr Strauss has repeatedly insisted on the need for consultation with the moderate native . . . and asked for a *volkskongres** to discuss the entire problem dispassionately.

Using the Party's slogan 'Vote United Party to be free and for the right to vote again', United Party members all over the country were making ineffectual speeches similar to Helen's. The National Party simply asked the electorate to 'Vote National for the sake of Afrikanerdom and a white man's South Africa', and contented itself with demonstrating to its supporters that it had made a successful start in implementing apartheid. If returned to power, it would fulfil the *volkswil* and take steps to place the sovereignty of the *volk* and Parliament beyond any doubt. The bogies of Afrikaner nationalism, current and perennial, were brought out and dusted down. The electorate was assured that the Government would protect white South Africa against an alarming alliance consisting of 'the Mau Mau, the United Nations, the Communists and the liberalists'. 'South Africa', declared the

*National Convention.

C

Minister of Justice, emphasizing the monolithic unity of Nationalism, 'does not deserve a government of the so-called United
Front with its United Party of all sorts . . .'[8]

The country went to the polls on 15 April, and the National
Party increased its representation from 79 seats to 94 while the
United Party's seats were reduced from 65 to 57 and Labour
from 6 to 5.[9] The Nationalists were jubilant. *Die Vaderland* wrote:
'Night is falling on the United Party. Full day is breaking for
the National Party', and *Die Burger* triumphantly called the
election '. . . our most glorious hour'. For the United Front
workers the results were a terrible awakening. The majority of its
supporters had sincerely believed that the 1948 election was a
reversible aberration. By maximizing anti-Nationalist support –
and in its urban strongholds the United Party with its newly
efficient organization doubled and sometimes nearly trebled its
majorities – they had believed they had a real chance of defeating
the Government. The massive anti-government protest meetings
sponsored by the Torch Commando had created an atmosphere
of euphoria and had misled the Opposition into over-estimating
the strength of its own support outside the areas of traditional
anti-National sentiment. But the Front had failed to convert the
rest of the electorate to a different political point of view, and,
worse still, had ignored the alarm of the mass of the *platteland*
Afrikaners at the aggressive militance of Torch. These voters
had responded to the National Party's 'call to the blood' and had
closed their ranks behind the Government. The election spelt the
death of the UDF, and the Torch Commando, having lost its
raison d'être, disintegrated. The more radical of its members
joined the newly formed, multi-racial Liberal Party led by
Margaret Ballinger, an outspoken Natives' Representative in the
Assembly. Others disappeared into the cul-de-sac of a Natal-
based splinter group called the Union Federal Party. The battered
United Party was left to lick its wounds, its always precarious
unity further weakened by its second electoral defeat at the hands
of the Nationalists.

A. E. P. Robinson, the United Party member for Langlaagte
(Johannesburg), a leading United Party front-bencher, had, due
to redelimitation, lost his seat by a small margin. Helen, still far
from enthusiastic about a parliamentary career and believing

Robinson to be a very much more valuable member of the Party than herself, offered to resign Houghton in his favour. Deeply touched, he nevertheless refused, telling her that it was not right for the Party to lose her services. 'The Party leadership', he said, 'was convinced that she would be a welcome and strong addition to the parliamentary team.' Helen then approached Strauss with the same offer, hoping that he might be able to induce the ex-member for Langlaagte to change his mind: but Robinson, while as he said, fully appreciating her generosity, was adamant.[10]

Shortly after the election, Dr Malan had ingeniously attempted to drive a further wedge into the United Party's crumbling unity. '. . . It is', he said, 'only regrettable that liberalism has penetrated so deeply into the United Party that one can distinguish between a right and a left wing.' On the other hand, the National Party would, he asserted, always be prepared to hold discussions with any section of the Opposition except its left wing.[11] Strauss called a meeting of the new United Party caucus in Pretoria to formulate strategy to combat this kind of attack. Here the reluctant member for Houghton met for the first time her fellow-recruits to the back benches: Jan Steytler, an Afrikaans doctor representing Queenstown in the Eastern Cape; Ray Swart, a former United Party Youth Leader, and, as representative for Zululand, one of the youngest members of Parliament; Townley Owen-Williams, the excitable member for Durban (Musgrave), described by himself in his election manifesto as '. . . a man who is prepared to take the practical consequences of a moral outlook and who wishes to introduce a little cold logic and commonsense into a welter of emotional prejudice'. With John Cope and 'Sakkies' Fourie, these new members, shortly to be joined after a by-election in November by Ronald Butcher, member for Durban (Berea), soon fell into a working relationship founded on the initial conviction that the electorate had given them a mandate to insist upon the retention of the Coloureds on the Common Roll. They came to the Pretoria meeting believing that the Party intended carrying on the Constitutional fight. Jan Steytler, in particular, voiced their feelings when, addressing the meeting, he said: '. . . we have just fought an election on the basis of retaining the Common Roll for the Coloureds and I look upon this as a mandate from my constituents to adhere to the policies which I . . . believe

. . . are fundamental to the United Party'. But the new members had been misled, probably by the enthusiasm of Torch sympathizers, invariably in a majority at election meetings, into believing that the issue of the Coloured vote was a linch-pin of party policy. At Pretoria they were taken aback to find that a strong conservative element, led by Bailey Bekker, the Transvaal Leader, and supported by an outspoken group of members,* appeared to have the firm intention of selling the Coloureds down the river. Obliquely attacking Strauss's leadership by alleging that they had not been consulted on the formation of the United Democratic Front, this group now demanded a radical re-orientation of party policy. The only way to election victory, they said, taking up a time-honoured South African political stance, was to move to the right rather than to the left, and, although they left it unsaid, they were clearly suggesting some form of compromise with the National Party over the Coloured vote. Strauss defended his leadership by appointing the Cape and Natal leaders, de Villiers Graaff and Douglas Mitchell, to investigate Bekker's accusations against him. He avoided adopting a clear policy stand on the Coloured vote question by issuing a vague statement in which the Party re-dedicated itself to the principle of national unity on the basis of 'a broad South Africanism and of co-operation with non-Europeans'.

Despite the already visible rifts in the defeated Party, Helen returned to Johannesburg confident about its future. Through her inexperience she failed to recognize the full significance of the right wing's covert hostility to Strauss's leadership and believed that the Party's avoidance of a definite position on the Coloured vote issue would resolve itself at the first caucus meeting in Cape Town. And having met the other new back-benchers and heard Jan Steytler speak, she realized that there were sufficient liberally inclined members to form an influential 'reform' core within the caucus. On this last point she was right. The seven new members, initially brought together by one shared principle, quickly became known, through their unyielding and vocal opposition to apartheid, as the United Party's 'liberal' back-bench, and in 1959 it was they who were to lead the exodus from the

*Arthur Barlow (Hospital), Frank Waring (Orange Grove), Blaar Coetzee (North Rand), Abraham Jonker (Gardens).

flesh-pots of the official opposition caucus into the Progressive wilderness.

Helen spent the next six weeks making her preparations for her departure for Cape Town. She placed her house and family in the hands of 'Haakie', her Dutch housekeeper. She resigned her post at the University and made her final report as Honorary Information Officer to the Women's Council, blaming the election defeat on unfavourable delimitation rather than bad organization or lack of voter support. At the end of June, full of excitement and apprehension, she left for Cape Town and the Opening of Parliament.

The first session of the Eleventh Union Parliament opened in winter, and a Cape winter with its sea mists, steady drizzle, dank, dripping foliage and cold, grey seas, can be very depressing. Having nowhere to live in Cape Town, Helen first stayed, because of its proximity to Parliament, at the Mount Nelson Hotel – a vast and ornate edifice which has been likened to a Union Castle luxury liner permanently grounded at the foot of Table Mountain. But the hotel proved as cheerless as the Cape winter. Helen felt disorientated and uprooted, and only began to settle down when she moved to the more modern Clifton Hotel. From the Clifton she wrote more cheerfully to Mosie: 'Hotel is fine – when I'm there. Views very rewarding . . . I have a quiet drink and watch the sea at sunset when [I am] home.'[12]

Her initial depression extended to Parliament itself. Once the excitement generated by the official Opening on 3 July 1953 was over, and Mosie, described by his wife as 'a lonely little baldhead among all those nodding plumes' as he watched the proceedings from the Wives' Gallery, had returned to Johannesburg, Helen began to feel more and more lonely. Part of the blame for this lay with the United Party's Chief Whip, Jack Higgerty, who, pre-occupied with internal caucus tensions, failed either to bring the new back-benchers together with the other members, or to instruct them in their parliamentary duties, responsibilities and rights. After two weeks in Parliament, Helen, in desperation, even had to ask him to introduce her to the Speaker, a function which Higgerty should automatically have performed. In spite of her initial contact with the new back-benchers in Pretoria she was still only on nodding terms with them.

Higgerty's inattention, unfriendly though it appeared to Helen, was explicable. The dissension which had first manifested itself at the Pretoria meeting in May had grown during June. Shrewdly sensing the growing discord within the Opposition and still lacking his necessary two-thirds majority to disenfranchise the Coloureds, Dr Malan continued his overtures to the United Party's more obviously conservative members, assuring them that they would be welcome on the Nationalist benches, while, within the United Party itself, members exacerbated the confusion by making widely disparate public statements about their party's attitude to the Coloured voters.

At the caucus meeting, traditionally held on the eve of the Opening of Parliament, the new back-benchers became aware that a possible compromise on the Coloured franchise, which in May they had believed to be mere kite flying, was in fact under serious consideration by a large section of the Party. In an address to the caucus Bailey Bekker asked members to examine closely the reasons for the Nationalists' second electoral victory. He believed that the Party's insistence on retention of the Coloureds on the Common Roll was unpopular with the conservative *platteland* electorate. Provided that the Government could suggest a formula for circumnavigating the constitutional issue, he told the caucus, the Party should accept the need for compromise or at least for a drastic revision of policy. Here was an issue with which Helen could come to grips. Bekker's pragmatic approach to what she saw as a fundamental moral principle was a challenge.

She wrote to Mosie in early July:

I wanted to put your mind at rest about my apparent unhappiness. I have settled down now and feel that I am really fulfilling a very necessary function in the caucus – things are very tricky at the moment and I find that someone has to help organize opposition to the section that appears bent on 'negotiations' at the time when the UP was really coming out well on the Constitutional crisis, the idiots!! Needless to say there's more to it than has come out in the papers . . . I am thoroughly unpopular with the Blaar Coetzee, Waring element (Bailey is one of them too) but I couldn't care less because I know I am on solid ground and that there is a very good element in the caucus that thinks the way I do.[13]

Thus Helen found a challenge in consolidating opposition to Bekker within the caucus: she also found that she no longer had time to be depressed since her days were crammed with routine work. She had 'like the rest of you cynical tax payers', she informed her constituents much later, 'always thought that lolling around on the benches was a pretty easy way of extracting £1400 per annum from the Treasury'. Instead, she found, she told Mosie,

... that I ... have hardly a moment to myself ... I have been put on the Select Committee to study the Women's Disabilities Bill for opening my big mouth ... the Public Accounts Committee three mornings a week, caucus on another, Management (i.e. who will speak on what each day) every day at 12 and Party group meetings (Native Affairs, Labour and Commerce) on other mornings. Have to be in the House all afternoon (new girl must sit and learn) and from next week we have Night Sittings three times per week. So not much time to answer mail, prepare speeches, study Bills, let alone get into mischief.[14]

As one of four women members, Helen shared an office with veteran Member for Jeppe, Bertha Solomon, and an ultra-conservative back-bencher from Drakensberg (Natal), Sannie van Niekerk. (The other woman MP, Margaret Ballinger, by virtue of her position as a Natives' Representative and as the Liberal Party leader, had an office to herself.) The three ladies thus flung together found that their close proximity generated tension. Bertha Solomon had achieved her life-long aim early in the session with the passing of the Removal of the Legal Disabilities of Women Act, and felt that she was, in her own words, 'entitled to sit back and take a bit of a break'. Sannie van Niekerk – nicknamed by Helen the Dragon of the Drakensberg* – resented this attitude and used, Helen recalls, to 'come in sniffing and go out sniffing'. Helen became a kind of buffer between the other two women. In the mornings all three would assemble in the office, Bertha chattering and gossiping, Helen frantically trying to write speeches and the formidable Mrs van Niekerk glaring silently at them both. In the evenings Bertha, always meticulous in matters of dress, would change her clothes in the office, evoking once an infuriated hiss from Sannie: 'This is a Lady Members' study, not a Ladies' Dressing Room.' 'Weally,' lisped Bertha to Helen, 'I do think I'm

*A play on the English meaning of the Afrikaans word Draken=a Dragon.

entitled to wespect. After all, I've been here much longer than *that* woman.'

Helen, whom the *platteland*-bred Sannie despised and mistrusted as an intellectual liberal, stood high in Bertha Solomon's esteem: although she emphasized that she was not a feminist, she chose to make her traditionally non-controversial maiden speech in support of Mrs Solomon's Bill.[15] She was unfortunate that her début came on Budget Day: her speech was overshadowed by that of the Minister of Finance and consequently received no attention from the Press.

My maiden speech was of course an anti-climax after the Budget – the Press Gallery empty as all the boys were busy getting their Budget stories to their papers. But I think I spoke well and my nervous system stood up to the strain very well – hardly a 'palp' to my amazement . . . Poor old Bertha was most put out on account of her most glorious hour being overlaid, so to speak, by the Budget . . . but I really was rather glad, because chaining myself to the railings at Joubert Park [central Johannesburg] isn't really my line of country and I'd rather be given publicity – if any – over a more vital subject.[16]

The chance was coming. In his speech from the Throne the Governor-General, Dr E. J. Jansen, had stipulated that the session would be devoted to extending apartheid legislation. There would, firstly, be a Joint Sitting of both Houses in an attempt to circumvent the entrenched clauses with a view to placing the Coloured voters on a separate roll. In addition, the Government intended passing several major Bills, including one to transfer black education from the control of the Department of Education to that of the Department of Native Affairs. Other measures designed to extend apartheid into the fabric of South African life were a Bill introducing a new process for settling black industrial disputes alternative to, and separate from, the trade union movement; a Bill to set up a statutory body empowered to remove Blacks from the 'black spots', or African townships in white areas of Johannesburg, and re-settle them outside the city, and finally a Bill enabling the Government to override a recent Supreme Court decision which made it illegal not to provide separate but equal facilities for different race groups. 'Such a decision', said the Minister of Justice in a rare moment of candour, 'threatens the implementation of apartheid because to provide equal facilities is impossible and impractable.'[17]

The Government's implacable determination to extend apartheid imposed intense strain upon the United Party, now divided into three clearly discernible groups – a conservative agrarian Afrikaner wing led by Bailey Bekker, a centre backed by English-speaking financiers and industrialists led by Harry Oppenheimer, and a small but increasingly vocal liberal wing centred around the new back-benchers. Each group was battling to influence Strauss, who by now had shown himself to be more of an ineffectual chairman than a party leader. The Tuesday morning caucus meetings became a long series of wrangles over policy and the Party's attitude to apartheid legislation.

When the first Joint Sitting of the session was convened in July 1953 to debate the removal of the Coloureds from the Common Roll, the United Party, maintaining its pre-election stand, moved an amendment at the Second Reading rejecting the principle of the Bill and asking for a Select Committee to consider the entire non-European problem (Strauss also suggested that consultation with non-Europeans themselves might be beneficial). The impact of the amendment was, however, lost when both Bailey Bekker and Arthur Barlow took it upon themselves to carry the United Party's suggestion even further by appealing for the colour problem to be lifted out of politics, an act which would make it possible, they informed Parliament, for the United Party to co-operate with the Government in the implementation of its policies.

The row that immediately erupted within the United Party caucus was violent. In an attempt to justify their action, the conservatives argued that the Coloured vote was unimportant to the Party and for the sake of a greater South African unity a compromise agreement had to be reached with the Nationalists. And the following weekend it became known that, in an attempt to reach an understanding with the Nationalists, three emissaries of the conservative wing, Barlow, Waring and a prominent front-bencher, P. V. Pocock, had been to Groote Schuur, Dr Malan's official residence, to 'drink coffee' with him.

Speculation as to the possibility of a major United Party defection to the National Party mounted. The liberals were appalled. In particular, Helen's violent contempt for the pusillanimity of the Party's right and her reiterated argument that the United Party had a mandate from its voters to honour its promises to the Coloureds and that the Coloured vote was not theirs to barter with, focused conservative attention upon her and earned her the bitter enmity of the right wing.

Strauss, torn between the liberals' angry insistence on no-compromise and the conservatives' attempts at *toenadering*,* wrote a letter (whose contents were never made public) to Malan setting out terms which he believed would enable an agreement to be reached between their parties over the Coloured franchise. Cautious negotiations opened between the two parties and Bekker again attempted to challenge Strauss's leadership by bringing up the vague charges he had raised at the meeting in Pretoria in May. Had he simply attacked Strauss over the Party's attitude to the Coloured vote, the outcome might have been quite different. But the Central Executive, the Union Head Committee and the caucus itself – with the liberals rallying strongly in favour of Strauss – once more rejected his transparently fabricated charges and passed a vote of confidence in their leader, the only dissenting votes being those of Bekker, Coetzee and Jonker.

When the Joint Sitting resumed in mid-September no accommodation had been reached between the two parties. Malan, his eye firmly fixed on the dissident conservatives, appealed in Parliament for twelve or thirteen 'right-minded' United Party members to help him remove the Coloureds from the Common Roll. Bekker requested Strauss to allow the United Party a free vote, a request which Strauss refused, claiming, probably correctly, that the postponement of the Joint Sitting had been no more than a clumsy endeavour by the Nationalists to split the United Party. At the third reading of the South Africa Act Amendment Bill, the Government failed to achieve its two-thirds majority.

Malan now introduced an Appeal Court Bill, designed to create a special division of the Supreme Court Appellate Division which would deal only with constitutional affairs. Bekker, now firmly established as the leader of the United Party dissidents, made a speech from the floor of the House violently attacking what he called the United Party's 'ultra liberals', such as Helen, for

*Coming together, i.e. for the purposes of coalition.

forcing it to 'deviate from the traditional Hertzog–Smuts path', and took it upon himself to beg Malan not to go ahead with the Bill. This was too much for the United Party caucus. It was decided that the 'day-to-day' loyalty grudgingly offered by Bekker, Waring, Coetzee, Barlow and Jonker (Helen in a speech to the caucus compared their attitude to promising one's wife 'night-by-night loyalty') could no longer be tolerated and Waring, Barlow and Coetzee were expelled from the caucus. Jonker and Bekker resigned to join them.

The departure of the five rebels from the caucus, and subsequently from the Party, was regarded as a triumph for the liberal wing. Helen wrote:

I am sure the tide of events is turning in our favour . . . The UP's task . . . is to present a clear alternative to the Nationalists' policy of repression . . . I do believe that it is vitally necessary to plan in a progressive direction, not to allow emotional ideology to cloud the basic economic issues that so greatly affect the welfare of the entire population, and to seek the goodwill and co-operation of the non-Europeans.[18]

But while the constitutional clash and the United Party's internal difficulties appeared to take up most of its members' time, in Parliament itself apartheid legislation continued to flow steadily on to the Statute Book.

Helen, who had been put on the Public Accounts Committee and made Secretary of the United Party's Labour Group, was also appointed, to her great pleasure, to the Party's Native Affairs Group under the benevolent chairmanship of Douglas Smit, member for East London (City) and a former Minister of Native Affairs in the Smuts government. Although the committee itself mirrored the divisions within the caucus, Smit, whom Helen described as a 'grand old man', was an excellent chairman and meticulous in the performance of his duties. He saw to it that the newer members were fully instructed in the implications of each Bill. He taught them how to move effective amendments, but most of all he prepared them to meet with equanimity and with courage the vicious onslaughts that the Minister of Native Affairs, Dr Hendrik Frensch Verwoerd, was preparing to make upon the lives of black South Africans.

Through the vast bureaucratic organ of the Department of Native Affairs, through the multitude of Native Laws which, already numerous in 1948, had proliferated alarmingly after the National Party came into power, Verwoerd controlled the lives of Blacks everywhere. He himself was a frightening figure. A doctor of psychology, one of Malan's earliest supporters, a former editor of the pro-Republican Transvaal Nationalist newspaper, *Die Transvaler*, and a close friend and confidant of the National Party's Transvaal Leader, J. G. Strijdom, he alone was felt by Strijdom (who in turn convinced the less *kragdadige** Malan) to possess the ability, ingenuity and force to convert the apartheid policy from theory into practice. His was not a prepossessing personality: his light grey eyes seemed opaque; his soft feminine mouth wore a perpetual smile even when making the most apocalyptic threats. Though a mediocre orator, he had a mesmeric effect upon supporters and opponents alike, as, speaking often for hours on end without notes, he would develop long, involved, but apparently highly logical sequences of arguments. He terrified Helen when she first found herself in a confrontation with him. She has since remarked that such was the hypnotic effect of his personality that she often had to remind herself that, since his basic premises were false, the arguments he was so painstakingly constructing were false too.

From 1950 onwards Verwoerd, with the apartheid theoretician Willi Eiselen as his Departmental Secretary, had been revolutionizing the Department of Native Affairs, transforming apartheid from a crude policy of *wit baasskap* into a more defensible philosophy of 'separate development' in which he envisaged a number of ethnic African homelands, gradually evolving into independent States which ultimately would link up with white South Africa in a confederation of self-governing units. He divided apartheid's transitional period into three stages: first, a continuation and even an increase in the flow of migrant Africans into white urban areas to meet white labour demands; second, the point of saturation when the labour needs were fully met and the flow stopped; and, finally, the period of exodus, when African labour would be replaced gradually by Whites and Africans would be repatriated

---

*Strong, powerful.

to their now developed homelands. This would be the climax and fulfilment of the ideal.[19]

In his first two years as Minister, Verwoerd abolished the Natives' Representative Council, the advisory body which had been established in 1936 as a sop to the disenfranchised Cape Africans. This action completed, he set about dealing with the weakest link in his proposed apartheid chain – the urban Africans. Once the Group Areas Act of 1950 was on the Statute Book, Verwoerd expedited the passing of a series of complementary laws through Parliament. These were the Prevention of Illegal Squatting Act[20] the Native Laws Amendment Act,[21] and the Natives (Abolition of Passes and Co-ordination of Documents) Act.[22] By the beginning of the 1953 session, the controls on urban Africans had been successfully tightened. Further pressure would now be brought to bear through increased regulation of African labour and education.

The first move in this next stage was the introduction of the Native Labour (Settlement of Disputes) Bill,[23] creating arbitration machinery which, the Minister of Labour, B. J. Schoeman, claimed, would cause African workers to have no interest in the formation of trade unions.[24] The Government's true intention was once and for all to prevent urbanized Africans from forming such unions. Schoeman considered that the Whites would be committing race suicide if they give them such an incentive.[25]

As one of the United Party's spokesmen on Economic Affairs, Helen attacked the Bill on the grounds that, as Africans were 'rapidly becoming aware that it is in their interests to organize and to act collectively . . . it is essential that Native trade unions be accepted as part of the industrial structure so that better and more responsible Native workers would be attracted into them and into the leadership of such trade unions'. The migratory labour system, she continued, militated very strongly against Native trade unions because of the high labour turnover and she drew attention to the rapidly emerging African urban proletariat, whose needs and aspirations were being ignored at the peril of the dominant race.[26] Helen's arguments indicated the trend of thought the more progressive members of the United Party were beginning to take in stressing the need for recognition of urban Africans as an integral part of South Africa's economy.

However, once one of their amendments had been accepted by the Minister, the United Party did not oppose the third reading of the Bill. The new law reinforced the foundations of South Africa's industrial legislation as it affected Blacks. It re-defined the term 'employee' as it appeared in the Industrial Conciliation Act of 1937*[27] so as to exclude all Africans, prevented registered trade unions from having African members and prohibited strikes by African employees as well as sympathetic strikes by workers of other racial groups. It provided for the setting up of separate industrial conciliation machinery for certain categories of African workers. While not prohibiting African trade unions, it denied them official recognition and status, thus placing them at a considerable disadvantage when negotiating with employers.[28]

The acceptance of the amended Bill increased Helen's slowly growing dissatisfaction with the United Party.

It is an unrealistic measure. To refuse recognition to the Native trade unions, to hope they will die when the Natives are becoming more and more integrated into industrial life, is futile. We will find that these trade unions will fall into the hands of the less responsible elements among Native leaders . . . [when they could have] been guided and controlled and made useful instruments of peace and order.[29]

The last apartheid measure to be introduced into Parliament by Verwoerd in 1953 was the Bantu Education Act,[30] the fruits of a commission of inquiry headed by Eiselen, which had reported in 1951, conveniently advising that African education be placed under the control of the Minister of Native Affairs – *Die Groot Induna*† – as Verwoerd so proudly called himself. This education would be suited to a Bantu‡ environment, would be based on tribal ethics and would be taught through the medium of the different ethnic languages.[31] The report effectively paved the way for the abolition of missionary influence, which had long annoyed the Nationalists, who claimed that the church schools (almost the

*Re-enactment and amendment of the Act of 1924 (see p. 20 'Propolitical').

†The Big Chief. Reportedly Verwoerd's own description of himself at this time to his wife. (A. Hepple)

‡When Verwoerd became Minister of Native Affairs the collective noun Bantu (the people) came into vogue in Nationalist and subsequently general parlance to describe the African population of South Africa, succeeding 'Native', which itself had succeeded 'Kaffir'.

only sources of African education in the rural areas) were turning out 'black Englishmen' imbued with a set of philosophical and ethical values they could not appreciate. This view was commonly held in South Africa even outside the National Party in the early fifties, where even a progressive journal could write: '. . . the academically educated non-European, with no roots in reality and his head full of book-learning, can be a most irritating person. He can also be a social misfit and a political danger.'[32]

Introducing the Bill Verwoerd assured the House that although he had no intention of creating a personal empire by taking upon himself the onerous task of administering Native education, he felt that the Native Affairs Department knew better than any other department what was good for Africans. The present system of education, he assured the House, simply led to feelings of frustration and hostility. Bantu Education would teach Africans 'from childhood that equality with Europeans is not for them'.[33] The United Party managed to oppose this Bill without further internal discussion. Even the conservative elements could not argue with the liberal view, as expressed by Helen, that it '. . . is quite futile to try and keep Natives in a perpetual intellectual twilight and lead them back to a tribal Eden'. However, in spite of all the Opposition's efforts, the Bill was passed and came into force on 1 January 1954.

As the 1953 session drew to a close in October, the Government made yet another attempt to disenfranchise the Coloureds. On 2 October a Second Joint Sitting was called to introduce a short Bill restricted to the separate representation of Coloured voters. Strauss, fortified by the defection of the Bekker group, reiterated the United Party's principles on the Coloured franchise – consultation and co-operation with the Coloureds and the removal of the 'non-European problem' from the political arena. He demanded that the Government cease tampering with the independence of the courts and with the entrenched clauses of the South Africa Act. Having made his point, he allowed the United Party to vote at the Bill's second reading, with the Government in favour of a Select Committee which would study the whole question of the coloured franchise and report its findings to the next session. On that co-operative and faintly hopeful note the session ended.

Helen returned to Johannesburg. She had established a name

for herself as a clear and concise debater, whose only fault, if fault it could be called, was the use of too many back-up statistics. ('You read too many books,' the Minister of Labour had accused her.) At her first report-back meeting, an innovation she introduced and which subsequently became traditional in the Houghton constituency, she said: 'I was surprised at the completely absorbing nature of the work. There is also a tendency which I am determined to guard against – of becoming cloistered in the atmosphere of the House, of forgetting the outside world.'[34]

Her experience in the caucus had led her to believe that the liberal wing was in the ascendant within the United Party. This belief seemed to be borne out when, at the Party's Transvaal Congress in late October, Bekker, attempting to vindicate his own and his supporters' actions in *toenadering* with the Government and challenging Strauss's leadership, appealed to the Party's *platteland* supporters not to deviate from the traditional United Party conservative path. The Transvaal liberals rallied sufficient support to have Bekker expelled from the Party by a small majority. His supporters formed a short-lived splinter-group called first the Independent United Party and subsequently the Conservative Party, before coming to rest in their spiritual home on the Nationalist benches. Because they had refused to resign their seats on leaving the Party, the triumphant liberals, determined never again to allow conservative deserters to retain hard-fought United Party seats, together with Max Borkum, the chairman of the Witwatersrand Action Committee, drafted the following pledge to be inserted on all Transvaal candidate nomination forms: 'If, in due course, I am elected to fill the vacancy and thereafter cease to be a member of the United Party, I will resign my seat.'

Flushed with their victory, they had no idea how ironically this pledge was to rebound on them later. But Helen and her fellow-reformists were confident that Strauss, grateful for the support they had given him throughout the Bekker crisis, would listen to them with sympathy and lend his support to their efforts to metamorphose the political philosophy of the United Party. The disastrous scale of their self-deception was soon to be made clear to them.

Helen told her constituents:

It was a difficult session, with its background of political intrigue. If it has cleared the air and removed from our ranks those who are uncomfortable in opposition, who look for short cuts, who think they can play politics with the Nats, it will have served a purpose. I hope we will return to Cape Town on 29 January, smaller in numbers but stronger in resolve, determined at all costs to maintain our integrity and our principles. Only by so doing can we justify the faith of over three-quarters of a million voters.[35]

Chapter Four 1954-5

Helen faced her second session of Parliament in a completely different frame of mind. She had gained in experience and self-confidence and her own constituency had remained unaffected by the internal strife generated within the Party by the conservative revolt. 'Your solidarity', she told her committee, 'is . . . of enormous value since it enables me to speak confidently, secure in the knowledge of your support.' She was now an acknowledged leading member of what the Nationalists disparagingly referred to as 'the liberalistic circle' and which Helen preferred to call 'the progressive group' within the United Party; those members who, since they had entered Parliament in 1953 had implacably opposed every move towards apartheid and, with one voice, had expressed an identical principle: no compromise with the Nationalists. 'I have been described as a liberal by members of the Government,' Helen said at this time. 'If you talk about principles to them you immediately become a liberal.'[1] The purging of the conservatives had temporarily terminated the internecine warfare within the Party's ranks and, at long last, she felt it would be able to function efficiently as an Opposition. This belief was largely borne out through the session as the Party consistently presented articulate opposition to the Government's continuing avalanche of apartheid legislation.

That the liberals were indeed effectively influencing Strauss's thinking became apparent during the 1954 Part Appropriation Debate when Professor 'Sakkies' Fourie made his momentous (at least in South African political eyes) 'economic integration' speech.

He asked a startled House:

What is the meaning of integration except pure co-operation? [This] movement, this process of co-operation commenced in the days of van

Riebeeck, has grown and become stronger and bigger until this very day, and it has by no means ended . . . The only salvation of our future . . . is that we should continue with and have a great deal more economic integration or co-operation.

Immediately a National Party member rose and asked whether this meant that economic integration 'must necessarily lead to political integration?' Without hesitation Fourie replied: 'Yes . . . one cannot support economic integration and imagine that one can forever maintain political disintegration or political apartheid.'[2]

Helen adopted Fourie's concept of economic integration developing it with the clarity which the Nationalists so disliked. She declared:

The United Party believes that South Africa depends on . . . two pillars, European enterprise and skill on one hand and the availability of Native labour on the other . . . The Government has decided to put aside its original idea of total apartheid . . . except in the nightmarish dreams of the Minister of Native Affairs . . . He finds that apartheid will be realized in the 'long run'. I would remind him of the words of the famous British economist . . . 'in the long run we are all dead!' . . . The pity of it is that if the present Minister is allowed to pursue his way unchecked, many of us will be dead in the short run, because the policy he is implementing now, in order to attain success in 200 years . . . is making it utterly impossible for Europeans and non-Europeans to live in amity in this part of the continent of Africa.

She then launched a savage attack on Verwoerd, who, she said:

should stop trying to fool the public by quoting little deviations from the norm in order to prove he is managing to stop integration . . . The test of the degree of economic integration is not the number of workless Natives who are ejected from the towns but the number of Natives who are employed in industry and on the mines and in domestic service and on European farms, and no amount of evasive action by the Government can prove anything but that integration has taken place at an increasing rate over the last fifteen years, and especially for the last six years, due to industrial expansion . . . The Government cannot continue to refuse to recognize the existence of a permanently urbanized Native labour force, and the natural consequence of that is to realize that Natives in urban areas have to have certain property rights and certain rights of ownership . . . It is utterly impossible to continue to employ the Native and then behave as if he is not here.[3]

That Helen and the other progressives should logically expand and extend 'Sakkies' Fourie's belief in economic integration was only to be expected. But that Strauss, when challenged to state where he stood by the Government, should unequivocally support Fourie, was less expected. To Helen's surprise and delight, her leader announced that

. . . the ultimate political rights and the ultimate position of the non-European will still have to be faced and defined . . . we are prepared to make that experiment. We are prepared to take that forward step and we are prepared to see whether African people, when you give them that opportunity, are prepared to learn and understand the demands of democracy.[4]

Helen's elation was understandable. For the first time since its defeat in 1948, the United Party seemed to be developing a policy which offered a clear-cut alternative to apartheid. Strauss was making no attempt to placate his right wing and had appointed one committee in each of the provinces to review and explore the Party's Native policy and report with their recommendations to the Union Congress in November. It was perhaps an advantage to them that the National Party's policy had been newly enunciated with uncompromising clarity by Verwoerd early in the parliamentary session. 'Apartheid', the Minister said, 'comprises a whole multiplicity of phenomena. It comprises the political sphere; it is necessary in the social sphere; it is aimed at in Church matters; it is relevant to every sphere of life.'[5] In answer, Strauss declared: 'The United Party is not afraid of searching our hearts . . . and of testing and re-testing our non-European policy against the circumstances and the facts of today and tomorrow, in order to see that we get only what is best for South Africa.'[6]

At last, Helen thought, the Party was beginning to wake up and appreciate the logical consequences of black economic integration. She told her constituents:

It has been said and rightly so . . . that the economic integration of the Native is a fact and not a policy. And of course, it is an ineluctable fact. More than two-thirds of the Natives live outside the Native Reserves – three million of them on European farms and two million of them in the so-called European urban areas. That many of them are migratory workers who come and go between town and country does not affect the basic issue. These people are all integrated into our economic structure. . . .[7]

Helen was too junior a member of the Party hierarchy to be appointed to the Transvaal's investigating committee. She was disappointed – but only slightly. As secretary of the Party's Labour Group, she was fully engaged in planning the Party's attack on the Industrial Conciliation Bill due to come before Parliament, and in addition Smit had chosen her to be one of the main speakers against Verwoerd's two new apartheid Bills – the Native Trust and Land Amendment Bill[8] and the Natives Resettlement Bill.[9]

Bernard Friedman, liberal front-bencher for Hillbrow in assessing the first of these Bills, said: 'This Government, like Abraham Lincoln, has discovered that a society cannot exist half slave and half free, but unlike Abraham Lincoln, their remedy is to make us all slaves.'[10] Helen reacted even more strongly. The Native Trust and Land Amendment Bill was abolishing a very important principle – the obligation imposed by the original legislation upon the Minister of Native Affairs to find alternative accommodation for displaced Africans. She abhorred the Government's cynicism:

You cannot just divide up Native labour as if Natives were beasts! This Act is clearly a form of forced labour. Natives can now be driven off European land and since the Reserves are full and access to the towns is barred by a variety of laws which restrict the mobility of Natives, those driven off will perforce have to accept employment on farms on any conditions the farmers care to offer.[11]

But she kept her real anger for the second measure – the highly contentious Western Areas Removals Scheme or Natives Resettlement Bill (popularly known as the 'Black Spots Bill'). The Bill's origins lay in the recommendations of the Mentz Commission, which some two and a half years previously had produced a scheme for the removal of the inhabitants of the Western Native Township, an African location which, due to Johannesburg's rapid post-war growth, had become a 'black spot' surrounded by predominantly white residential suburbs, to Meadowlands, a new location some fifteen miles to the south, on the outskirts of the city. It was probably not coincidental that F. Mentz, the chairman of the Commission, was the MP for Westdene, a Johannesburg constituency which bordered on the Western Areas. On the surface the Mentz Commission's arguments were logical. Three of the four townships destined to be evacuated were grossly over-crowded,* with an average of 150 people per acre of shanties. There was hardly a spot of green anywhere. Thin dogs scavenged in the dusty roads and backyards, which in summer became seas of mud. Innumerable grubby little shops and shebeens flourished. In spite of their fearful squalor, these areas were prized by the Africans for one reason and one reason alone: within the Western Areas they could own freehold houses. It was this fact rather than philanthropic ideas of slum clearance which was behind the National Party's insistence on implementing the Western Areas Removal Scheme. 'There must be no confusion of thinking that a location counts as a black patch,' declared Verwoerd categorically. 'It is the ownership of land which determines whether it is a European area or not.'

It was this combination of forced removal and loss of freehold privileges for Africans which made the Bill both odious and emotive to large numbers of urban Opposition supporters. Helen received hundreds of postcards and letters from her constituents demanding that she should use every weapon at her disposal to fight the removals. She took, she said, great pleasure in complying with her constituents' requests since they represented her own personal feelings concerning the Bill.

In her speech Helen was at great pains to stress that the United Party did not, as some National Party members claimed, object to mass slum clearance nor, obviously, to improved living con-ditions for Africans, but to the fact that the Government was clearing the Western Areas:

. . . not because they were slums, not even because they were adjacent to European residential areas, but because Natives owned the land.

She quoted Verwoerd's infamous epigram: '. . . the presence of the Native does not mean the permanency of the individual'.

---

*The Western Native Township itself was a respectable municipal housing scheme. The other locations concerned, Sophiatown, Martindale and Newclare, could not be called anything but slums.

That remark is tantamount to saying that he recognizes that there is oxygen in the air, but he does not recognize that he breathes it, because exactly the same thing applies as far as the permanency of the Native in European areas is concerned. Whether the Minister recognizes it or not, whether he likes it or not, the Natives are in the towns and they are in the towns to stay . . .[12]

While other United Party speakers, such as Marais Steyn, quibbled about the finer legal points of the removals, even stressing (for the benefit of the poorer white electorate, whose residential areas often adjoined African townships) that the Party was still pledged to wholesale removals in principle, subject to several conditions which did not exclude compulsion, Helen made it clear that her primary concern was the real suffering and injustice to which thousands of Africans were about to be subjected. Her unequivocal stand and her demand that Verwoerd should '. . . as a simple matter of elementary justice . . . grant . . . freehold for freehold [since] . . . these people are no migrant workers, but people who have saved, who have scraped and who have finally managed to buy themselves a little piece of land in one of the very few areas where they are allowed to buy land'[13] earned her the soubriquet 'Salvation Army lassie' from the Independent United Party member, Arthur Barlow, while Frank Waring insinuated that Helen's impassioned speech was made to salve her liberal conscience. 'To me', he said, 'a man's property is as important to him as his liberty, but of course the hon. Member for Houghton has not got any worries about property.'[14] He went on to charge that the United Party had fallen into the hands of 'a lot of young people who have peculiar ideas about liberalism'.

Verwoerd could only answer the Opposition attacks with the old defence of *swart gevaar*. He thundered that the United Party, controlled by its liberal wing, would not only go so far as making 850 morgen (1785 acres) near Johannesburg available for ownership of Natives but would not exclude a single inch of the area of white South Africa,[15] a statement which evoked a panic-stricken rejoinder from the United Party front bench to the effect that the Party had no intention of allowing Natives to acquire freehold rights in European areas.[16]

Helen had been greatly stimulated by this debate, easily the most heated of the session. Her aggressive assault on the 'Black

Spots Bill' firmly fixed her deep concern with justice in the minds of the members opposite and she had learnt to shrug off the anti-semitic *sotto voce* wisecracks which emanated from the 'kitchen' of the House (the area of the cross-benches acoustically and visually 'dead' to the Speaker) and which so infuriated her Natal bench-mate, Ronnie Butcher. She was also learning that riposte and mimicry were far more effective weapons than the furious outbursts of temper which had marked her early political career. She was becoming absorbed by the question of the extension of economic and political rights for Blacks and spoke increasingly frequently on Native affairs, but her main areas of concern were still economic affairs and immigration. The Western Areas Removal Scheme had aroused bitter anger in her but it was the Industrial Conciliation Amendment Bill which she considered the most significant measure introduced that session.

The Government had designed this far-reaching measure to extend the legislative colour bar to the manufacturing industry. Its most controversial clause (clause 77) enabled the Minister to set aside certain jobs for persons of different races; to limit the strike weapon; to forbid inter-racial trade unions and to establish industrial tribunals with wide powers. Introducing the Bill, the Minister of Labour admitted that the Government's first consideration was not to maintain economic laws but 'to ensure the continued existence of the European race in South Africa'.

In Helen's view fear was in fact the motivating force behind the introduction of the Industrial Conciliation Bill. The Suppression of Communism Act[17] – amended that very session as part of the Government's sedulity in loophole plugging – had already quietly removed a number of trade union leaders from the industrial scene, but even more legislation would be required if the Government was to tighten its grip on organized labour and to continue its plan of circumscribing the trade unions' control of their membership. Helen told the House that the Government had introduced the Bill in order to protect a certain class of European workers which required artificial protection if it was to hold its own against competition from non-Europeans. 'The bald fact,' she said, 'is that in a dynamic society we cannot give security to all groups at any point in time.' Clause 77 she described as an untimely extension of Hertzog's 'civilized labour' policy. 'Listening to the Minister, we would believe that the spectre of poor Whiteism is again stalking about the country, that Europeans are being displaced right and left by non-Europeans and that the entire economy of the country is crashing to ruins.'[18] Would it not be better to subsidize the 'marginal' Whites than to hamstring industry which, at this stage of South Africa's development, should be completely flexible? The majority of Whites were surely adequately protected by the customary colour bar, the 'rate for the job' and apprenticeship regulations. Conservative though it appeared to many labour leaders, Helen's speech was too advanced for many of her own party's supporters: as Morris Kentridge, who represented a Johannesburg working-class constituency put it, 'she was . . . casting a great number of pearls, economic pearls, before people with closed and prejudiced minds'. The Government remained adamant in its desire to extend the industrial colour bar and the Bill was referred to a Select Committee.

In spite of the ever-tightening grip of the National Party's apartheid measures on black and white South Africans, at the close of the 1954 parliamentary session Helen was still sanguine about the future. Her friends and constituents who assumed that she must find the United Party's lack of success depressing were quickly corrected. She told them:

I do not find parliamentary work frustrating because whether Nationalist bills are passed or not is not the issue. Naturally it is infuriating and saddening to find that logical argument is met with blank indifference or with emotional tirades or even just with monotonous repetition of interjections such as 'Mau Mau' from the hon. Member for Cradock [G. F. H. Bekker]. The real issue however is still whether or not the official Opposition to the Nationalists is functioning – the presentation to the country of a point of view that is the opposite of a narrow sectionalism which is fear-ridden and in relation to the racial problem is blind to the realities of the economic requirements of the Union. As long as we still have such an Opposition functioning, the parliamentary democratic system serves an invaluable purpose in South Africa. I am very pleased indeed to be able to report that the United Party fulfilled the role of a responsible official Opposition during the last session by standing firmly on principle and voting against the Government on every contentious issue that arose.[19]

Helen's attitude at this stage of her political career may possibly be seen as a triumph of hope over experience. The United Party at its National Congress in Bloemfontein in November was due to 'unveil' its new Native Policy. Something more positive than past attitudes, Helen believed, was bound to manifest itself. She should have been forewarned by a survey carried out that May by the Witwatersrand General Council of the United Party to discover the attitude of its rank-and-file to 'economic integration' and the extension of political rights to Africans. The Executive Committee reported that ignorance of the meaning of the phrase 'economic integration' had led to fear and suspicion and in some instances hostility. 76 per cent of the people questioned were in favour of Whites representing Africans in Parliament, and 71 per cent were against the extension of political rights to the Africans.

But Strauss had taken an unexpectedly firm line in Parliament on economic integration. His appointment of the four provincial committees to review and report on United Party policy seemed to be a positive step in the direction so ardently desired by the liberals. It was true that since that date he had made no further statements in favour of economic integration, nor had he corrected the public outcries of ultra-conservatives such as Senator Steenkamp and Major van der Byl, who headed the policy-making committees and who, in company with the other right-wingers, repeatedly repudiated the philosophy of economic integration. It was also true that on the eve of the provincial elections, when the Party found itself under heavy attack for its alleged liberalism from the National Party and from its own *platteland* MPs and supporters who found economic integration unpalatable and unacceptable, that the Transvaal leader, Henry Tucker, had stated unambiguously that the United Party was pledged irrevocably to white leadership in South Africa. 'Only irresponsible people', he had said, 'talk about granting any political rights to the Natives, which, at this stage, is to divorce the South African situation from reality.' But at Congress, the liberals believed, Strauss would publicly repudiate the conservatives and reiterate his support for them.

By the time Congress opened on 16 November 1954, Helen's former experience was beginning to have the edge over her future hope. In August the United Party had been roundly defeated in the provincial elections by the National Party.[20] A new ground-swell of anti-Strauss opposition was beginning to develop. It was being channelled by several conservatives into a revolt against the Party's 'pro-liberal' line.

In his opening address to Congress, Strauss again postulated his belief in economic integration. 'The wagon of our economy', he declared, 'must run on all four wheels (land, labour, capital and production)' but (and here in one sentence he blasted the liberals' hopes) '. . . from the point of view of practical states-manship, a measure of differentiation, separation and even considered discrimination might reflect a much more realistic and enlightened approach under present conditions.'[21] Strauss's caution enabled him for the time being to impose some semblance of unity upon the Party. On the following day its new Native Policy was smugly proclaimed as 'In economic affairs – integration, properly controlled; in political relations – guidance; in social and residential policies – separation; in all things – justice and fair dealings.'[22]

The sops flung to the liberals were three: economic integration as the basis of party policy; a concession of African freehold rights in urban areas; and a proposal to increase the number of African representatives in the Senate from four to six and to allow what were described as 'advanced non-Europeans' to take part in the election of these Senators.

This lip-service paid, the Party policy-makers then had no hesitation in declaring that as the Native peoples had not reached a stage of development to exercise the full democratic rights of citizenship, the Party would direct itself towards determining the best method of consultation with the non-Europeans through the medium of those Natives who, by virtue of their education, development and adoption of Western standards were thought best able to interpret the needs of the mass of the Native peoples in a 'responsible manner'.[23]

In habitual United Party fashion the leadership had succeeded in satisfying all factions. Conservatives, middle-of-the-road men, liberals, all supported the new Native Policy, each reading into it what they themselves most wished to see. The essential flaw in the liberals' thinking at this time appears to have been a belief that even minor concessions by the conservative elements would still enable a progressive advance to take place. The conservatives on the contrary felt that the limit to concession-making had finally been reached. Almost they said with Luther '*Hier stehe Ich : Ich kann nicht anders*'. Members must no longer be allowed to deviate from the official party line without risking the charge of disloyalty or breaking faith. At their instigation this resolution was now put before the Congress:

That the Native Policy of the United Party, as decided upon by the Union Congress, be adhered to, disseminated and propagated by all members of the Party, and any public statement made by a member of the Party which conflicts with this duly accepted policy shall be dealt with as an act hostile to the interests of the Party.

The inexperienced liberals remained sublimely unaware of the fact that they had been out-manoeuvered, outflanked and out-gunned by the conservative faction. To a man they voted for the resolution. Looking back in 1974, Helen appreciated that their failure to add any rider to this affirmation of loyalty – perhaps, to the effect that, to them, the new policy was no more than a signpost pointing the way to further political advances – tied their hands and circumscribed their future influence within the Party.

The thunderclouds of *kragdadigheid** were building up over South Africa. In October 1954 the ageing Dr Malan announced his impending resignation as Prime Minister. For fifty days the country hung upon the decision of the National Party caucus as it chose its new leader. English-speaking South Africa hoped for the election of the elderly, moderate Havenga or the temperate Cape Leader, T. E. Donges, but the caucus, after six years of cautious inching towards apartheid, was no longer in the mood for moderation: they wanted an implacable hard-liner. Choosing the Transvaal leader, the 'Lion of the North,' J. G. Strijdom† they had exactly the man they needed. *Die Volksblad* wrote:

At last we will see the final settlement of the question of the Coloured vote with which is bound up the question of relations between Parlia-

---

*Power, in a particularly aggressive sense.
†Strijdom is sometimes spelt Strydom, even in Hansard. The author has opted for the former spelling.

ment and the courts; further extension of the positive apartheid policy of which total development of the Reserves and the incorporation of the Protectorates [Swaziland, Basutoland and Bechuanaland] form a part; the acceleration of the tempo of preparation aimed at a Republic which in the comparatively near future will become a matter of practical politics.[24]

The editor of *Die Volksblad* spoke for the whole of Nationalist Afrikanerdom. His editorial predicted with extraordinary accuracy the course the Government was to pursue under its new leader.

Dr Malan, on the verge of resignation, had been content to hand the settlement of the Coloured vote issue to his successor. The Select Committee appointed at the end of the 1953 session had failed in its attempts to reconcile the differences between the Government and the United Party, which, fortified by all the evidence presented against separate representation, had steadfastly refused to change its attitude. The United Party was sure, said Helen, that '. . . the Government only need cease its efforts to remove the 100-year-old franchise privileges from the Coloureds and the "crisis" will disappear'. During the 1954 session Dr Malan had once again tried to remove the Coloureds from the Common Roll – this time by employing strictly constitutional means.[25] Although the Government came closer than ever before to its two-thirds majority, thanks, Helen claimed to the floor-crossing antics of the Barlow–Bekker Group, it still failed to achieve the desired majority. As the disconsolate Independent United Party members trudged back to the Opposition benches after the division, Helen quipped 'Was your journey really necessary?' Following the Government's defeat, Strijdom, not yet Prime Minister, in conjunction with the other National Party Provincial leaders, issued the following statement:

The South African nation will not tolerate such a state of constitutional slavery into which the United Party seeks to plunge it . . . The struggle will be waged to the end . . . This is a clarion call to take up the struggle for the most sacred rights of a nation as it exercises those rights through its Parliament.[26]

In January 1955 in his speech from the Throne the Governor-General stressed Strijdom's determination to terminate the whole crisis once and for all. Parliament would, he said, at the appropriate time be asked to give consideration to the separate representation of voters and to the question of the sovereignty of Parliament.[27]

Strijdom for the first three months of the session stayed in the background, allowing his lieutenants to steer legislation through Parliament. Verwoerd, now the second most powerful man in the Cabinet, dominated the session with his Native (Urban Areas) Amendment Bill, one particular section of which, 4(b), was designed to do away with what Verwoerd called 'those locations in the sky', leaving five resident African servants to each block of flats unless the flat-owner had specific permission to house more. Verwoerd based his case on the fact that more Africans were already housed in a few blocks of flats in the Johannesburg suburb of Killarney than in the locations of many small towns. Unless the Government took immediate action, he claimed that there would be more than 30 000 Africans living on the tops of flats in the one square mile which made up the densely populated area of Johannesburg known as Hospital Hill.

The fact that her constituents in Houghton, many of whom were flat-dwellers, were urging her to oppose the Native (Urban Areas) Amendment Bill in general, and Section 4(b) in particular, played only a small part in the stand that Helen took against it. Feeling that the evils of the system arose as a direct result of the Minister's own policy of employment of migratory labour, she stormed at the Government benches:

It is no good begging Europeans in the name of residential and social segregation to make the supreme sacrifice of going without their early morning tea served by Native servants . . . Members of the other side must search their consciences a little more carefully before coming up with this argument. They must do away with all farm labourers living on the farms . . . They should then be prepared to make the real sacrifice of doing without their domestic servants in order to carry out full residential and social apartheid . . . It is high time, that the hon. Member the Minister stopped constantly introducing measures like this which increase the prevailing feelings of uneasiness and unrest among the non-European peoples . . .[28]

Apart from this attack, the 'famous and notorious member for Houghton' and her fellow-liberals were lying low. Their silence and depression were more than explicable. The adoption of its

new Native Policy in Bloemfontein had failed to provide the hoped-
for injection of fresh and vigorous thinking into the United Party
and Strauss and his front-benchers put up a sadly lethargic and
ineffectual performance. Indeed, when the Minister of Justice
banned all public meetings in Johannesburg and Roodepoort one
day before the Western Areas removals were scheduled to start,
on the grounds that the Congress movements were planning to
make 'blood flow in the streets of Sophiatown', Strauss's concern
with the ban appeared to be not that the Minister of Justice was
exercising what the Labour Party leader had no hesitation in
calling 'vast tyrannical powers . . . to suppress a small group of
agitators', but that the Government's action would be misrepre-
sented in the foreign press. He stated:

There can be no question at this stage of any criticism of the Government . . . in regard to this particular banning order . . . Once a law
has been constitutionally passed, I think it is the duty of the citizens
of the State to give obedience to that law and to accept that law in a
proper law-abiding spirit . . . [but] . . . a wrong impression [might] . . .
serve as some kind of foundation for statements which might injure
and do harm to our country.[29]*

From the liberal standpoint, Strauss's attitude was unforeseeably
weak-kneed, but worse was yet to come. On 21 February the
Minister of Justice Introduced the Criminal Procedure and
Evidence Amendment Bill.[30] This Bill which, *inter alia*, allowed
police to shoot a suspected thief, no matter how trivial the theft,
if there was no other means of apprehending him, and which
also introduced corporal punishment for first offence thefts, was
opposed by the United Party caucus, for divergent reasons as
was so usual in that disunited body. The right wing objections
were raised in classical form by Douglas Mitchell who announced
that he was not going to vote for the right of a non-European
constable to search his house;[31] the liberals' objection lay in their
belief that such blanket powers for the police would move South

*The removals passed off peacefully. Two thousand police armed with Sten
guns cordoned off the area and the Sophiatown Africans went to Meadowlands
in Army lorries. Verwoerd told the House that the removals 'went like clockwork
. . . the Natives went singing from Sophiatown to Meadowlands'. Leo Lovell,
Labour MP for Benoni, commented, 'I would also sing if there were 2000 police
standing by.'

Africa a step nearer to becoming a police state, while the moderates took pains to explain that while they did not believe that the Government was planning a police state, it would end up with one if it were not careful.

Strauss appointed Sir de Villiers Graaff, the Party's Cape leader, chairman of its Justice Group and heir-presumptive to the national leadership to lead the Party's attack on the Bill. Throughout the second reading debate and the Committee stage, Graaff displayed considerable coolness as he weathered the attacks levelled at the United Party from the Government, who accused it of favouring sabotage, and from the Independent United Party, who took the line that the major cities in South Africa were in a state of siege and that to oppose the Bill was to lead the country into anarchy. Arthur Barlow spoke of Johannesburg as an armed camp where shootings took place every day, claiming that his own constituency had the highest murder rate in the country. Helen, who played only a minor role in the debate, observed: 'I would point out that if the hon. Member would bother to put his nose in his constituency, the murder rate would go up by one.'

After hours of heated argument, it was finally agreed by the divided United Party caucus that Graaff would move amendments to the Bill's two most contentious clauses (the shooting on sight and the corporal punishment for the first offence clauses) which, if accepted by the Government, would allow the United Party to vote with it at the third reading.

At the Report stage of the Bill, the Minister of Justice sprang a surprise on the United Party by announcing several amendments to the Bill, including built-in safeguards to the offending clauses. But he did not accept the United Party's amendments. Graaff stood up and re-outlined his party's objections. While he was speaking, the Secretary of the Party's Justice Group, Douglas Smit leant across and handed him a note detailing the arguments he should use in his speech. Graaff glanced casually at it and abruptly declared:

Apart from those objections which I have summarized, this Bill, running into well over sixty clauses, introduces a large number of desirable improvements in the Criminal Law and Procedure in South Africa. On that account, despite the objections which we have, it will nevertheless receive our support at the third reading.[32]

Graaff had misread the heading of Smit's message ('*Notes for third reading*') as 'Vote for third reading'. The Opposition benches dissolved in uproar. The back-benchers shouted at Graaff, who, empurpled, abruptly sat down. Townley Owen-Williams, scheduled to speak next, remembers thinking how this typified the Party's lack of principle. Graaff's action seemed to him to signal the end of his own political career. Through the National and Independent United Party's roars of laughter, Blaar Coetzee was to be heard congratulating the Minister of Justice on having persuaded the United Party that the police state as evidenced by the Bill was the best thing in the interests of South Africa. When the embarrassed Higgerty had finished trying to explain to the House that Graaff had made a genuine mistake and that the United Party had decided despite the fact that certain amendments had been accepted by the Minister, to vote against the Bill at the third reading, the Minister of Justice exclaimed, 'This is just too funny for words!'[33]

The liberal wing were less amused. For Helen personally, Graaff's blunder, his failure to listen to caucus discussion and to adhere to caucus decision, confirmed for her what she had for some time thought of him. In his bid for leadership, he appeared too eager to please all the factions in the Party, and his favourite catch-phrase, 'When in doubt, leave out!' underlined the extreme caution of his political philosophy. But while she was still wondering what her attitude should be towards him and pondering whether despite his deplorable tendency to vacillation she should consider supporting his leadership bid, she and her co-thinkers were dealt yet another and even worse blow.

Shortly before the Easter recess, the Minister of Justice introduced the Appellate Division Quorum Bill[34] to the House. 'The Government wants a strong court to hear its case,' he said in an oblique reference to the Separate Representation of Voters legislation. Once the Quorum Bill became law, Strijdom fulfilled his promise to the National Party electorate. On 23 May 1955 he introduced the Senate Bill,[35] which recognized what he claimed to be the mandate already given to the Government at four elections in regard to the separate representation of voters and at two elections in regard to the sovereignty of Parliament.[36] In fact

D

Strijdom, well aware that there was no legal way in which he could obtain a two-thirds majority, had cynically decided to pack the Senate with National Party nominees. The United Party immediately attacked the Government's action and Strauss claimed that the Bill would not only make a mockery of Parliament, but would render it a mere tool in the hands of the 'political bosses' of the country.[37] Helen added her voice:

South Africa is in the position that existed in Germany in the 1930s . . . The destruction of our old Senate is of course not analagous to the burning down of the Reichstag, but it is certainly going to be packed to suffocation with Nationalist candidates who will form 85 per cent of the inmates of the Other Place . . . Members have said that the Coloured franchise was a side issue as far as this Bill is concerned . . . As regards the contents of the Bill and [its] immediate effects, this Bill and the entrenched clauses, it may be that the Coloured franchise is a side issue, but there is an aspect of the Coloured franchise embodied in this measure which is not a side issue at all, and that is the effect on future race relations in South Africa if the franchise is removed from the minority group of the Coloured people by this type of two-thirds majority . . . 'When we lose faith in the system, we lose faith in everything we fight and stand for.'[38]

Helen's concluding quotation summed up what many South Africans outside Parliament were thinking. The Government's action roused English-speaking South Africans to demonstrate their hostility to it in a manner reminiscent of the Torch Commando days, and the women of the newly formed Black Sash[39] marched in silent protest through the streets of South African cities. The Bill even caused disquiet among Nationalists. Thirteen professors and senior lecturers from Pretoria University resigned in protest and even *Die Burger* wrote: 'No right-thinking person can approve of the Senate Bill as seen by itself. It is acceptable to the Nationalists and to Nationalist sympathizers only as a possible means of ending the completely untenable position created by the United Party in relation to the Coloured Vote.' But despite the antipathy the Bill aroused, the United Party, to Helen's dismay and to the consternation of its electorate, after years of rigorous opposition to the separate representation of voters, did an abrupt about-face.

For some time prior to the introduction of the Senate Bill, both the Independent United Party and the Government had been repeatedly asking Strauss to clarify his party's attitude to the replacement of the Coloureds on the Common Roll should it be returned to power. The Opposition leader continually evaded answering this question, so that finally the liberals, puzzled and infuriated by his inability to give an unequivocal affirmative to his questioners, persuaded Jan Steytler to raise the matter in caucus. Strauss, refusing to commit himself, offered them the palliative of a committee consisting of Douglas Mitchell, the conservative Natal leader, de Villiers Graaff and Bernard Friedman, the witty, principled and liberal front-bench member for Hillbrow (Johannesburg), to interview caucus members individually in order to assess their feelings on the separate representation of voters. This committee discovered a solid block, excluding only the liberal wing, which felt that the Coloureds had been the 'political football' of the Whites for too long and that, once they were removed from the Roll, there should be no consideration of their re-enfranchisement. Within days its findings were confirmed when Senator Connan told the Cape Head Committee that if the Party persisted with its policy of Coloured re-enfranchisement it would lose every Cape *platteland* vote. This was all Strauss needed to hear. Unmindful of his promise made only four years earlier to restore the Coloureds to the Common Roll on the Party's return to power, he told the caucus on 13 June 1955 that the consideration of the question of the Coloured franchise was both premature and hypothetical. The relieved conservatives now felt at liberty to assure the *platteland* electorate that the Party had freed itself from any binding commitment to the Coloureds. Friedman, staggered by Strauss's opportunism and lack of principle, hastened to contact the other liberals. 'Such an abandonment of principle', he told a hastily convened meeting, 'deprives the struggle we have waged over the constitutional issue of its moral basis. It renders [it] absolutely meaningless.' The eight dissidents then approached Strauss to tell him that unless he could give his unequivocal assurance that the Party would honour its 1951 pledge to the Coloureds, they would be forced to resign. To their consternation, Strauss apparently acting on conservative advice, decided to treat their concern with the issue as a revolt against his leadership. They were met by bland indifference and

180907

a flat refusal to discuss the matter. The eight left Strauss's office to draft their resignation statement for the Press. Strauss's son-in-law, Zach de Beer, who was not at this time openly identified with the liberal group, informed Harry Oppenheimer of their action. Oppenheimer at once left Johannesburg for Cape Town and told Strauss that the Party could ill afford to lose such capable and dedicated members. 'If they go, I will have to reconsider my position', he is reported to have said. Once again flung into indecision, Strauss fell back upon his usual expedient of appointing yet another committee, this time composed of a more moderate group comprising Oppenheimer, De Beer, Hughes and Lawrence, in order to try to find common ground between the leadership and the dissidents. The new committee avoided approaching Friedman, whom they realized would accept nothing less than an unequivocal 'Yes' from Strauss and who was already suspected of having leaked news of the crisis to the Press. Friedman's statement read:

The question has been put squarely to the United Party, whether, on being returned to power, it would restore the Coloured voter to the Common Roll should the National Party Government succeed in removing them.

In my opinion, the only possible answer on such a fundamental question of principle is a clear and unequivocal 'Yes'. The statements issued by Mr Strauss on behalf of the United Party will inevitably be interpreted as a serious departure from the strong stand which has hitherto been maintained by the United Party and will deprive the struggle the party has waged over the constitutional issue of its moral basis.[40]

Friedman's action was widely applauded. He left Cape Town and, on 27 June 1955, resigned from the United Party and prepared to fight a by-election as an Independent candidate in his constituency of Hillbrow.*

Helen felt very uneasy at her failure to resign with Friedman.

---

*In the by-election his slogan was 'Oppose, not Appease'. A minute of the Witwatersrand General Council of the UP at this time reads: 'Unfortunately, Dr Friedman, by his melodramatic gesture, created a diversion which but for the splendid enterprise and self-sacrifice of our womenfolk [a reference to the Black Sash?] would have relegated the evils of the Senate Act to the political background.'

Inexperience led her to believe Oppenheimer's assurance that change could only be effected through the caucus. On 16 June (the day the Senate Bill passed its third reading in the Upper House) she said in Parliament:

I want to make clear my position . . . My interpretation of [Strauss's statement of 13 June] . . . is that we stand by the principle by which we have always stood, the retention of the Coloured voter on the Common Roll. We are against group representation as a principle, and we stand also for undoing the grave injustice which will be done to the Coloured people when this Government succeeds in removing the Coloured people from the Common voter's Roll . . . I say that it, at this stage, enables me to state unequivocally that we will return the Coloured voters when we are able to the Common voter's Roll.[41]

One after another, the seven liberals made similar statements in attempts to vindicate their behaviour to themselves and to the country at large.

The Houghton Divisional Committee had been planning to resign *en bloc* alongside Helen. When she recanted they sent her an urgent telegram asking her to explain herself to them. She immediately went to Johannesburg and at a meeting used Oppenheimer's arguments to persuade them to support her. She addressed the angry and resentful members:

The entire Nationalist philosophy is orientated to narrow sectional control of South Africa and while we turn our frustrations in on ourselves, the Nationalists are busy consolidating themselves. And they are immensely encouraged in their work by our internecine warfare and the split forces of the Opposition . . . Those who have had a shot at formulating policies – say in the smaller parties like the Liberals and [the] Labour Party – know perfectly well that even in such smaller councils it is extremely difficult to lay down hard and fast and inflexible lines acceptable to all their members . . . those people who use the phrase that the United Party is no different from the Nats . . . should pause and think. Of course we all feel frustrated and angry because there seems little that we can do to unseat the Nats. And this frustration manifests itself most clearly in the so-called safe United Party seats – one does not find it in the marginal or Nationalist seats where the small band of stalwarts face and fight the Nationalists every day in ordinary walks of life and are therefore not torn by internecine warfare. Their emotional reactions to the Nationalists have an outlet. Ours are turned in on ourselves, and we spend so much time trying to get a clear definition of political 'peace aims' that we forget that the 'political war' is nowhere near a satisfactory conclusion. I do not want to imply that I believe that the United Party should advance only an anti-Nationalist policy without any alternative policy of its own. I believe it must forcibly advance an alternative policy.

She then reiterated the United Party's new Native Policy, asserting that she believed that its principles were concepts which could be built upon. Admittedly, she told her committee, they might not go far enough, but as far as she was concerned party policy was not inflexible and she saw nothing to prevent anyone within the councils of the Party from advocating changes.

I myself have advanced ideas at Congresses which have not proved acceptable to the general body of Congress. This does not mean that I am precluded from advancing such ideas again at later Congresses. And since I feel that my ideas are based on sound economics, I am sure that one day they will prove acceptable. But meanwhile I must conform to accepted policies. Does this make me dishonest? I think not. I like to think it shows a sense of responsibility to those people who nominated me for this seat. As long as I stay in politics I shall continue to fight within the Party for my ideals and for the ideals for which I believe you want me to fight.[42]

The committee accepted her apologia and passed a vote of confidence in her, but she herself was experiencing serious doubts about the validity of her reasoning. She had asked her committee if her conformity made her dishonest. She believed it did not, although she still had serious misgivings. She had written to Joyce Harris of the Black Sash on 18 June:

I have just gone through the worst week of my life . . . I know too that whatever decision I may have taken would have led to regrets and questions and recriminations. It would have been far easier, however, to have gone out in a blaze of glory – the climate of disapproval for the UP could not have been better for such a gesture. But there were other considerations. My original decision to enter politics had one main objective, to bolster up the sagging remains of the major Opposition Party. It is still my task to try and do that. But there was also the consideration due to my friends, such as 'Sakkies' Fourie and Jan Steytler, who are far more important to the political future of SA than I in my favourable 'liberal' seat. Moreover, unlike Barn, I was not convinced that this is a sell-out. That there are people in the Party who don't give a tuppenny damn about our pledges to the Coloureds or any other pledges, I am quite aware. But these were not the people who persuaded us not to smash the Party – indeed, they would have been happy to have seen us go. We were persuaded by people like Harry Oppenheimer, Gray Hughes and others whom I respect and who also are very concerned about the non-European problem. . . .

Of the seven liberals, it had been Helen who had reasoned most strongly in favour of resignation. Probity now demanded that she resign; but political expediency coupled with her own in-experience gave victory to the siren voices of Oppenheimer and the *middel-pad* men. She stipulated, however, that neither she nor any of her committee were prepared to assist any candidate which the Party, now massing its not inconsiderable strength against the rebel, might nominate in Hillbrow. Despite heavy pressure from the Transvaal leadership for the liberals' public support for its candidate, a noted conservative, Senator Louis Steenkamp, Helen and the other liberal members salved their conscience and their pride by remaining aloof from the struggle.*

In fact, rather than remain in Johannesburg during Steen-kamp's by-election campaign, Helen went with Ellen Hellmann and Hansi Pollak on a fact-finding tour of the Central African Federation and the Belgian Congo. Of the three-week tour, Helen most remembers the ubiquitous choking red dust which might almost have symbolized the fog of erroneous impressions garnered by her group. She met Garfield Todd, Prime Minister of Southern Rhodesia, and came away from her interview with him impressed by the depth and quality of his faith in the future potential and stability of the young Federation. Todd's political philosophy, based on what she described as the '. . . somewhat intangible ingredient of . . . faith . . . and firm determination to increase the settled White population by means of a vigorous immigration policy [at this time still a hobby horse of Helen's], the maintenance of harmonious race relations, and the fullest

---

*In a low poll (58 per cent) Steenkamp defeated Friedman by 641 votes on 14 September 1955. The *Rand Daily Mail* which had promised Friedman its support, came out on the morning of the by-election with the advice: 'A vote for Friedman is a vote for the Nationalists' and this undoubtedly was one of the causes of his defeat.

possible utilization of its resources, both human and material'
found its appeal for her in delimitating a path she would have
liked the United Party to follow. As she saw it, the Federation's
official policy of 'partnership' was an excellent one, since it did
not envisage any immediate or radical change in the existing
relationship between the races, yet eschewed a policy of perpetual
white domination with no outlet for the aspirations of the Blacks.
But however impressed she was with Todd's vision, she returned
from her tour fully aware that both the Rhodesias and the Congo
had great problems to face in the not-too-far-distant future. She
believed that the Central African Federation would have to
translate its partnership concept into something more tangible
if the aspirations of the African population were to be realized
and its confidence maintained. The Congo, governed on traditional
colonial lines from Brussels, and where no section of the population had any political rights, raised other problems. If the Belgian
colons began pressing for political representation, the thorny
question of rights for the Africans would be raised too. Helen
prophesied difficulties for the Belgian Government, but she
believed that all the pressures for self-determination would come
from the Whites.[43] How, at that time, could she believe that when
self-determination came, it would come, not for the *colons* but
for the Blacks? Nor could Helen have foreseen the disastrous
effect the subsequent Congolese upheaval would have in hardening
South African political attitudes. (Ellen Hellmann was even more
misled. She reported to the SAIRR '[There is] . . . no territory
where there is a greater economy of words and theory, a more
unsentimental, realistic and practical approach than the Congo . . .
When the question of political rights becomes pressing, the Bel-
gians will tackle it in the practical sane manner that characterizes
their present conduct.')[44]

Helen returned from her journey 'up North' refreshed in spirit
and more determined than ever to press for liberal reform within
the United Party. Whatever she felt privately about her decision
to stay in the Party, publicly she made her intentions quite
clear. A suggestion in the *Forum* magazine that the liberal elements
within the United Party should quit it and join the Liberal Party
or form an independent group was scornfully rejected by her.
'This article', she wrote, 'reminds me of the complaint of an

old-fashioned gentleman who dislikes the pace of modern traffic and wishes we could return to the pony-and-trap days.'

Her case was that not only must the United Party win new supporters but it must retain those it already had. Should the so-called liberals be removed because of their progressive tendencies from their constituencies, the Party would lose some of its hardest workers. She firmly believed that within the ranks of the United Party's supporters, even among the politically apathetic, growing numbers of people yearned for the Party to attack the Government on every possible score including its apartheid policy. These people accepted traditional residential and social segregation and, while wishing to maintain white leadership, realized that South Africa would have to adjust her policies to bring them into line with both the economic realities of the situation and the thinking of the civilized world. Such voters should have a voice representing them, not in the wilderness but in Parliament. So she and her fellow-liberals stayed where they were, hoping to be able to convince their colleagues that their point of view had validity. Their option was to get out and go it alone with about as much influence on future events as a hermit on a mountain top. Perhaps it might be braver to go into the wilderness, but, on the other hand, was it really a good idea to get out of hearing distance of everybody?

She was to add to this argument at her 1955 report-back meeting, when her intention appears to have been that of preparing her constituents for the coming battle with the United Party conservatives. She and her co-liberals had already publicly served notice on the leadership that any further deviation from its pledges to maintain existing statutory black rights would mean their breaking with the Party. This action had effectively set them apart from those members of the caucus who had conveniently placed quite another interpretation on Strauss's statement of 13 June, and who felt that at last the Party was released from any binding pledges made since Union to black South Africans. Helen told her constituents:

I am not among those who think the Nationalists are in for good. The Union is but part of the vast continent of Africa and policies being worked out north of the Limpopo must inevitably have their reaction here. We cannot hope to maintain our position as the leading industrial country in Africa unless we make adjustments more in keeping with the forward steps being taken elsewhere . . . prosperity and solvency can in the long run be maintained only in an atmosphere of racial co-operation . . . We [the United Party] have to present the country with alternative policies, based not only on solid economic grounds but also on solid moral grounds. To a large extent the basis for such alternative policies has been established. We wish to maintain our strong links with the Commonwealth. We desire a unified South African nation governed constitutionally and not despotically. And by accepting economic integration, we recognize that the non-European cannot forever be denied rights and responsibilities. Most important of all, our policy is not rigid and inflexible and if it does not go far enough for some of us, there is nothing to prevent us from advancing other ideas and advocating changes.[45]

In this deep conviction that the liberals had a key role to play in the United Party, she had forgotten one thing. The liberals might be bound together by a community of moral interest but although they were identified in the public mind as a cohesive group, their great weakness lay in the fact that they worked and thought as individuals, lacking a common strategy. It was this failing that the right wing was now about to exploit. Its first step, directed by Douglas Mitchell, was to decide that the ineffectual and vacillating Strauss must go, and, if he were to be replaced, that the perfect tool for the particular ends of the right wing lay to hand in de Villiers Graaff.

Graaff, enormously wealthy, scion of an old Cape family, was a man of great personal charm, had a wonderfully persuasive platform manner and a large popular following both with members of the caucus and in the Party's grass roots. Mitchell had correctly assessed his political leanings as essentially conservative, although both moderates and liberals believed him to be a *middel-pad* man. Neither Oppenheimer nor Lawrence, preoccupied with holding the centre together, raised any objection to Mitchell's plans. Both liked Graaff and believed him to be the ideal man to hold the balance between left and right, while even the liberals, disturbed though they had been by Graaff's inept handling of the Criminal Procedures Act, preferred him to Strauss who had let them down so indefensibly.

Mitchell's manoeuvring paid off. Neither the centre nor the left appreciated that his ploy in supplanting Strauss with Graaff was no more than a preliminary to shedding the liberals. Shortly after Friedman's resignation from the caucus, one conservative was overheard in the lobby of the House exulting to another '*Nou sal ons hulle kry*'.* And as though that were a signal, Mitchell's four-year campaign to oust the liberals from the Party began.

*Now we'll get them.

'The coming session of Parliament will be historic, for no less a reason than that the trenches for the foundation of the South African republic are being dug. The final vestiges of British supremacy in South Africa are about to be wiped out.'[1] This triumphant prognostication came in December 1955 from G. F. van L. Froneman. And, indeed, four-fifths of the five-month 1956 session were directly concerned with the practical implementation of the grand design of apartheid. Helen told a Johannesburg lunch-club audience that there were two reasons for the deluge of ideological legislation falling upon the Assembly. Firstly, the Government wanted to collect a 'good stock of talking points for its supporters to distract their attention from the sad graveyard hopes presented by the Tomlinson Report',[2] and secondly it wanted in the pre-election period of 1957 to devote itself to bread-and-butter matters which, having been neglected throughout the session, would by then be assuming greater importance in the eyes of the electorate. With the legislation proposed under the Industrial Conciliation Bill, the Bantu Education Amendment Bill, the Native Administration Amendment Bill, the Natives (Prohibition of Interdicts) Bill, the Native Urban Areas Amendment Bill, the Group Areas Amendment Bill and the Population Registration Amendment Bill,[3] the Government declared it was 'preserving White civilization in South Africa'. The actual purpose of all these was to deprive Blacks of still more of their already drastically limited rights. The Bills restricted freedom of movement of Africans; deprived them of ready access to the courts and compelled them to send their children only to government-approved schools. Helen condemned the measures roundly, stating that they 'jangled the nerves of everybody who has a care or thought for democracy'. The Bills, she declared increased the already vast powers of the indefatigable Verwoerd and constituted a flagrant violation of fundamental democratic practices. 'Those measures enacted in the name of apartheid are a formidable series of Bills designed to deprive the non-Europeans of their rights by statutory doses.'[4]

The 1956 session also saw the end of the six-year battle to remove the Coloureds from the Common Roll and to deprive them of their right to sit in the Cape Provincial Council. At a Joint Sitting held on 15 February, Strijdom achieved his goal. 'Subject', he said, 'only to the supreme sovereignty of God, Parliament as the instrument of the people through which they give expression to their will and desires in the political sphere is the highest authority, as far as State institutions are concerned, to which all, and consequently also the courts, are and must be subordinate.'[5] The Labour Party refused to participate in the Joint Sitting, claiming that it was a farce, and while the United Party fought, as was expected, the South Africa Act Amendment Bill,[6] its attack lacked vigour. But whatever it might have done, the Opposition stood no chance against the Government whose ranks, thanks to the Senate Act, were swollen to 172 members against the Opposition's 70. The Bill became law on 1 March 1956. All the members of the United Party's liberal wing spoke during the Joint-Sitting debate, refuting the claim of the Minister of Justice, who in January noted the liberals' marked silence during the No Confidence Debate and jeered: 'Where are those members at the wailing wall . . . who got up here last year and made a solemn confession of faith . . . have they also been "zipped" now?' To some extent his taunts were justified. In common with the other liberals, Helen stressed that she associated herself with the United Party's comments on the Bill '. . . as regards its moral implications, as regards its effects on race relations, and particularly as regards its effects on South Africa . . . It is a bad Bill. It has had a bad past and will have a bad future.' But she was also at pains to emphasize that she thought:

. . . we have seldom seen a finer display of unity than has displayed itself in this Party during this debate. I am not denying that there are varying shades of opinion in this Party, there always have been and I hope there always will be, because we are a democratic party. I would rather belong to a party which allows and encourages variations of opinion than to a party like the National Party which adopts the principle of 'When Pa turns, we all turn', and much worse, at every gyration somebody has got to stand up and thank 'Pa'.*[7]

Having failed to stop the South Africa Act Amendment Bill and what Helen termed its 'ugly step-sister', the Separate Representation of Voters Amendment Bill[8] the United Party placed its final hope in the Courts. 'We are doing our best', Helen told her constituents, 'to have the Senate Act declared invalid and despatch all those superfluous gentlemen back to the remote corners they came from.'[9] But the Party's efforts were in vain. The Cape Provincial Division first rejected the appeal and the Appellate Division of the Supreme Court dismissed it finally by ten to one, Chief Justice Schreiner dissenting.

Once the Government had thus buried the last remnants of the Cape liberal tradition, the United Party recovered some of its old form. Helen's own debating prowess had increased considerably in the three years she had been in Parliament and although she preferred to speak more and more on Bills dealing with race relations, as Secretary of the Party's Labour Group she had become a major spokesman on industrial affairs. When the revised Industrial Conciliation Bill[10] now a mammoth measure of eighty-eight clauses, came before Parliament in January she made an important speech, attacking the Bill and claiming that

nothing could be more calculated to stagnate and indeed halt industrial progress than the introduction of a rigid structure into an industry which should be flexible . . . [We have] . . . pointed out over and over again that the extension of jobs for one race does not mean that the other race will go jobless, that White labour and non-White labour are not necessarily competitive to each other, but that they are complementary to each other . . . That is why I said that I was unperturbed that economic forces were breaking down the customary colour bar . . . The National Party are gloomy pessimists. They think that South Africa has got before it only the choice between economic suicide and racial suicide . . . We . . . have a completely different idea. We see . . . the path of gradual development of our economic possibilities and resources, and the utilization of all our resources, capital and labour, manpower and management, using both White and non-White labour

*She was referring to the curious habit of National Party back-benchers who on the conclusion of any Ministerial speech spring to their feet with a cry of *'Dank die Minister'* (Thank the Minister).

to its fullest potentialities, and at the same time living in racial peace and amity with the rest of our fellow South Africans.[11]

Unlike some of the other liberals who prevaricated when taxed on whether they would like to see the industrial colour bar dropped, Helen never hesitated with an unequivocal 'Yes'. Her open and marked liberalism made her a favourite target for government and conservative attacks. Bailey Bekker unpleasantly observed of her during the debate on the Bill:

If the hon. Member were to consult her conscience, she would go into the wilderness because that may be the brave thing to do, but she would rather remain here. That is why she does not wear a black sash outside, because it is very much warmer than wearing a black sash outside and much more comfortable to sit in this House with its air-conditioning.[12]

At the committee stage of the Bill, while Helen was describing as absurd the Government's contention that Coloureds were unfit to sit on trades union executives, the Minister of Labour interjected 'Sez you'. 'Well,' said Helen, infuriated by the puerile level of this kind of attack, 'who "sez" better, you or I! If that is not a school-room debating society interjection, then I do not know what it is, and that coming from a Minister. He is a younger Minister than I am a Member so that possibly accounts for it.'[13] (It was not long before she was to become sufficiently experienced to ignore such low-level comments.) But despite the United Party's strenuously fought and well-argued attacks and despite the Labour Party's marathon struggle against it, the Bill, which had occupied the House's time almost continuously from the beginning of the session until the Easter Recess, was passed without a single amending clause being accepted by the Government.

As the session drew to its close the United Party with marked vigour condemned Verwoerd's 'Native Bills' and in debating the Tomlinson Commission's findings used the Commission's own facts and figures to prove that it would be impossible to implement total apartheid. Strauss briefly took a liberal line by asking whether the Government wanted Africans in the white areas of South Africa to become a hate-ridden, unsettled proletariat, seething with resentment at injustice and oppression, or a contented community integrated with proper safeguards into the South African economy. He questioned the morality of Whites accepting all the economic fruits, and wealth which had been accumulated as a result of the labour of the non-Europeans who had, he said, been given nothing in return. He concluded his speech by declaring that 'the future of the non-European is the challenge to all white South Africa'.

But both this moment of liberalism and the Party's seeming recovery were illusory. Throughout the session, the caucus discussions on every piece of legislation ended by becoming heated, violent arguments over the Party's course of action and even a minimally controversial subject – whether to support the Government over pay increases for parliamentary representatives – evoked, said Helen, much heart-searching and acrimonious debate. On this particular issue the caucus eventually decided by a majority vote that it had no option but to accept the Government's terms. And those members, like Helen, who voted against such acceptance, were forced to abide by the majority decision, lest they split the Party from top to bottom.

The Party had set out its Native Policy and its economic integration policy in numerous pamphlets that were lengthy and verbose, and left much interpretation open to the reader. Even so staunch a supporter as the *Cape Argus* wrote: 'The Party has not yet found a true compass or direction. Goals gleam and beckon on the distant horizon but there is no straight path to them. Whichever way the Party moves they seem to remain just as far off and just as unattainable.'[14] The *'Jakkals het twee gate'** approach of its members taking one policy line in the urban areas and another in the *platteland* was increasing daily. While Helen and her fellow-liberals were exhorting English-speaking South Africans to stop treating politics as a profession and political matters with the indifference and contempt of the past, and to play a full part in the political life of the country, accepting the necessity of giving Blacks a 'definite and secure place in the economic life of South Africa', the conservatives were pushing quite a different line. Backed by Louis Steenkamp, Douglas Mitchell preached *kafferboetie*† propaganda in which he accused the National Party of doing too much for the Blacks by spending unnecessary sums on their education and giving them preferential

*A fox has two earths.
†A derogatory Afrikaans term for negrophile.

[*sic*] treatment in the Reserves: a tactic which, the conservatives claimed, won the United Party converts in the *platteland* and which even moved the Prime Minister to comment:

. . . the propagandists of the United Party do not shrink from expounding the Government's non-European policy to the conservative voter of the *platteland* in terms which are the very opposite of what they tell the liberalist voter in the town. The former is told that the Government pampers the non-European and spends too much money on them. The latter [the townsman] is told, on the other hand, that there never has been a worse oppressor of the non-European than the present Government and that much too little is being spent on the non-European.[15]

Strauss appeared incapable of arresting Mitchell's reactionary course. As the 1956 session drew to its close, it became obvious that the strain of the past eight years had been too great for him. He appeared physically unwell and was, in fact, suffering from jaundice, although he himself did not then realize this. He began avoiding his colleagues; was often absent from the House and several times failed to address scheduled meetings. Party supporters began to complain of a lack of dynamic leadership. The conservatives took advantage of Strauss's behaviour to 'white ant' him. At the Provincial Congresses held before the main Congress, none of which were attended by Strauss, it was subtly hinted that the leader was heading for a nervous breakdown, and delegates to the Union Congress were persuaded that he had lost interest in the leadership. Shortly before the Union Congress, scheduled to be held on 20–22 November 1956, Strauss wrote to the Party's union secretary, enclosing with his letter the reports of two doctors, both recommending a protracted holiday abroad. He emphasized that within three months he would be fully fit and eligible for re-election as leader. Part of the letter read:

You might, as is your right, elect a new leader. If you were to decide to follow this course, as being in the interests of the party in view of the imminence of the next session of Parliament and the nearness of the General Election, I would not criticize nor complain but would give my full support to your choice.

This paragraph made him vulnerable to the conservatives' carefully laid strategy. Before he departed for Europe, Strauss was assured by several senior conservative party members that his re-election was a certainty and that he was not to trouble himself about the leadership issue. But as soon as he set out on his travels, the Central Executive, the body responsible for making the Party's most important decisions, implemented its plan to depose him. The Congress's Steering Committee was composed of Jack Higgerty, the Chief Whip, Sir de Villiers Graaff, deputizing for Strauss, Henry Tucker, the Transvaal leader, Douglas Mitchell and Senator H. G. 'Wolfie' Swart, the newly elected Orange Free State leader, all *bloedsappe*, all members of the Central Executive. Throughout Tuesday, 20 November, they formulated their plans and by evening had unanimously 'officially' decided that Strauss must go. On Wednesday, 21 November, with Harry Lawrence in the chair, the Congress went into closed session to discuss the leadership question. First the Chief Whip, then the Provincial leaders one after the other spoke. Tucker told Congress that the Head Committee had advised Strauss to attend the Congress but that, ignoring their advice, he had preferred to go to Europe for a holiday. He also claimed that he had informed Strauss that since he could no longer guide the United Party through its difficulties, he should resign. Next came de Villiers Graaff. Refraining from personal comment on Strauss, he emphasized the important pre-election period that lay ahead. Instead, he said, of the Party being run by the Central Executive Committee, it was essential that it should have a strong, vigorous leader. Douglas Mitchell followed Graaff. Waving a piece of paper which he claimed was a medical report, he told the delegates that Strauss was a mentally sick man who could no longer hold down the party leadership. He derided the suggestion of the leader's illness with the crude observation: 'If Strauss is well enough to go to Europe, he is well enough to come to Bloemfontein',* which caused gentle Douglas Smit to object on a point of order and the Chairman to call the speaker to order. 'Wolfie' Swart now addressed the delegates. His was only another variation of the theme. 'Strauss commands', he said, 'less than 30 per cent of the Party's support. If I were Strauss I would resign.' The Provincial leaders set the

*In fact all the Central Executive members knew that Strauss had had jaundice. Graaff had even written to Oppenheimer: 'Straussie has gone down with jaundice' (11 October 1956).

tone for the ensuing debate, which raged for six hours, briefly interrupted by the discovery made by an African cleaner that a 'baas' (who claimed to be a National Party Jeugbond leader but seems in fact to have been a reporter from *Die Volksblad*)* was hiding under the platform. His discovery caused a temporary diversion until he was ejected covered in dust and cobwebs. In his absence, their reasoning that a change in leadership was essential if the Party was to be revitalized before the election prevailed. A resolution was proposed that

. . . while Congress expresses deep sympathy with Mr Strauss in his present indisposition and heartily wishes him a complete recovery, and looks forward to the day when he will be able to resume his service as an MP . . . it considers that in view of the grave position confronting South Africa at the present juncture and the efforts demanded to eliminate them, the best interests of South Africa, the United Party itself will be served by relieving him of responsibilities which are inherent in the leadership of the United Party and decides that a new leader will be elected.[16]

Only two MPs and seven delegates voted against the resolution. 'Sakkies' Fourie most vehemently opposed it, protesting strongly at Douglas Mitchell's insinuation of a mental collapse. 'Why kick a dog when he is down?' he demanded. 'In all justice we must hear the other side. You cannot sack a leader who is not here to defend himself.' Fourie protested in vain.[17] Once the Congress had accepted the 'change of leadership' resolution, Harry Lawrence called for nominations for a new leader. Loud cries of 'Div Graaff' rose from several of the 500 delegates in the Hall and without being officially seconded Graaff was unanimously elected new leader of the United Party. While the majority of the delegates were singing 'For He's a Jolly Good Fellow' and cheering, Helen experienced grave misgivings. She had not supported Fourie because she had never forgiven her leader for his behaviour the previous year and was not prepared, she now admits, 'to lift a finger to save Strauss's bacon'. However, it was unquestionable that Graaff's election held grave implications for the liberal wing. Those delegates who had voted for him were attracted by his

---

*It was never actually established who the 'spy' was but coincidentally the following day, *Die Volksblad* carried an entire report of the secret session up to the moment of discovery.

commanding personality, his obvious sincerity and his personal charm, and were convinced that he would burgeon into a strong decisive personality who would give the Party the impetus it so desperately needed. In his acceptance speech, he told Congress that he envisaged himself as a new type of leader, less of an individualist, more a chairman-in-committee. Nevertheless, Helen felt that those who had supported his candidature had been deceived. To her Graaff, a cautious man, appeared essentially conservative in outlook. She knew him, too, to be irresolute, a man who to avoid dispute preferred to follow a neutral path and because of this, she believed that the liberal wing's hopes for reform from within would suffer. Moreover, Graaff owed a debt of gratitude to those conservatives who had brought him to power and who, now that they had installed the leader of their choice, were intent on asserting themselves.

One of Graaff's first acts as leader was to confirm the appointment (made originally by Strauss) of a Constitutional Committee. Composed of fifteen members, its object, among others, was to draw up a constitutional policy for the Party which would 'restore a sense of security to all people who live in the Union, whatever their colour or creed'. Although she was now less junior, Helen was not invited to sit on the committee, her views being too outspokenly liberal for Graaff and the Central Executive. She was, however, more relieved than disappointed and told a reporter that she intended spending the recess with her children. 'I also want to see my friends, bring my golf handicap back to eleven and keep my bridge up. All have suffered considerably lately . . . Sewing? No, I'm afraid I'm completely undomesticated.'

The close of 1956 marked a new turning point in South African politics. In early November the Prime Minister assured his supporters that the National Party's fundamental aim was still the preservation of white racial purity and cultural identity through apartheid.

South Africa is our only home and fatherland and here we must remain either to survive and preserve what is ours, or to go under and be destroyed as a result of being swamped or absorbed and assassinated by the non-White . . . When . . . we are dealing with an issue that forms the very basis or cornerstone of our people's life, our national safety demands of all good citizens adherence and submission to our traditional way of life. Any aberration from this clearly demarcated path must be regarded as dangerous because it must clearly strike at the very roots of our national existence and imperil our safety.[18]

It was manifest that the Government had no intention of allowing its *status quo* to be imperilled and, now fully reinforced by its impressive array of restrictive legislation, was planning to move against the growing black protest movements. In April the Minister of Justice had hinted to Parliament that the police had uncovered a treasonable plot and he expected about 200 people to be charged. 'Something very unpleasant', he claimed, 'had been avoided.' After a lapse of eight months the scepticism of opposition supporters, many of whom had derided the Minister's hints as being no more than *rooi gevaar* propaganda and Nationalist tub-thumping, was shattered when on 5 December, in a series of pre-dawn raids, over 140 people of all races, including L. B. Lee-Warden, the Natives' Representative for the Western Cape, ex-Chief Albert Luthuli, the President General of the African National Congress, and Dr G. M. Naicker, President of the South African Indian Congress, were arrested. To the accompaniment of scenes of violence, in which crowds of Africans stoned the police, who fired on them in retaliation, the preparatory examination was opened in the Johannesburg Drill Hall. The State declared that its basis for the high treason charge 'will be incitement and preparation for the overthrowing of the existing state by revolutionary methods including violence – and the establishment of a so-called people's democracy on the basis of the Eastern European Communist satellite states and China'. The defence counsel accused the Government of trying to stifle free speech when he said 'Criticism of the policies of the Government and all that the accused believe is implicit in their definition of the oft-misused word "democracy".'[19]

It was against this background of the Treason Trial, the Johannesburg bus boycott,[20] sporadic outbreaks of violence in the rural areas as government officials started the enforcement of the carrying by African women of reference books, and a noticeable increase in black political solidarity, that Parliament reassembled on 18 January 1957 for its last full session before the 1958 general election. It was again a mammoth session. Ninety-five Bills came before Parliament and eighty-three were enacted. While the previous session had concentrated on legislation designed to bring about political apartheid, the legislation of the 1957 session was aimed more at cultural and educational targets, as the Government attempted to complete what Helen called 'its crazy misshapen jigsaw puzzle'.[21] Assessing the Party's performance after the session, Helen claimed that 'Sir Div and his fifty-nine rugged individualists had put up the best show possible and that morally, we won every debate'. That the morale of the United Party's parliamentary team had been boosted by the election of Graaff as its new leader was unquestionable. For the first time in many years the Party could be seen to be opposing the apartheid legislation without continually looking over its shoulder. In its battle it was ably supported by both the Labour Party and by the Natives' Representatives. The Conservative Party now no longer existed. Describing its demise, Helen said:

In 1956 . . . its members used up the valuable time allotted to the Opposition by Mr Speaker by spending those hours castigating the UP and defending the Government. They wore out the carpet in the House in their innumerable expeditions across the floor to vote with the Nationalists. One of their number, Abraham Jonker, finally realized what a waste of energy the return journey was, packed his goods and trekked forever.

By the end of 1957, the Conservative Party had committed what Helen called harakiri. 'With the exception of Mr Blaar Coetzee,' she said, 'who found his spiritual home among the Nats, [they] sit in dispirited fragments on the cross-benches . . . [they] have acted in what I can only describe as a "now they're with us, now they're not" fashion. Mostly not.'[22] Eventually, of the original Conservatives Coetzee, Waring and Jonker joined the Nationalists and the remainder faded from the political scene.

At the outset of the session the United Party caucus launched a two-pronged attack on the Government. Its first strategy was to expose the National Party's hypocrisy as far as their so-called *volkseenheid** aim was concerned. From the No Confidence debate onward, it concentrated on exposing the educational and immigra-

*National unity.

tion policies of the Government, orientated as they were in the interests of sectional Nationalism. Helen observed:

Afrikaans-speaking children must be kraaled off from their English-speaking compatriots lest they be contaminated by British liberalism and immigrants should not be welcomed lest they dilute Nationalism. Not that the Nationalists need worry over much about immigrants . . . the net four hundred that we gained last year, were offset by the fatal accidents in 1956 on our roads . . .[23]

The United Party's second major line of attack was to pin-point Verwoerd as Public Enemy Number One. Verwoerd had been Minister of Native Affairs for seven years, during which he had succeeded in forcing South Africa's ten million Blacks into an administrative and legislative strait-jacket. His evolving pattern of apartheid had reduced their mobility to the barest minimum. Under his rule Blacks were no longer able to seek the best market for their labour; they were prevented from receiving the same education as the Whites and even their freedom of worship was restricted. No other Minister of Native Affairs in South Africa's history had invested himself with such arbitrary powers. As one commentator put it, 'It is no exaggeration to say that he rules a vast black empire almost independent of Parliament.'[24] Throughout the Budget debate and on each Ministerial Vote, the United Party sustained its continuous attack upon the extent of this private empire, whose net Helen claimed was cast so wide that there was hardly an aspect of South Africa's economic life on which it did not impinge. She attacked it for slowing down industrial development, and what the Minister of Economic Affairs called 'a healthy state of consolidation' (the fact that the national income of the country had reached a plateau), she called 'a very unhealthy state of calcification'. The country's economy, she said, was 'gradually grinding down because of the administration of the Government'.[25] The shortage of overseas capital and the lack of skilled labour were all directly attributable to the suspicion with which South Africa was regarded by the outside world as a result of the implementation of Verwoerd's apartheid policy, which, she said, was completely out of keeping with the development of a modern industrial state. The only government reaction was a witticism by B. J. Vorster, who said: '. . . if the difference between her and the Liberal Party is a matter of tempo, then the Liberal Party must be very fast'. And all that the Opposition as a whole could arouse from the Government were the two stock retorts that the United Party and the English-language Press were setting out to sabotage South Africa by their criticism of the Government and that, in its blind worship of *die Mammon van die geldmag,** the United Party was prepared to sacrifice white civilization.

Two Bills, the Native Laws Amendment Bill[26] and the Nursing Amendment Bill,[27] preoccupied Helen during the session.

The first Bill, made notorious by its clause 29, contained much more than just a section prohibiting Africans from attending churches situated in white areas. It also attempted to minimize any social contact between the races by making it possible for the Minister to prohibit all gatherings at which Whites and Blacks were present. It was, however, the Church clause, affecting as it did the fundamental concept of freedom of worship, which roused countrywide protest from both Church and laymen and took the Government by surprise with the vehemence of the opposition. Helen wrote:

I am pretty certain that not even the prolific Dr Verwoerd himself had any idea of the wrath that would descend on him when this measure was tabled. I have a happy mental image of the Doctor presenting this Bill to his caucus. Imagine the scene . . . a room packed with Nats . . . some 165 prize specimens of the people's choice, gathered together . . . 'Order', shouts the Chief Whip and Dr Verwoerd takes the floor, and tells his bored colleagues that he has a little Bill he proposes to introduce . . . nothing special, just an amending Bill to tighten up influx control of Natives into towns, and to see that *sosiale integrasie* is controlled. No new principles, in fact. Everybody cries *Hoor Hoor* and the Doctor departs, smiling blandly, and tables his little bombshell. Well, I am sure even he was surprised at the fall-out it created. Hasty amendments, which just made matters worse, by putting the onus on the Native church-goer instead of on the Church itself. Dutch Reform delegations hastening to Cape Town, gloomy Nat. MPs in the Lobby.[28]

Debate on the Bill was marred by anti-semitic attacks by National Party members. One claimed that it was 'an impertinence for Jewish members to lay down the law to a House consisting mainly

*Lit = Mammon of money power.

of Christians', while Blaar Coetzee exceeded even himself by declaring 'there is only one principle in the clause . . . control over the influx of Natives, just as there is control over the influx of Jews into certain areas to attend synagogue.'[29] The United Party, together with the other Opposition groups, put up a magnificent performance. They fought every clause of the Bill, highlighting not only the Church clause but the other restrictions on the daily life of urban Africans which it so heavily increased. In the Report stage Helen hammered at Verwoerd incessantly, pointing out that every law

which is introduced to try and stem the influx of Natives into the urban areas has failed and it has failed for the simple reason that it is fighting economic forces . . . On the one hand industry needs more Native labour in the towns and at the same time the poverty factor is driving these people out of the rural areas . . . What the Minister must try to do is to realize that labour will flow to those areas where it is required despite anything which the Minister may do.[30]

Helen's persistence, like that of other Opposition speakers, in cross-examining Verwoerd, often forced him to display a remarkable and quite unusual degree of argumentative logic. While he seldom modified any of his legislation, he was prepared painstakingly to explain every aspect of his Bills, arguing for hours on end about the points raised by the Opposition. His laboured arguments were brilliant compared with those of B. J. Vorster whose only retort to Helen's attack was: '. . . My grandmother had a parrot which made much more intelligent remarks.'[31]

None of the Opposition's arguments and motions of closure had any effect, although it took Verwoerd eighty-six hours to pass the Bill through the House. Helen commented later, 'Dr Verwoerd seems to have no contact with urban Natives – he dashes around holding tribal *indabas** and being presented with white heifers. But he just looks blank when one tries to talk about rights for urban Natives . . .'

Helen spoke into the closing hours of the session. The United Party Whips had given her the task of winding up its debate on the Nursing Amendment Bill, a great honour for a back-bencher and an acknowledgement of her ability to make some impact on

*Councils (Zulu).

the Government. She returned to Johannesburg, she said, 'punch drunk' and deafened by division bells. As she told her constituents, 'Those of you who have witnessed a division in Parliament will understand why I cried "No" when my front bell rang this morning.' There had been a stage in the past week where she had feared that she would have to miss her report-back meeting but throughout the week she had been accosted by anxious Nationalists in the lobby, crying imploringly, *'Mevrou, bly stil, asseblief, ons wil maar huis toe gaan.'** 'Well,' she said 'we finally did *"bly stil"* but not, I can assure you, until the last Bill had been fought and the last word said on every conceivable subject.'

In 1956 Helen had prognosticated that the election would be fought on bread-and-butter issues but her experiences in the 1957 session now led her to appreciate that the Government's election platform would once again be *swart gevaar*, while the mystique of Afrikaner nationalism was still powerful medicine. Nevertheless she believed that the United Party could put up a good fight if at its special pre-election Union Congress, it demonstrated once and for all to the electorate that it was moving towards greater reform in its colour policy. The liberal wing had a valuable ally in Oppenheimer, who, as a member of the Constitutional Committee, had been pressing for direct Coloured and African representation in the Senate through Senators of their own race. What Helen did not know was that Oppenheimer's original plan had been put on one side by the Committee and was doomed never to reach the Special Union Congress for discussion. Shortly before Congress, addressing the Krugersdorp Women's Council of the Party, she had said:

The time is coming when the non-Europeans must be given a share in running the country. There must, however, be differentiation between the educated Native and his tribal counterpart . . . There must be legitimate concessions which must be made because the Natives are entitled to certain rights and responsibilities . . . The policy of apartheid has been achieved only at the price of seven years of strife but economic apartheid is a different matter . . . [you] . . . cannot unscramble eggs which were scrambled 300 years ago.[32]

Graaff gave her the lie. In his opening address on the eve of

*. . . Please keep quiet, we want to go home.

Congress, standing under two huge golden keys – the latest United Party emblem representing prosperity – 'big, calm Graaff' dressed in the baggy suit which enhanced his appeal to the *platteland* members, delivered a speech which alarmed the liberals and set a 'White supremacy' tone for the Congress. 'The United Party', he pronounced, 'is certainly not seeking power to preside at the dissolution of the Western way of life by handing inordinate powers to those not fit to exercise them.'[33]

Die Burger claimed with some truth that the Congress was 'one long song of self-praise and excuses to sing "For He's a Jolly Good Fellow" to Sir de Villiers Graaff' and commented: 'One is almost prompted to ask whether it is a gala or an election congress.' Helen felt some sympathy with the Nationalist editor's views. She roundly condemned the adulation which surrounded 'Div' and refused to rise when he entered caucus meetings, bringing upon herself a rebuke from the Chief Whip, while the fulsomeness of the Central Executive's motion of confidence in the leader, caused her to scribble on her Congress agenda, 'He should have made us kneel down.'

With the election in mind, Graaff's long-awaited and extremely complicated Senate plan proved to be nothing more than a firm entrenchment of white supremacy. Before any legislation of a fundamental nature could be passed, it was to have not only the consent of a majority of the Senate, but a majority of the Senate as it represented Whites. In effect this gave double assurance that no major change of the constitution could be effected without the consent of the majority of the white electorate.[34]

From the floor of Congress it was suggested by some delegates that Indians, too, should be represented in the Senate and that Coloureds and Africans should be allowed to elect members of their own racial group. Graaff, when the Constitutional Committee had proposed a similar plan to the Central Executive – which had split evenly over the decision – had, as chairman, voted against it. He now again rejected the request. But to pacify the liberals he announced that the Party would restore the franchise to those 50 000 Coloureds who were originally removed from the Common Roll, 'a step', he claimed, 'which will do much to retain the friendship of the Cape Coloured people'. On the other hand, the Party proposed raising the qualified franchise qualifications for new Coloured voters in the Cape and Natal and would not extend the franchise to the Coloureds in the Orange Free State and the Transvaal.

'Graaff was downright firm with any move that would have caused splinter groups in the Party, especially towards any move that would have alienated the *platteland* – he wanted his way and he got it',[35] claimed one delegate after the Congress. Graaff's firmness had its effect. Oppenheimer, to whom the liberals had looked to give them a lead, moved a resolution in which he asked the electorate to support the United Party, a party, he said, that stood for 'white unity, white leadership with justice, for freedom of the dignity of the individual and for government in the true spirit of democracy'. Faced with Oppenheimer's lack of force and with a general election pending, the liberals, realizing that any obvious difference of opinion would fatally weaken the Opposition, preferred not to force the colour issue. During the short two week pre-election session nothing more interesting than Graaff's cumbersome No Confidence motion took place – a motion in which he meticulously listed the Government's misdeeds and underlined the fact that its pre-occupation with race was progressively slowing the country's economy.

The following debates were uniformly dreary, neither of the two parties showing any sign of being 'campaign conscious'. Parliament was prorogued on 12 February and Helen returned to Johannesburg to fight an election as a member of a party for which, by now, she felt little or no enthusiasm. The General Secretary of the United Party, J. L. Horak, had spoken of 'its hard-working and inspiring leadership and its morale, very good and getting better', and it was the optimistic conviction of the majority of its members that the Party was on the verge of toppling the Government, a curious propaganda myth that it somehow managed to put across to its supporters right up to the 1974 election. But it had become obvious to Helen that the electorate was moving more and more to the right, and in addition, she knew that the recent Delimitation Commission would create extra Nationalist seats. There was also Graaff's continuing obsession with the *platteland* – where, admittedly, each constituency possessed two or three thousand *bloedsappe*, ineffectual in terms of votes but providing a large part of the Party's funds – to be faced since

she had every reason to suppose that it was an increasing source
of dissatisfaction to the younger urban voters who saw in the
Party's avowed 'White supremacy' policy nothing more than a
diluted form of Nationalism.

At the end of 1957 the liberal group sustained yet another blow
when Oppenheimer was forced by the death of his father, Sir
Ernest, to resign his seat in order to assume the chairmanship
of the Anglo American Corporation. Oppenheimer had been a
moderating influence on Graaff and in him had lain the liberals'
chief hope of eventually reforming the Party from within. 'I was
sick of it all and ready to give up,' Helen remembers. But she was
persuaded by the argument of her Divisional Committee that the
liberal United Party members should continue with their efforts
to capture the Party for liberally minded South Africans, and by
the pleas of her fellow liberal MPs not to desert them, and,
reluctantly, she accepted the Houghton nomination and signed
the 'Borkum' pledge which after the Bekker group's defection
had been brought into general use in the Transvaal.

Helen was once more given control of the Witwatersrand
Region's postal vote organization. Her liberal views were an
embarrassment to the conservative Transvaal leadership, and as
far as possible she was kept off election platforms on the grounds
that her Afrikaans was inadequate. She was, however, permitted
to make one election speech in Benoni, where a three-cornered
election was being fought against the National and the Labour
parties.

At its 1956 Congress the United Party had confirmed an earlier
executive committee decision that the next general election would
be fought on the strength of the Party's own 'tested and accepted'
policies without inter-party pacts. Shortly before the 1958 general
election, an approach was made to two of the Labour MPs,
Alex Hepple and Leo Lovell, to persuade them to join the United
Party, an offer which both declined unhesitatingly. They declared:

Once we joined the United Party we would be prevented from maintaining our unrelenting opposition to Nationalist extremism. We would
become victims of political expediency . . . It should be known that
on many occasions individual members of the UP caucus tell us
privately that they support and admire our unequivocal opposition to
objectionable Nationalist measures, but cannot vote with us against the

Government because they are bound by caucus decisions, often taken for tactical reasons . . . Neither of us desires to join that unhappy and frustrated band of UP members who are constantly held in check by their less progressive colleagues.[36]

Benoni was a seat in which the United Party–Labour pact had operated and Leo Lovell had held it for five years against the Nationalists without United Party intervention. Now the United Party put up a candidate and it was ironical that Helen was sent to speak in his support. Although she both liked and admired Lovell as a parliamentarian, she felt that party loyalty gave her no choice. Having refused the United Party's offer, Lovell used as election propaganda the fact that he was 'no Blaar Coetzee' and had 'no ambition to appear in South Africa's museum of political turncoats'. Helen felt this to be an unfair comparison since for several years the United and Labour parties had successfully operated their pact and the Labour Party members only retained their urban seats by virtue of the United Party's favour. Nevertheless, on the Benoni platform she devoted as little time as possible to discussing Lovell. She told her audience what an excellent parliamentarian he was and how sadly he would be missed, but that in the hard game of politics the reality of the situation was that Benoni was potentially a United Party seat and no party voluntarily gave up its seat to a representative of another party, no matter how able that representative was. She went on to devote the rest of her speech to an effective attack on the Nationalists, but Lovell was bitterly convinced that it was Helen's intervention which ultimately won the seat for the United Party and did not forgive her for nearly twenty years.

The campaign in the country was acrimoniously fought. While the United Party called for 'bread-and-butter' issues before ideology, the National Party had no hesitation in fighting its campaign on the two platforms of *swart gevaar* and Afrikaner unity. 'Vote for the Nationalists – or death', said the Prime Minister, and told the country in his final election address that a vote for the United Party and its policy of economic integration, would lead inexorably to political integration and the destruction of the white race in South Africa, while the National Party's policy of apartheid (which he claimed was both fair and just) would secure its survival. The second line of attack was the usual hypnotic call to Afrikaner unity as expressed in a leading article in *Die Trans-valer*: 'The tribal drum beats for every *rasegte** person . . . [and] when the National Party beats the tribal drum, it causes a voice to be heard which its people trust – the voice of the good shepherd who knows his own and whom his own know.' It had become, Strijdom implied, almost treasonable not to vote for the Government. The United Party's emphasis that two-thirds of its candidates had Afrikaans names and its claims that its 'roots lay deep in the history of the Afrikaner and in his cultural heritage'[37] provided no effective counter pull. While delimitation had adversely affected the Opposition, its great weakness lay in the fact that the greater part of the anti-Nationalist electorate could not see the potential danger of the heavy assaults by the Government on the status of Blacks which was breeding bitter racial antagonism and feeding the fires of black nationalism. These essentially reactionary voters tended to approve Nationalist colour policies, however much they deplored Nationalist attacks on their own position as non-Afrikaners. The United Party's aim, when it was not wooing the Afrikaans-speaking vote, had been the espousal of the cause of those Whites who were aggrieved by Nationalist republicanism and language policies. It had resurrected the hoary issues of the flag and the national anthem, and made standpoints on white taxation and Afrikaans/English school segregation while evading as far as possible the crucial issues of race relations.

In an attempt to pressurize the electorate, the African National Congress called for a stay-at-home and strikes by Africans to ensure that this time their demands would be heard. The Government responded by banning ANC members and meetings or gatherings of more than ten Africans in any major city, and used the United Party's silence on the issue to claim that under a United Party government the ANC would be able to achieve its aims. Graaff's statement that 'The United Party will not tolerate disorder, illegal action or economic blackmail for the redress of political grievances'[38] came too late. When the country voted on 16 April 1958 the United Party was severely defeated while all the minor parties and the independents were wiped out.[39] Graaff himself was defeated in Hottentots-Holland[40] to the accompaniment of derisive catcalls and jeers from Nationalist supporters

*Thoroughbred or pure-blooded.

and the unconcealed tears of his *bloedsappe* supporters. His attitude seems to have been considerably hardened by the circumstances of his defeat which showed him that the electorate were uninterested in a more liberal accommodation of Black and White in South Africa. From this time he openly espoused the conservative line of white supremacy as being the only policy generally acceptable to the electorate. The Hottentots-Holland defeat put paid to whatever expectations of reform the liberals continued to entertain. Virtually imprisoned as they were within a conservative party, there was not the smallest chance that any attention would be paid to their demands for urgent radical change.

Helen, who had undergone an emergency operation at the beginning of July, missed the first month of the new session. 'It saddens me', she observed, 'on reflection to think that my last words may well have been "Please phone Higgerty".' On her return to Cape Town she wrote, in the patronizing tones of a newly-promoted fifth former:

Our new back-benchers [among them Colin Eglin, Clive van Ryneveld and Boris Wilson][41] were over their teething troubles . . . [they] had a better initiating session than the 1953 vintage – most of our first session was spent in bitter caucus brawls over the Bekker issue and the ensuing sessions were not made easier by the violent sniping from Coetzee, Jonker and Co. who nestled like cankers on the Opposition benches.[42]

The fact that the caucus infighting of recent years did not immediately recur was remarkable in view of the Party's third successive electoral defeat. Following the election post mortem, the leadership had issued a bland statement to the effect that it was satisfied with its policy and saw no reason for changing it. Its supporters, the statement continued, were 'still in good heart' and there was 'a surprising amount of confidence about the future'. For a while the liberal wing speculated that the Party's crushing defeat would force Graaff to call for some revision of policy. But as the session wore on, the leader neither asked for nor encouraged any discussion on possible changes.

The session itself was mainly devoted to financial affairs while only two Bills of any importance were passed. The first was the

Electoral Laws (Amendment) Act[43] which lowered the voting age to eighteen. Helen described the Bill as 'the most obvious political cynicism of the worst type'. It was clear that apart from the electoral advantages to the Government of enfranchising more members of the larger white population group, the ground was being prepared for a Nationalist victory in the long-awaited referendum on the Republic issue, which the last electoral victory had brought significantly closer. She also found it a sad thing that the Government should be contemplating measures of this sort, when they were not contemplating an extension of the franchise to people only on the grounds of their colour.[44]

The second Bill, the Natives Taxation and Development (Amendment) Bill,[45] was fought by the United Party on the obvious grounds that a tax burden was being placed on people least able to bear it. In her speech on the second reading, Helen pointed out that more than half the urban Africans earned less than £15 a month while the poverty datum line was £23. It was, she said, the normal concept in every modern state that the richer members of the community should contribute according to their ability to pay and that they should support the poor people in their essential requirements.[46]

The 1958 session was truncated by the death on 25 August of Strijdom, who had been ill for some time. There were three contenders for the premiership. The first, Dr Verwoerd, despite his short parliamentary career and negligible personal following within the caucus, had built himself up as an Afrikaner extremist and the strong man of Transvaal Nationalist politics. The second contender was T. E. Donges, the suave, softly spoken Cape leader, whose English education and background had deceived English-speaking South Africans into believing him to be a moderate, although he in fact had been one of the architects of apartheid and had steered through Parliament such legislation as the High Court of Parliament Act, the Population Registration Act and the Group Areas Act. The third was C. R. Swart, leader of the Party in the Orange Free State, who as a temporary compromise had been made Acting Prime Minister. Helen pointed out to her constituents that it was not in the nature of the National Party '. . . to want wishy-washy compromises – the man who is the most *kragdadig* will win every time'.[47] Her assessment was correct. The National

E

Party caucus voted on 2 September. In the first round Swart was eliminated and in the second Verwoerd was elected leader by ninety-eight votes to seventy-five. Speaking on the steps of Parliament, shortly afterwards, the new Prime Minister said, 'I believe that the will of God was revealed in the ballot.'[48]

Of the new Prime Minister, Helen said

Personally I would rather have Verwoerd, who admittedly is mad, but at least genuinely believes in his mad schemes . . .* And I would rather have Verwoerd because it is hard enough as it is to keep English-speaking people politically conscious, and with Donges as Prime Minister, they would have lulled themselves into a complete coma.

She also dismissed the rumour, commonly held both within the United Party and by English-speaking South Africans at large, that Verwoerd's fanaticism and authoritarianism would wreck the National Party.

I wish that this wishful nonsense would be dissipated. The reason why I say this is that Afrikaner unity is still the driving force in this country and will continue to be so until the Republic is achieved. No Nationalist worth his salt will split Afrikaner unity until this main objective has been attained . . . So until the Republic – South Africa will have the mixture as before only more bitter. Not a very rosy future, I'm afraid. One day when emotional issues become less pressing South Africa may grow up sufficiently to have political differences based on economic issues and not racial issues.[49]

The growing concern of Helen's fellow MPs as week followed week during the session and still no mention was made by Graaff of a policy review mirrored her assessment of the situation. The liberals continued to hope that the Party leadership, having pandered to the fears and prejudices of the electorate and still having been defeated, would realize the necessity not only of accepting economic integration as an irreversible process but also of accepting the logical implications of economic integration as an essential feature of a progressive 'Native' policy. The conservatives, on the other hand, were pinning their hopes on a positive swing to the far right. This situation persisted until almost the last week of the session, when a new MP, A. I. D. Brown, finally asked Graaff

*Verwoerd once said, 'I never have a nagging doubt of wondering whether I might be wrong.'

in caucus, whether he was going to give members an opportunity of reappraising the Party's policies. To both the liberals' and the conservatives' relief Graaff replied that he intended setting up a committee which, during the parliamentary recess, would be asked to examine policy and to discuss the best ways and means of propagating it. He was at great pains to stress that he personally believed there was nothing basically wrong with party policy as it stood, only that it had been wrongly and unsuccessfully presented to the electorate. The promised committee initially consisted of three conservatives, Marais Steyn, Frans Cronje and Vause Raw, with Zach de Beer representing the moderates and Boris Wilson the liberals. John Cope, the secretary of the Native Affairs Group, now asked Graaff to appoint him to the committee, believing that whoever held the middle ground of the Party would be in a position of strength in the crisis he was convinced was impending over 'Native' policy. He was also convinced that the inequitable balance of the committee could only precipitate another situation similar to that which had led to the resignation of Bern Friedman. Cope, before going to Graaff, had failed to discuss his intention with his fellow-liberals and Helen, angered by his apparent lack of integrity, called Cope, within his hearing, 'Graaff's jackal', cut him in the lobby and once when Cope sat down beside her in the caucus room, moved and sat elsewhere. Her attitude was emulated by the other liberals, and apart from Boris Wilson, who remained friendly with Cope, he was ostracized by the liberal group until the final split.

While the recess committee sat, having extreme difficulty with its brief since it could not come to an agreement on what exactly United Party policy was, the dichotomy between conservative and liberal attitudes was becoming increasingly apparent even to the rank-and-file of the Party. In the tactical manoeuvring between the two wings, all the victories were going to the conservatives. Under Louis Steenkamp's generalship, Ray Swart had been removed as chairman of the United Party's Youth wing. A counter-attack by the Natal liberals attempted to unseat Douglas Mitchell as provincial leader but was heavily defeated when he outfaced what he called 'that loose group' by refusing to leave the hall when the election for provincial leader was taking place. He was re-elected, much to the liberals' discomfiture, by an enormous majority. In June 1958 the Witwatersrand General Council of the Party, once more firmly under the control of the conservatives, passed a resolution strongly critical of its MPs, demanding that, 'all party bodies and members shall publicize, propagate and live up to the ideals of *true South Africanism*' (a party jargon phrase for unquestioning obedience to the dictates of the leadership). At the Transvaal Congress held in October a strongly worded resolution from Houghton, prompted by Helen, that the Party cease trying to make capital out of government expenditure on African education and essential services, as it had deplorably done during the election, was shelved by being referred to the Central Executive for discussion, while a resolution calling for consultation with 'responsible representatives of the non-Europeans to press for a basis for inter-racial representation for all South Africans irrespective of colour' was side-tracked by an amendment calling on delegates to endorse the colour policy of the Party as adopted by the Union Congress of 1954. No resolution related to any of South Africa's major political problems. Indeed, a delegate from the *platteland* constituency of Wakkerstroom claimed that the United Party had lost three elections on the colour issue. 'The Native baby is Dr Verwoerd's baby and we should confine ourselves to talking about the White,' he affirmed.[50]

Such statements brought a response from Harry Lawrence, one of the few remaining members of the pre-1948 cabinet, who, for the first time, publicly indicated that his views were more progressive than had been suspected by even the liberal members. He wrote in the *Star* in November 1958:

Either, we are a multi-racial country or we are not. If we are, then the non-European section must be accorded their rights. I am not thinking necessarily of political rights at the moment. But attempts by this Government to diminish and reject these rights must be resisted now ... I do not think the United Party can evade this question. We are not a pale shadow of the Nationalist Party and deserve neither respect nor credit if we do not make our position clear-cut and unambiguous.[51]

At about the same time the liberal wing scored a local triumph when Jan Steytler, the member for Queenstown, described by an enthusiastic journalist as the 'battling Doctor, an athletic, lantern-faced, restless member', was elected as the Cape leader of the

Party, despite attempts by Graaff to influence the Cape Congress in favour of either the conservative Jack Connan or the moderate Zach de Beer, both of whom withdrew in Steytler's favour.

But these minor victories only served to disguise a growing undercurrent of feeling against the United Party liberals in Parliament, at their provincial Congresses and even within their own regions. And this deep-rooted conservative reaction within the Party was in itself being used by the designers of a deep-laid plan which was meanwhile being hatched to drive out the liberals, and which was scheduled by its chief architect, Douglas Mitchell, to come to fruition at the Party's National Congress at Bloemfontein in August 1959. At the instigation of the Central Executive a special committee was formed consisting of four prominent conservatives, Vause Raw, R. B. Badenhorst-Durrant, J. D. Opperman and J. L. Horak, with official instructions to fan out across South Africa collecting funds for the Party in every corner of the country. Fund-raising was its ostensible *raison d'être*, rallying anti-liberal support was its real function.

Chapter Six 1959: The Split

The fifty-three United Party MPs gathered in Cape Town in January 1959 for their pre-parliamentary caucus meeting, the great majority of them unaware of the purpose of Raw's and Durrant's peregrinations about the backveld, which were to have such momentous consequences before the year was out. They could scarcely have known that their party, which had been through so many crises in the last long decade of opposition, was about to be precipitated into a crisis greater than any it had faced since Smuts' defeat. For eleven years they had been content to drift in the wake of the Government, mouthing empirical objections to apartheid and offering the electorate little more as a substitute than the 1954 'Native Policy', and latterly the 1957 Senate Plan. But the lines of battle were being drawn between the conservative and liberal factions, despite the ignorance of the liberals of the tactics being employed against them and the indifference of the 'centre' group, which saw no pressing need to clarify colour policy in the light of the Government's failure to define apartheid in any positive way. As 1958 drew to its close, however, hints that the Nationalists were about to elevate their ideology into a concrete doctrine should have given the Opposition policy-makers cause for alarm. At the Orange Free State National Party Congress in October, the New Minister of Bantu Administration and Development,[1] M. D. C. de Wet Nel, declared in an *ex cathedra* style, 'Give me two years and I will create a new South Africa.'[2] Shortly afterwards, going into more detail, the Minister of the Interior said:

The National Party has never altered its policy to abolish representation of Natives in the House of Assembly . . . the matter will again be considered as soon as the pattern of our apartheid policy in this connection has unfolded and developed to such an extent that the Natives' own forms of government in their own areas under our principle of guardianship have in our opinion progressed sufficiently.[3]

Dr Verwoerd's theory that apartheid had now evolved to such an extent that South Africa was ready for the next stage of its implementation came as a bombshell to the majority of the United Party, which had never seen the Prime Minister's deeply held beliefs as more than party propaganda rather cleverly expressed. At their first meeting the caucus pressed Graaff to reveal the Recess Committee's findings. He reluctantly explained that the committee had failed to produce a unanimous recommendation. Five of its six members – Zach de Beer, Marais Steyn, J. Hamilton-Russell, John Cope and Boris Wilson – suggested that the Party face up to the implications of the multi-racial nature of South Africa and accept the eventual representation of Blacks by Blacks in the Assembly. Vause Raw, however, in a minority report, indicated his violent opposition to this more liberal approach, stressing the conservatives' firmly held belief that the Party had lost the 1958 election only because its policy veered too far in a radical direction. When presenting his report he stated verbally that should the Party consider any form of extension of franchise rights to Africans, he for one would have no hesitation in splitting it from top to bottom.[4] Graaff felt, not for the first time, that the whole matter of policy exposition should be shelved for the time being. Unfortunately for him, Verwoerd's reply to his motion of no confidence in the Government on 27 January 1959 preempted him.

'Our attitude', Verwoerd said, 'is that matters have now reached the stage where we can proceed to the next stage of our positive plan of development . . . namely to establish a clearer separation in the political field than exists today.' And, as a first step, the Government intended removing the Natives' Representatives from Parliament, since their continued existence there, Verwoerd claimed, could only serve to confuse Africans as to where the true focus of African political power lay. He continued:

We must ensure that the outside world realizes, and that the Bantu realizes, that a new period is dawning, a period in which the white man will move away from discrimination against the Bantu as far as his own areas are concerned; and that the white man is leading him through the first stage towards full development . . . We are no longer going to give the Bantu representation in the white Parliament because the white Parliament, after all, is the governing body of the white man in his own areas, but the white man with his Parliament will carry out his duties of guardianship over the Bantu in the Bantu areas and will give them the opportunity to develop fully in these areas, everyone knows what the future possibilities are.[5]

This terrifyingly clear exposition of the Government's plans created consternation in the United Party hierarchy. Its members were uncomfortably aware that a clear definition of their own party policy was urgently required as a counter, but Graaff's response indicated his in-built caution. It was unwise to reply to Verwoerd's aggressive speech immediately without caucus advice, he said, and he felt that it would be to his and to the Party's benefit if the Tuesday morning meetings of the Native Affairs Group were for the time being to be attended by all caucus members, who would there be given the opportunity to voice their individual views on 'Native policy'. With a consensus, he would then present the Party's response to Verwoerd's so-called 'new vision'. So every Tuesday throughout the session the entire United Party caucus assembled to express itself on the most emotive issue of South African politics. It was not long before this exercise in democracy produced three groups with profoundly differing views. One, clearly, was made up of the liberals (or progressives, as they were now openly calling themselves); another avoided original thought and seemed content to leave policy decisions to Graaff: most significantly, however, the experiment gave birth to a new cohesive array of conservatives, who for the first time began to organize themselves openly into a conscious anti-liberal formation.[6]

For almost a year now individual conservatives within the Party had been developing a view that advantage should be taken of Verwoerd's determination to implement geographical apartheid to disengage from the unfulfilled but still embarrassing obligations of the 1936 Land Act. Before the 1958 election Douglas Mitchell had made use of the popular argument that agricultural land in African hands soon ceased to be economically productive. There was truth in such statements, due to the inevitable overcrowding and over-stocking of the land and to the traditional and hopelessly unscientific farming methods of tribal Africans, and Mitchell's arguments won him many votes in Northern Zululand, where numerous white-owned farms had been theoretically scheduled to be handed over to African occupation in terms of the 1936 Act. But now the United Party right wing received more ammunition as the Government began to take the land issue far above the level of agricultural economics.

Just before the Easter recess the Minister of Bantu Administration, introducing the Promotion of Bantu Self-Government Bill[7] described apartheid as '. . . a divine task which has to be implemented and fulfilled systematically . . . The desire to manage their own affairs exists in the hearts of the Bantu population, just as it exists in the hearts of all other nations in the world . . . These matters lie near the soul of the nation and no safety valve in the world can smother it forever . . .'[8] Later in the same debate Verwoerd announced that the Government was fully prepared to accept full independence for the Bantustans as the ultimate consequence of its policy. 'South Africa', he said, 'is on the eve of a very great decision, a very difficult decision and it is not the time to rant and rave and inspire fear.'

Verwoerd's speech gave Mitchell cause to alter his line of attack. 'The Government', he said bluntly, 'intends selling Oom Piet van der Merwe's farm to the kaffirs.'[9] It had never been, he claimed, the intention of the United Party when it regained power to purchase land in order to hand it over to independent black states. Louis Steenkamp, Jack Basson and other conservatives, in speeches both in and out of Parliament declared that if the Government purchased land for Africans under its new policy it would be guilty of treachery to white South Africa, while in the Assembly Vause Raw, in a dramatically emotional outburst which typified the attitudes of the United Party right wing, cried:

What right has this foreign Prime Minister,* who is not the descendant of a single person who has made any sacrifice for South Africa, to give this country of ours away? Where on this map, Mr Speaker, is that Blood River[10] which we celebrate, that Blood River for which so many tears have been wept, and so many wonderful phrases have been

---

*A reference to Verwoerd's Dutch origins.

written, that Blood River where the White man established his supremacy in South Africa, that Blood River of which they boast? They are
giving back that Blood River without a fight, without a shot fired in
anger, they are giving it back to the Black man from whom it was wrested.[11]

Such blatant *swart gevaar* tactics offended even the more
orthodox moderate United Party members. Douglas Smit expressed his utter dismay at Mitchell's attitude. He would, he said,
never be party to breaking faith with the Africans over an Act
which had been passed by a United Party government. The
progressives, naturally, were considerably more vocal. Helen,
going far beyond the land issue, demanded as an alternative to
apartheid that the Party should accept the implications of a
multi-racial community and press for both the retention of the
Natives' Representatives and the extension of the black franchise.
Her standpoint was supported by those other progressives referred
to by her as 'the class of '53' as well as by newer back-benchers
like Boris Wilson. For the first time during the Tuesday morning
meetings Colin Eglin and Zach de Beer, both of whom were close
to Graaff and who were regarded by the progressives as being his
'blue-eyed' boys, emerged as liberally inclined, as well as, more
surprisingly, Harry Lawrence, who had been believed to be more
consistently moderate. Eleven days before the final caucus
meeting on 'Native Policy' was scheduled to be held, he had
submitted a memorandum to Graaff in which he suggested that
the Party had to seek a practical policy between the extremes of
complete territorial apartheid and full equality of Black and White.

Either we agree with [Dr Verwoerd] or we do not. If not, we should
have the courage, the wisdom, the faith and the far-sightedness to
give the country our alternatives – not in detail, because details flow
from wise consultation with all those affected, but in principle. The
over-riding principle which has already been accepted by the United
Party is that the Africans both within and without the Reserves must
have representation in the central Parliament.

Lawrence went on to detail his belief that the United Party should
be prepared to face up to the principles of eventual multi-racial
participation in South Africa. He pointed out that the 1954
United Party Native Policy emphasized that political rights were
not only dependent on the vote.

In dealing with this Bantustan Bill we should be prepared to implement this outlook. My formula for peaceful co-operative co-existence in South Africa can be summed up in three words: Consultation, extension [of political rights], and participation.

Consultation with the Africans should include, *inter alia*, questions such as the Pass Laws – particularly in regard to African women – in relation to influx control; migrant labour; the amendment of Native Urban Areas legislation; and freehold rights in urban areas. What is so essential is to create the climate for co-operation. At present we are poles apart. If a cultured African such as ex-Chief Luthuli were to appear on a United Party platform, we would have a barrage of criticism from the Nationalists. Has not the time arrived when we should defy this ?[12]

But Graaff was not prepared to defy the conservative opinions of the electorate. At the final caucus meeting before the Promotion of Bantu Self-Government Bill debate, he finally committed himself. The United Party, he said, saw the Bantustans as a gigantic potential fifth column, and stood for 'the maintenance of *white leadership with justice** in an integrated society'. Maintenance of white leadership would depend on the sincere willingness and desire of the Whites to share the fruits of Western civilization with those non-Whites who developed the capacity for accepting and carrying the joint responsibility for the country's future well-being. Only when the Africans had undergone a long period of training in the ways and responsibilities of democracy could claims to greater rights be entertained and then only with the agreement of a decisive majority of the electorate . . . Meanwhile the white group must be strengthened numerically by immigration, and the Party would ensure that the Cape Coloured community was restored to what he called 'its traditional status as an appendage of the white race'.[13]

He also indicated that the United Party intended increasing African representation in the Senate to six and suggested that Native representation should not only continue for Africans in the Cape but that it should be extended to the northern provinces as well, subject to the approval of the Party Congress.

The majority of progressives found this alternative to Verwoerd's Bantustans depressingly indecisive and insufficiently committed.

*Author's italics.

However at Graaff's express request they did not, as Harry Lawrence wrote, 'make an issue of [their] differences when the need for unity in [the] ranks – was paramount'. Once again Lawrence stood out as the progressives' spokesman.

> Verwoerd's aims require the posing of a clear alternative, an alternative, moreover, which must rest on sound moral and ethical grounds, which must not involve permanent discrimination for all time . . . our attitude as a Party should be based on the recognition of the permanent multi-racial character of our country, and on the acceptance of all the implications of a multi-racial state – with due regard to the hitherto mutually accepted social conventions which have formed a South African tradition, and to the understandable determination of the minority of White South Africans to fulfil their mission of leadership which has made past development of the country possible . . . You will remember that I urged to you, and to Caucus, that the three principles which we should have to endorse, and sooner or later implement, were real consultation, extension of rights, and participation by non-Europeans in our legislative bodies.

Lawrence went on to make it clear that Graaff had been unable to satisfy him fully on the first and second points and not at all on the third. 'Without', he said, 'departing from the basis of party policy as I understand it in terms of the 1954 Congress statement, I propose to continue in public and in private to press for their acceptance by the Party.'[14]

In Harry Lawrence, an influential front-bencher, a former Minister of Justice under Smuts and a brilliant and acerbic debater, the progressives had clearly gained a notable ally. Their manoeuvres were also receiving tacit support from Harry Oppenheimer, who, although no longer in active politics, played an important role behind the scenes in the United Party. Oppenheimer was kept closely informed of progressive attitudes and of events within the caucus by de Beer and Eglin. To Lawrence, who had copied his letter to Graaff to him, he wrote:

> I was very interested in your letter to Div with which I entirely agree. I had a long talk with Zach and Colin. Naturally I am in sympathy with their (and I take it your) ideas and if a break cannot be avoided would – as you know – be on that side of the fence. I had a talk with Div and was pretty frank. I feel very sorry for him – he looks worn out and worried. Is there any hope of keeping him on the side of the angels?

I am not optimistic – he seems convinced that the only thing is to accept or appear to accept, the Nat. view on race relations and hope to distract them on some other question.[15]

The unresolved internecine conflict was beginning to embitter Helen, who for the first time seriously began to question her own role as a member of the United Party. During the long-drawn-out debate on the Extension of University Education Bill[16] (an important apartheid measure described by the Government as being 'designed to prevent a spirit of equality arising' and to obstruct 'the dangerous influence of liberalism which is using the universities as its breeding place'),[17] she asked the rhetorical question '. . . whether the Opposition is not indeed rendering a disservice to the country by our very presence in the House. I feel more and more that we are simply providing the Government with a cloak of respectability, because in South Africa we are no longer enjoying a system of parliamentary democracy . . .' And yet in her attacks on this Bill, as well as on the other apartheid legislation that came before the House that session, she maintained more than any other Opposition member, a sustained logical and unrelenting pressure on the Government. The Universities Bill she described as 'a snare and a delusion and an attempt by the Government to impose its bigoted way of thinking on one of the last bastions of independent thought in South Africa'. She argued the need for extending education to the Blacks by opening the concept of Western civilization to them, allowing them to benefit from the accumulated wisdom and learning of the centuries.

The way to improve cultural achievements of under-developed people is to put them into contact with better developed people, and not to withdraw that contact from them. How do you teach mathematics in terms of Bantu culture? With cowrie shells . . . I suppose the Minister of Native Administration, who is always talking about trees and acorns, will tell us to teach economics in terms of diminishing returns of milk from milch cows . . .

In an anecdote calculated to infuriate the Nationalist soul, Helen recalled that the best essay she had ever read on the poor white problem was written by an African student,* and emphasized her

---

*A Mozambiquan named Eduardo Mondlane, later to be founder of FRELIMO.

feeling that since the so-called 'open' universities were one of the remaining few places where young Whites could meet Blacks on any level other than that of master and servant it was '. . . important that young white South Africans realize that there are non-white South Africans who are their intellectual superiors'.[18]

Helen was beginning to make a name for herself with speeches like these, and when the Government imposed the 'guillotine' on the Industrial Conciliation Amendment Bill,[19] it was left to her to sum up the United Party's attitude. She castigated the Government's misconception that increased employment of black workers in semi-skilled jobs inevitably led to white unemployment, and pointed out that the white workers they believed were being displaced by Blacks had in fact moved to better-paid jobs, higher up the industrial scale; that overall the number of Europeans employed in private industry had increased during the past twenty years while the ratio of Whites to Blacks employed in industry over the same period had changed to only an insignificant extent. She stressed that it was not the 'civilized labour' policy of the twenties that had solved the poor white problem, but the great industrial expansion of the 1930s which followed South Africa's departure from the Gold Standard, the rise in the price of gold, the increased economic activity engendered by World War II, and the opening up of the Orange Free State goldfields which had led to an immense increase in the country's national income, shared by all sections of its economically integrated population. She pointed out that if white workers wished to maintain their high standards of living and wage levels they should realize that they could achieve this by increasing their productivity rather than relying on artificial protection. And, while conceding that there might be some white workers who needed such protection, she pleaded with the Government to accept that the choice facing South Africa involved neither economic nor racial suicide but a possibility of developing the country's vast resources and potential with the full co-operation of all the racial groups. The only response she evoked from the Government benches was to hear herself described as a friend of the Soviet Union and almost in the same breath, the United Party called an '*onderdrukker van die arbeider*'.* 'We [the United Party] are therefore', said Helen, 'both

*Oppressor of the worker.

capitalists and Communists at the same time; I find it impossible to answer that argument.'

Debate throughout the 1959 session took place in an atmosphere of heated racialism – not only towards its end, White–Black racialism (which in the early months of the session, the Government had ruthlessly suppressed, during an apparent attempt to convince Nationalist intellectuals and the outside world that apartheid was not entirely immoral) – but in the form of unpleasant sniping between the white groups. As the session drew to a close, the Government appeared to recollect the impending provincial elections in September and, as if sensing a need to rally the *volk* (some of whom were openly dismayed by Verwoerd's new policy), suddenly released its back-benchers to indulge in one of their favourite pastimes, an orgy of *engelsehaat*, anti-semitism and *rooi gevaar*.* This kind of deliberate outburst was, and still is, a tried Nationalist pre-election manoeuvre, the disparate cultures of the electorate lending themselves to emotive responses, sustained by newspaper editorials. Real issues at such times become relegated to the background. Now, of all the Opposition members, Helen drew the most concentrated fire from the Government benches, possibly because she was a woman and Jewish, but more probably because they recognized that she had made a decision to take an uncompromising stand against apartheid, unlike the majority of the United Party's members who, whatever their private views, were publicly still toeing the party line.

Late in the session, prompted by reports from the liberal lawyer Joel Carlson of Africans being press-ganged into working on farms in lieu of prosecution for trivial offences, Helen asked the Deputy Minister of Bantu Administration, F. E. Mentz, for his comments on the allegation. He replied that not one African had been forced into farm labour under the conditions described by Carlson. In a subsequent statement, however, the Minister himself let slip that in 1958 over 2500 Africans had been sent to farms in precisely these circumstances. Speaking four times in one debate, Helen launched a savage attack on the Government, accusing Mentz of giving false information to the House. She made it quite clear that she was not attacking the farmers or the labour tenant system as such, 'although', she said, 'I think there are abuses under

*Anglophobia and red danger, i.e. Communism.

that system . . . I am attacking farmers who committed abuses, and I am attacking the way in which the system has been implemented and the lack of supervision by the Department.' In replying, the Minister of Bantu Administration first employed the well-known tactic of the generalized smear.

I do not know whether the honourable member for Houghton has ever in her whole life been on a farm, but now she is the mouthpiece of the United Party, and she has launched this attack. She is very concerned about this scheme but she knows very well that she is the mouthpiece of the Black Sash . . . the Opposition is allocating special time to her so that she can carry on with this campaign of besmirching the farmers.

But when Boris Wilson supported Helen's charges and her call for a properly constituted judicial enquiry into the matter, a blast of racist abuse was loosed on them both from the Government back benches. They were told that, being Jews, they had no right to criticize farmers for ill-treating their African workers. Instances were quoted of Jewish farmers who had appeared in court in ill-treatment cases. (The florid and excitable J. F. Schoonbee, a farmer MP who introduced this line of defence, said: 'I just want to say that if I were today of Jewish descent, I would be the last person to raise the matter in the House.') When Helen persisted in condemning the evils of the system Schoonbee was heard to yell at her amid the uproar: 'Go and preach in the synagogue!' while an anonymous Nationalist interjected, 'We don't like your screeching Jewish voice.'[20] As if symbolizing the growing United Party schism, H. G. Swart, the United Party member for Florida and an Orange Free State farmer, sat dumb throughout the debate, and was singled out, to his evident embarrassment, for his silence by de Wet Nel.

It was attacks like these by Helen (in what Schoonbee called that 'tje-tje voice of hers') on aspects of the national *status quo*, however distasteful, and the reactions of the Government to them that earmarked her for violent attack, not only from the Nationalists themselves, but from the United Party conservatives, who were by now convinced that she (and the other liberals, notably Wilson and Cope) were doing the Party's cause among the *bloedsappe* untold harm. Raw and Durrant had done their work well on the farms and in the country dorps. The divisional

Top With her daughters Patricia and Frances 1953

Above Helen Suzman at the Opening of Parliament 1953

Top The Progressive Party members photographed in their basement office in the Assembly Building in 1960
Left to right (sitting) Helen Suzman, Boris Wilson, Ray Swart, Townley Owen-Williams, Harry Lawrence, Jan Steytler, John Cope, Colin Eglin, Ronald Butcher
(Standing) Clive van Ryneveld, Walter Stanford, Zach de Beer

Above The Progressive MPs after the General Election of 1974
(Left to right) Réné de Villiers, Colin Eglin, Gordon Waddell, Alex Boraine, Rupert Lorimer, Frederick van Zyl Slabbert *(In front)* Helen Suzman

Opposite Speaking at a Protest Meeting

Above General Election 1961: Patricia, Mosie, Helen and Frances

Above opposite **Rand Daily Mail** Mrs Suzman's Stilettos 1963

Below Opposite **Die Burger** 'I hear that there are dangerous patriotic ideas loose amongst you. But remember, as long as I am the *de facto* leader of this party, you will think the way I say.' (Helen with the Progressive members elected in 1974)

Top With Kenneth Kaunda, State House, Lusaka, Zambia 1970

Above With Chief Gatsha Buthelezi, 1973

Above opposite With Réné de Villiers during the announcement of election results April 1974

Opposite Houghton Polling Station April 1974

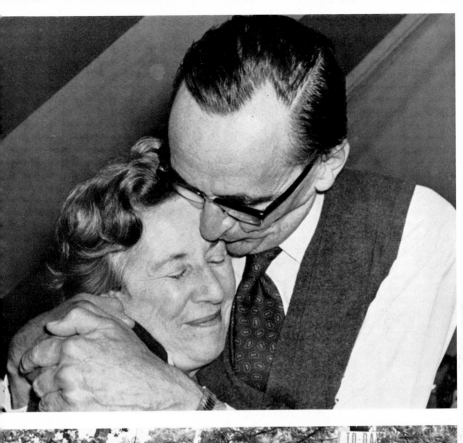

Hearing election results April 1974

committees of the *platteland* now had strict instructions to ensure that their full complements of delegates[21] attended the Union Congress in August, and, most importantly, that they knew their targets. Douglas Mitchell, meanwhile was assuring caucus meetings that he had every intention of forcing, through the introduction of a series of highly contentious Congress resolutions, a confrontation on the land issue. This, at last, was to be the lever by which the liberals were to be removed. Once Verwoerd's Bantustan policy came into effect, the conservatives considered the 1936 Land Act to have become irrelevant, since neither Hertzog nor Smuts had intended the African areas to be independent within a white South Africa. Mitchell's resolutions were intended to give these attitudes official status. The progressives felt such views, if adopted as official policy, to be one more shameful landmark in the Party's growing record of negations of pledges to the Blacks. It had broken faith with the Africans over the Cape franchise, and with the Coloureds over the Separate Representation of Voters Act. Many party members felt that the least it could now do was honour the grant of land it had made in lieu of the Cape Common Roll franchise. At the time of the 1936 Act Smuts had said: 'There is a tremendous risk that we would take away the rights of people who are entirely in the hands of the white population, and I think that we, as the ruling race, are bound to give them a fair substitution rather than see them lose their rights finally and absolutely.' To deny this firm commitment of the late leader was, the liberals felt, opportunism carried to intolerable lengths, and if the Party did not honour its 'fair substitute' it would indeed be hard for men and women of conscience to remain within it. But once again the progressives had formulated no concerted plan about what they would do if Mitchell's reactionary resolutions became party policy. Contrary to the strongly held conservative belief, they had no formal caucus of their own. Harry Lawrence, however, conferred with de Beer and Eglin shortly before leaving for a holiday in Europe in July. He told them that he was worried by the apparent rightward swing of the caucus and felt that if this mood persisted as he was sure it would, there was a strong likelihood of some form of schism at Congress. He hoped that neither Eglin nor de Beer would do anything rash or irresponsible, but, if Mitchell forced his land proposals through, he wanted them to know that he gave them virtual *carte blanche* to use his name as their supporter and if they left the Party he too would leave. And, in his capacity as leader of the Party in the Cape Province, Jan Steytler, who had asked the same two members to stay with him at his farm near Queenstown in the Eastern Cape Province on their way to Congress, warned them that at the Central Executive meeting held in Durban on 25–26 July, despite a plea from Graaff (aware of the feeling in the caucus and desperately trying to maintain the façade of unity) to defer the land issue, the Executive had insisted on keeping it forward. Indeed, Steytler, who strongly believed that the 1936 Act was morally binding on every white South African, found that at Executive meetings he, Graaff and Gray Hughes were in the minority, and even then both Graaff and Hughes felt that the Land Act was no longer altogether relevant in the face of changed National and United Party policy, although it should still be implemented for the purposes of the rehabilitation and re-settlement of as many as possible of the urban Blacks.

The four Transvaal progressive MPs had not consulted each other about the stand they were to take at Congress. 'Sakkies' Fourie was recuperating from a coronary thrombosis, Helen and John Cope were still hardly on speaking terms after Cope's performance over the Recess Committee, and Boris Wilson was more a friend of Cope's than of Helen's. But when discussing Houghton's tactics at Congress, Helen told her Divisional Committee of Douglas Mitchell's intentions of making a major issue of his land resolutions. She warned them that whatever happened at Congress, she would not tolerate any further departure from party principle, and indicated that any move in this direction could lead her to a break with the Party.

Indeed, most informed observers confidently expected Helen, Cope and Wilson to resign from the Party after the Congress. Graaff himself hoped that his three most troublesome MPs would go, closing the door on liberal interpretation of party policy and consolidating the Party in a more conservative mould: he even let their names fall in this context to his research assistant Mrs J. Beck, at this time, and also warned the chairman of South African Associated Newspapers, Clive Corder, who was about to leave on a trip to Europe, not to be upset if he heard that a few

MPs had left the Party. Thus with Graaff's tacit support the conservatives finished laying the groundwork for their plan. Vause Raw arranged with the Transvaal provincial organizer, Klaasie Viljoen, the strategic disposition of conservative supporters throughout the Bloemfontein City Hall, where the Congress was to take place, with instructions to catcall, boo and jeer any known progressive who spoke. At the Party's Natal Youth Congress held shortly before the main Congress the names of the three progressive members were freely bandied about as candidates for ejection at Bloemfontein. News of the planned purge was even published in the *Eastern Province Herald* on 31 July:

A plan to drive the 'progressive wing' out of the United Party is openly being discussed among conservative members . . . Mr Douglas Mitchell . . . is believed to be at the head of this 'get-rid-of-the-liberals' movement . . . A member of the conservative group . . . said the progressives would be driven from the Party at the Congress. He claims there is increasing support for the United Party on the *platteland* where Nationalists are disturbed by the implications of the Bantustan plan. 'To get rid of these liberals would win us many votes,' he said.[22]

On 11 August 800 United Party delegates converged on Bloemfontein, the unattractive judicial capital of South Africa set in the centre of the vast treeless Free State plain. Even the least informed were by now fully aware that the Party was on the verge of a major crisis. At the Head Committee meeting which preceded the Congress, Mitchell raised the land issue which, he observed, had been before the Central Executive twice before and had been debated for many hours, but had never been agreed upon. Despite Graaff's plea to him not to continue to press for a discussion, Mitchell informed the Committee that he had every intention of putting the whole issue before Congress. Reluctantly, Graaff, reiterating his disapproval, suggested that it be referred to Congress for an expression of opinion. Several resolutions on the other vexed questions of African representation and of separate voters' rolls, emanating from Natal and from the Orange Free State and Transvaal *platteland* constituencies, all of a noticeably conservative nature[23] were then considered by the Head Committee,[24] which could give no direction either to the constituencies or to the delegates concerned and eventually opted out by declining in any way to interfere with the presentation of the resolutions.

In his opening address on the eve of Congress, Graaff more or less repeated his statement in the Assembly Bantustan debate in May. The lesson for South Africa, he said, was that it was imperative that the white man should not abdicate his leadership. A surrender of white control over even a part of the Union would place Western civilization throughout the country in jeopardy, a situation, he claimed (with a quite remarkable lack of understanding), which was desired by Verwoerd. 'He wants to divest the white man of his responsibility in respect of certain groups of Native people by encouraging them to go it alone in undefined Bantu homelands,' accused Graaff. In contrast, the United Party policy of white leadership with justice was both realistic and responsible.

I certainly do not mean arrogant domination or crude *baasskap*. I mean the maintenance through the political influence of the white man of those principles which have developed in the Western world to preserve human dignity and to offer men full opportunity for self-realization as individuals . . . But for practical success, our Western democracy requires more than mere institutions of Parliament. It also requires an electorate experienced in self-administration . . .[25]

In effect, he gave the Party a guideline of civilized *baasskap* for South Africa in perpetuity, a policy which suited both moderates and conservatives and was repugnant only to the progressive wing.

Graaff, in his own words, had gone to Congress '. . . anxious to get the position in respect of white leadership cleared up, ask for approval of the policy statement I made during the Bantustan debate and get one or two worrying little matters like the qualification of Coloured voters and the purchase of land for Bantustans settled'.[26] In his opinion he had dealt with the position of white leadership in his Tuesday evening opening address and had made the position plain to his own satisfaction. On Wednesday morning his policy proposals were put as formal motions to Congress, divided at his own request into five parts, to be discussed together but voted on separately. These were:

1   That Natives in all four provinces would be given representation in the House of Assembly.

2 That Natives would be represented on the basis of a separate roll.

3 That the franchise on a separate roll would be primarily based on the 'responsible class' of Native.

4 That representation of Natives in the House of Assembly and the Senate would be by Europeans.

5 That these Natives' Representatives would number not more than eight.

A sixth formal motion followed, approving the policy statement generally and so enabling any delegate who disagreed with any one part of it to demonstrate acceptance of the statement overall. Finally, a seventh resolution, emanating from the Head Committee, commended Graaff for accepting that the future political relations between Europeans and Africans would be on the basis of group representation of Africans on the separate roll.[27]

The first point (regarding representation for Africans in all the provinces in the House of Assembly) was accepted unanimously. But as the debate moved on it became heated, and soon Helen, who had gone to Congress with her great friend Kathleen Mitchell, Houghton's City Councillor and MPC-elect, remarked it was 'a-buzz with hostility'. Even Graaff recalls that '. . . irrelevancies crept in. They turned largely on statements alleged to have been made by certain unnamed public representatives of the Party off the Party line and causing embarrassment. There were references to liberals and some quite stupid and provocative statements from people who should have known better.'[28] What was in fact happening was the beginning of the conservatives' attack on the liberals. Speeches began to take on a more and more venomous sound. When Louis Steenkamp finished proposing the seventh resolution, Eglin rose to express the progressives' view. He had, he said, always understood that the representation of Africans on a common or a separate roll was not a major issue with the Party and that members of Parliament were allowed to vote freely on it according to the dictates of their conscience.* At the time of the Separate Representation of Voters Act (the Government's first attempt to remove the Coloured franchise) the United Party had issued a minority report to the Select Committee of

---

*Eglin was referring to Article 6(b) of the United Party Principles.

Parliament, stating quite clearly that 'The almost universal experience of countries in which communal representation had been applied is that it tends to aggravate rather than to alleviate racial tension.'[29] Furthermore, Graaff, in the No Confidence debate in the session which had just ended, had said categorically that the United Party, if it came to power, would restore the Natives' Representatives, extend Native representation and appoint a Joint Select Committee to investigate, among other things, the possible introduction of proportional representation, a federal system or a common roll.

Now the conservative trap was sprung. As soon as Eglin finished speaking, as if on a signal, the assembled ranks burst into an uproar which raged for twelve hours, until eleven o'clock that night. The progressives rallied into a laager for the first time, forced into solidarity by the sheer intensity of the assault. Steytler, taking the chair at one stage, was greeted with jeers and cries of 'we will not have that ultra liberal'. Graaff seems to have made no attempt to stop the debate from degenerating into chaos, as discussion of his policy points became no more than excuses for savage attacks on the progressives by delegates who repeated monotonously the well-rehearsed theme that believers in the common roll were *kafferboeties* and 'liberalists' and should not be allowed to remain in the Party.[30] At one stage, Helen, who had just finished trying to defend the progressive standpoint to a sustained background of abuse and barracking, turned to Klaasie Viljoen (who had been openly boasting of his part in the organization of the disturbance) and likened his behaviour to that of a Nationalist demonstrator at an Opposition meeting: he laughed in her face. She exclaimed to Frans Cronje and Murray Hofmeyr who were sitting next to her: 'What a lot of bastards!' Cronje replied: 'Don't be such a starry-eyed idealist, Helen. You can only go as far as your electorate will let you and they won't let you go very far at all in this country.'

As the day wore on, the insults hurled at the progressives (and most particularly at Helen, as the representative of what was seen as an extremist viewpoint) became increasingly offensive. One conservative, Miles Warren, the MP for Kingwilliamstown, accused her in tones of hysteria of betraying the United Party by her liberalism. At this moment Ronald Butcher approached Graaff on the platform and asked: 'Why are you letting this happen? You know all these allegations are untrue. Why don't you stop them?' Graaff replied, with unruffled calm, 'I know they are. But when I have two dogs and they don't get on with each other, I just let them fight it out and then they are good friends after that.' Butcher returned to the floor to make a powerful appeal for inter-faction tolerance, only to be howled down by the majority. The delegates, for the most part right wing, and many of them primed by the propaganda of the Raw–Durrant expedition, were becoming inflamed by the emotional speeches of the conservative leaders. Even Graaff wrote shortly afterwards that he did not find it easy to describe the atmosphere accurately. It seemed to him that the bulk of delegates had come to Congress to take the step forward outlined by him in the Bantustan debate, but were upset to find there were delegates who wished to go further. By the end of the afternoon he had become, in his own words, 'a bit fed-up' and belatedly told the Congress that he considered some of the discussions to have overstepped the normal limits of debate, requesting the delegates to allow their fellows their democratic right to state their views fairly and openly.[31]

His appeal exercised some form of temporary check on the unbridled passions of the conservatives: the evening session continued in somewhat a quieter vein. Graaff summed up on each resolution before it was voted on, and of his policy points the first three were carried unanimously. When Leo Boyd, a moderate MPC from Natal, moved an amendment that representation of Africans in the Senate and in the House of Assembly be by any person regardless of colour, he found only thirty supporters, despite Graaff's comment that this step would have to come one day and that the Party could not hope to consult through people of a different race. Even then the cautious leader hastily qualified his viewpoint by emphasizing that he did not believe that the public was ready for such revolutionary suggestions at this stage in South Africa's development.

At last the debate ended and the resolutions were put to the vote. Leo Boyd had taken the calculated risk of assuring Graaff publicly on the progressives' behalf that although they would vote according to their consciences when the first five points were put individually, they would, in the interests of party unity, give him a *nem con* vote on the sixth (the policy statement as a whole). Boyd later wrote:

In making this gesture, I ran the risk of Colin Eglin and others saying that I had no mandate to speak for them [which was of course true]. Colin and Helen had consistently refused to agree to my suggestion that, having spoken against the five points we should leave it at that and not vote for or against those on which we disagreed.[32]

In the event, the sixth resolution was passed without a dissenting vote: although Boyd recalls that there were 'one or two' abstentions, no definite record of the voting exists.

Trouble arose again over the seventh resolution, that of the separate rolls. In view of the differing interpretations which had been placed upon it during the debate, Graaff asked the Congress to accept firstly that in future members of the Party on public platforms would not diverge from the official policy of separate representation for Natives and Europeans, nor plead publicly for Common Roll representation; and secondly that if the Party came to power and the Select Committee promised in terms of the 1954 policy statement which recommended Common Roll representation for Natives and Europeans, approval from Congress would be required before this measure could be placed on the Statute Book.[33] Sixteen of the progressive delegates voted against the resolution, which seemed to slam the door for ever on Common Roll representation and undoubtedly marked a clear new departure in United Party policy. They could not accept Graaff's argument that the change from common to separate roll was a temporary step made to placate public opinion, or his vague suggestions that the Party would first seek acceptance of a black policy based on separate roll representation, and on achieving power would at some undefined future date revert to the concept of a common roll.

When the vote had been taken, cries of treachery against the progressive dissidents rose from some delegates sitting immediately in front of and behind Helen and Leo Boyd. (It appears that Raw and Badenhorst-Durrant had deliberately placed themselves and their supporters in this area: Boyd recalls that during the voting Durrant turned round and stared fixedly at them every time a vote was taken.) Immediately after voting had taken place

on the last resolution a delegate demanded to know what discipli-
nary action would be taken against those members who had failed
to vote for all five points. Although it was ignored by the chairman,
Graaff took it upon himself to answer this question, assuring the
Congress that those members who had voted against any of the
resolutions were perfectly entitled to do so, and had his complete
confidence. He was sure that they would continue to work ami-
cably with him as they had done in the past.

Late on Wednesday night, when the exhausted delegates had
adjourned, Helen and several other progressives separately made
up their minds to leave the Party if Mitchell's land resolutions
were passed. Indeed, Helen only stayed in Bloemfontein at all for
the next day's session because she felt she had an obligation to her
constituents to endure what seemed bound to be another prolonged experience of jibes and abuse from the rampant conservatives.

Thursday morning and much of the afternoon were taken up
with routine and non-controversial work: an artificial calm prevailed as the delegates awaited the final confrontation. Late in the
afternoon Douglas Mitchell announced that he intended proposing
a resolution which was not on the agenda, and proceeded to read
it to the assembly. It was the ultimate bait for the progressives, to
which the previous day's attack had been only a prelude. He
read: 'This Congress of the United Party records that:

1 it is mindful of and maintains the pledge given by General
   Hertzog in 1936 to provide for the Bantu of the Union seven
   and a quarter million morgen of land under conditions which
   maintain that land as an integral part of the Union; and
2 expresses its entire opposition to the acquisition and alienation
   of more land for the Government's avowed purpose of giving
   it to Bantu tribes which under the Bantustan policy of the
   Government are to form independent sovereign Bantu states,
   whether such land is today Crown land or in private ownership; and
3 calls upon the Prime Minister forthwith to define the boundaries of the proposed new independent Bantu states for the
   information of South Africa.[34]

Graaff opened the debate by making it clear that while he

himself would not support the resolution, he would not regard it as questioning confidence in the Party leadership if it was passed, and to the best of his ability tried to put both sides of the question. He indicated that he would vote for further purchases of land because he feared that failure to do so might be misunderstood by the electorate. He felt additional land to be vitally important to the rehabilitation of the existing eroded and overcrowded African areas, but did not in fact believe that Verwoerd could stay in power long enough to make the implementation of his policy irreversible.[35] In conclusion, he appealed to Congress not to pass Mitchell's resolutions in order to gain the Party a temporary political advantage when there were party members and many supporters who felt a moral issue to be involved.

Graaff's step in speaking and voting against Mitchell was a curious one. Very few political leaders have ever made a public statement before a vote that if it went against them, they would not take it as a vote of no confidence in their leadership. It seems that it was only the regard the conservative rank-and-file had for Graaff, and the fact that Mitchell, Steenkamp and Raw can have had no desire to lose so compliant a figurehead, which enabled him to retain the leadership at all at this crucial juncture.

Mitchell now formally introduced the resolution in an inflammatory speech, claiming that if the United Party came to power it would honour its obligations, but until then it saw no reason for white money to be spent in the furtherance of government schemes. Raw and Steenkamp spoke in support and the conservatives began to rally behind them. A Boer War veteran, Jannie Landman from Newcastle, Natal, was heard to observe that he 'knew the Kaffirs, and there were three things to be kept from them: guns, brandy and the vote'. The Voortrekkers, said this uncompromising old delegate, had fought for South Africa with their blood and, since already one quarter of the land had been given to the kaffirs, they did not need an inch more.[36]

All in all, the conservatives were playing their hand with considerable expertise. Their resolution was so worded as to appeal to the ordinary delegates' sense of loyalty to the memory of Hertzog and Smuts, while contradicting the very essence of those statesmen's sop to the disenfranchised Africans. At the same time its last paragraph seemed to be an aggressive demand to the

Nationalist Government in the true spirit of a dynamic opposition. Its sting lay in the first words of the second paragraph, and was recognized by the progressives for what it was: a flat repudiation of Hertzog's solemn promise to the Africans to buy them land as a *quid pro quo*, firstly, for the loss of the vote, and also for their previous loss (in 1913) of the right to purchase land anywhere else in the Union.

A short but violently heated debate took place. The moral arguments put forward by the progressives came up against a blank wall. Abuse and recriminations were once more hurled about the hall. Eventually Graaff, still desperately trying to maintain the crumbling façade, asked Mitchell to waive his right of reply in return for his own waiver of the right to sum up. Mitchell agreed. The motion was put to the vote and carried by an over-overwhelming majority. Despite having voted against it Graaff appeared unperturbed. He wrote shortly afterwards to Lawrence that he did not believe that Congress's action precluded the Party, once returned to power, from purchasing every inch of land promised by General Hertzog for the extension of the reserves. He still believed that in Opposition the United Party should support the purchase of any land for enlarging the reserves in terms of the 1936 Act provided it was outside the boundaries of the areas destined by Verwoerd to become independent Bantustans. The Party would meanwhile continue to support the purchase of land for African housing and recreational facilities in the neighbourhood of the industrial areas and would support the spending of money for rehabilitation and development of the reserves.[37] He felt that what was involved was, in his own words, the suspension, as opposed to a breach, of a pledge.[38]

The vote was almost anti-climactic for the progressives. Without exception they had passed a personal Rubicon. Eglin and de Beer were sitting at the back of the hall when the voting took place, and when it was over they decided that rather than leave Bloemfontein that night as they were scheduled to do, they would stay in the city to discuss the action they must now take. De Beer left to cancel their flight bookings, and while he was out of the hall Sydney Waterson, a former cabinet minister and senior party member came up to Eglin, red-faced and agitated, saying, 'Look, Colin, I don't now what you fellows are going to do, but I'm getting out of the Party on this.' A few moments before he had said to Ronald Butcher: 'This is where I say "good-bye". I was a signatory of the 1936 Land Agreement with Hertzog and Smuts, and I will not dishonour my signature.' Eglin told Waterson that he would meet him later at the Bloemfontein Club, and when de Beer returned sent a note to Steytler asking him to join them. Steytler replied, 'It's happened. Meet me at Room 309, the Maitland Hotel, at 6.30 p.m.' Outside the Hall, de Beer and Eglin approached an agitated group of progressives including Townley Owen-Williams, Clive van Ryneveld and Douglas Smit and asked them to come to Steytler's meeting. Smit refused outright, saying, 'I'm not going to let Douglas Mitchell have the satisfaction of driving me out of the Party.' As they stood on the steps in the late afternoon sunshine, Ray Swart came up to them and said, 'I've had it': to which they replied in chorus, 'Come with us.'

Helen, followed by Kathleen Mitchell, had stormed out of the hall a few minutes before the others. In the foyer they met J. R. Neame, the political correspondent of the *Rand Daily Mail*. 'That's it', she told them, unconsciously echoing Steytler and Swart, 'I'm out.' They walked to her car, which was parked nearby, and Helen had just started the engine when in the driving mirror she saw Eglin, de Beer and Swart leave the City Hall together and stand on the steps talking excitedly with a growing number of delegates. 'Hang on,' she said to her passengers, 'something's happened.' She climbed out of the car and joined the group on the steps. 'I don't know what you're doing,' she said to them, 'but I'm getting out of this damned Party!' She recalls that they agreed with her and somebody proposed that they issue a statement. 'Don't do it on your own,' said Helen, 'because we all want to do the same thing. For God's sake let's act together.' They agreed to meet in Steytler's hotel room at 6.30 and to bring with them as many of the dissident progressives as they could find. John Cope passed them on his way out of the hall, but they ignored him, believing him to be a Graaff supporter and unlikely to agree with them. Cope and Wilson, the latter had left before Mitchell's resolution was debated, returned to Johannesburg ignorant of the impending break. Ronald Butcher and Lester Hall (a Natal MPC), both of whom had individually decided to resign, had also already left for Durban, and, stopping at Harrismith on the Natal border for the night, had their depression compounded when their hostess asked them if the liberals had been successfully ejected from the Party. 'What do you mean?' Butcher asked her. 'Oh, it's been common knowledge around here for weeks,' she replied. 'The Nationalists have been spreading it around.'

On their way to Steytler's hotel, Eglin and de Beer stopped at the Bloemfontein Club to collect Sidney Waterson. There they found J. P. Hamilton-Russell, MP for Wynberg, writing a letter of resignation to Graaff; Leo Boyd was also in the club. Throughout the Congress, Boyd had been advocating collective rather than individual action by the progressives and had also decided to spend the night in Bloemfontein. He asked if he could accompany Eglin, de Beer and Waterson, who demurred, saying that they wanted to consult Steytler alone and would telephone Boyd immediately anything transpired.

By 6.30 ten progressives were jammed into room 309 of the Maitland Hotel, involved in passionate argument, not so much about the fact that they were going to leave the Party but as to the method of doing it. A general consensus of opinion finally emerged, that, as a first step, Graaff should be informed of the group's intention to make a public statement on the land resolution. Steytler and Waterson were deputed to do this, if possible before Graaff left for Cape Town. They drove fast to the airport and found the Party leader awaiting the Cape Town flight in the departure lounge. In the ten minutes before his plane left they told him that a number of delegates were extremely upset about the Mitchell resolution, and, since this fact was almost certain to find its way into the Press, they did not want Graaff to discover a crisis in his own party in the morning newspapers. Graaff claims he told Steytler that as Cape chairman he had a responsibility to the Party and to the leadership to see that nothing untoward leaked to the Press. Waterson asked what advice he must give the dissidents, and Graaff instructed him to tell them to do nothing until they had had the opportunity of seeing him personally. He hoped they would come to Cape Town to do this within the next day or two.[39] The Cape Town flight was called and the two progressives returned gloomily to the hotel to find that the remainder of the group had drafted a statement, which had already been signed by Helen and de Beer. Helen recalls that in the mood of depression and disillusionment then possessing her she was prepared to sign anything. All she wanted, she said, was to get out of the Party and go home.

The statement read:

The United Party Union Congress today took a decision to oppose further purchases of land for Native settlement by the present Government. This is a clear breach of the promise given by the United Party Government in 1936, and as such a backward step from the 1954 statement of United Party policy. None of us can accept this decision. It is indicative of the general unwillingness of the Congress to face up to what we believe to be the increasingly urgent problems of our multi-racial country. For this reason we doubt whether we can any longer serve any honest and useful purpose as members of the Party and we have therefore to consider our position and to discuss it with Sir de Villiers Graaff. We have had no opportunity of consulting with other Party members who may share our views.[40]

Leo Boyd, who had by this time been brought over from the Club, opposed immediate publication of the statement. He was a cautious man, and its air of finality alarmed him. 'If', he asked, 'we are already so definite, for what purpose are we going to see Div?' He also found two other grounds for objection: firstly, the absence of Wilson, Cope and Butcher, who could be counted on to join the progressives if any split took place and who should have a chance to read the statement before it was published, and, secondly, and more importantly to Boyd, the fact that Graaff had not wanted the Mitchell resolution passed, and, indeed, had voted against it himself. Graaff had specifically asked Steytler and Waterson to meet him in Cape Town to discuss the matter and the personal loyalty owed by members to Graaff should, he felt, make them postpone publication until the leader had been given a chance to heal the breach. Boyd, as a member of the Natal Provincial Executive Committee probably did not fully comprehend the depth of dislike and contumely the majority of the progressive MPs by now felt for Graaff. At any rate, he soon capitulated in the face of arguments from Helen, de Beer and Eglin, none of whom was in a mood to brook any further delay. Graaff, they said, had had every opportunity both at Congress and during the earlier caucus meetings of taking a stronger line on the Mitchell resolution. They pointed out that, as leader, he must have known that feelings were running high, and had in fact received a letter from Harry Lawrence threatening to leave the Party caucus if Mitchell's resolution was passed. The rest of the group were unanimous. The statement was given to Neame, who had been waiting in the lobby of the hotel.

That night the news of the split spread like wildfire through South Africa. Graaff, at home in Cape Town, was rudely awakened from sleep by calls from various newspapers telling him of the publication of the statement. He refused to comment, saying that he was seeing Waterson and Steytler on the following Monday in his office. In the morning he summoned his remaining provincial leaders and spent a weekend of furious activity trying to rally forces on to his side. Waterson and Steytler, meanwhile, flew to Cape Town, while the remainder of the progressives returned to their respective homes, themselves whipping up support in their divisions and the surrounding regions.

On the 280-mile drive back to Johannesburg, Helen kept repeating to her companions, 'Now I've done it! Now I've done it!' While she knew her divisional committee would accept her action, she appreciated that the rank-and-file of the Houghton voters would have difficulty in understanding the issue. Certainly it was not as clear-cut as the question of the Coloured vote had been, but she was adamant that she was not going to give way once again on what she believed to be a fundamental moral principle. Apart from that, she now admits, she felt that she had reached the end of the road with the United Party. Immediately on her return to Johannesburg she called a meeting of the Houghton committee, to which Henry Tucker, the conservative Transvaal leader, was invited, and at which he was the first to speak. He claimed, using Graaff's own words, that no pledge had been broken, and that General Hertzog had made it clear that the 1936 undertaking to buy land was in no way connected with the franchise arrangements at that time, and was certainly not to be regarded as a *quid pro quo* for the Africans' right to vote on the Common Roll. He asked the Houghton Division to retain their loyalty to Graaff and the Party and not to destroy its chances of making an impact at the provincial elections. Helen when she rose to speak refuted his arguments point by point.

She began by analysing the facts of what she called the 'rather clouded 1936 land issue', starting with the principles laid down in the 1913 and 1936 Acts. She quoted General Hertzog's statement at the time of the passing of the second Act:

The Government wishes once more to give the assurance that it is its earnest desire to see that the obligation towards the Natives of the Union arising out of this Bill, in conjunction with the Representation of Natives Act recently passed by a Joint Sitting of both the Houses, shall be faithfully carried out, and trust that this statement will be regarded as sufficient guarantee of the same.

She pointed out that of the 17 750 000 morgen of land allocated to the Africans by the two Land Acts, 15 million morgen had already been acquired. It was not within the rights of the United Party to oppose the acquisition of the remaining 2 750 000 morgen, despite any new concept of what she termed 'pie in the sky' now being forced on the Africans by the Nationalists. The land should, in any case, have been acquired long before. Mitchell was making voting capital out of the fact that 200 000 morgen of the land still to be purchased were in Natal, made up either of Crown land or white farms, and that this had given the Natal United Party a local political advantage in the northern part of the province. Indeed, Vause Raw, speaking in support of the Mitchell resolution, had pointed out that five seats in Northern Natal could be vitally affected by such propaganda. She told her committee that she sincerely believed that the vast majority of delegates to the Congress who voted for the resolution had no clear understanding of its import, unlike Graaff, who had voted against it and had made it quite clear that in opposing the motion his belief was that the other issues involved far out-weighed any immediate political advantages that could be obtained.

'Thereafter', Helen wrote to a constituent, 'having heard my side of the story, the entire Committee of forty, with two exceptions [one of whom was Mrs Sophie Lyons, who six years earlier Helen had so assiduously wooed for support in the nomination campaign] resigned with me from the United Party.'[41]

Secure in the knowledge of divisional support, Helen flew to Cape Town on Monday, 17 August, to see Graaff. She felt inwardly that this was a waste of time, for she knew how much

Graaff disliked her. She was right. Of all the dissident members, Helen headed the list of those whom the leader secretly hoped would leave the Party. He let her go with no regrets: fourteen years later he confirmed that, despite her subsequent parliamentary performance, he was still convinced that he had been right.[42] With relief she returned to Johannesburg to wait on events, which were indeed happening fast and furiously.

De Beer and Eglin had gone straight from Bloemfontein to Johannesburg to enlist Oppenheimer's support for the split and had consequently failed, as Helen had not, to make the immediate and vitally necessary contact with their divisional committees in Cape Town. Their over-confidence in the support they expected proved a serious error of judgement: the Party leadership was able to appeal to the loyalty of the local officials to such an extent that when several days later the two MPs asked to address the committees they were refused permission. Graaff, advised by Mitchell, Tucker, Horak and 'Wolfie' Swart, refused to accept Hamilton-Russell's resignation on the grounds that he had not signed the dissidents' statement. He now busied himself seeking a weak link in the progressive chain, and found it in Sidney Waterson. In the course of a long talk, the persuasive leader succeeded in obtaining a complete recantation from Waterson, who later attempted to justify himself in a letter to Harry Lawrence.

Under our Parliamentary system there is only room for two big parties. Splinter parties have, without exception, failed to achieve anything and have faded out ingloriously. For practical purposes, therefore, it is a question of getting out altogether, or continuing the harrowing task, in which you and I have been engaged for so many years, of trying from within to make the Party face the facts of life.

I don't particularly want to retire at this stage and there is, of course, the major factor of Graaff himself. I have no doubt of his personal views . . . [and] . . . on balance, I have decided to stay where I am.[43]

Perhaps Waterson had been a *bloedsap* for too long: at any rate his loyalty to Party and leader was too strong to allow him to face up to the implications of a broken pledge to Hertzog's solemn undertaking to which he himself, unlike any of the other dissidents, had been a party.

For a while it looked as though Clive van Ryneveld, too, would

F

defect back to the United Party. After his interview with Graaff, who had always taken a personal interest in his career, he signed a humiliating retraction strongly reminiscent, as *Die Burger* commented, of a 'Moscow trial' confession, in which he said:

I have apologized to Sir de Villiers Graaff for having associated myself with the statement made after the Congress of Bloemfontein and have expressed my profound regret at any damage caused to the Party . . . In view of the difficult situation to which I have contributed I have tendered Sir de Villiers Graaff my resignation from the Party to accept or reject as he thinks fit.[44]

When Steytler heard of van Ryneveld's action, fearing there would be more retractions, he resigned from the Party forthwith without consulting the other dissidents. He was immediately joined by the entire Natal group, Butcher, Owen-Williams, Ray Swart and the two Provincial Councillors, Hall and Boyd. In the Transvaal, meanwhile, Helen formally resigned, now to be joined by John Cope and Boris Wilson, together with several MPCs and provincial candidates. In the Cape Eglin and de Beer followed suit and the next day, 'Sakkies' Fourie joined them. Two days after his retraction on 10 August, van Ryneveld wobbled back into the progressive group.[45]

Those who had taken the plunge experienced a buoyant sensation of being rejuvenated. Walter Stanford wrote at the time:

. . . Ronald [Butcher] said to me he feels as if a millstone had been removed from his neck. Zach and Colin are running about like two-year-olds with adrenalin injections. There is a definite atmosphere of something big happening – a date with destiny, as Ronald calls it. Jannie is dead certain he is right and feels intensely relieved.[46]

But the most important progressive remained out of touch on holiday in Italy. It was as vitally important for the dissidents as for the Party leadership to bring Harry Lawrence, as one of the Opposition's most influential members, over to their side. De Beer expressed this urgent need when he wrote to Lawrence: 'One thing we lack – a really senior parliamentarian. The implication is obvious. We have taken the whole future of progressive thought into our hands. We may stand or fall by what you do. I hope you will think it right to join us.'[47]

At the same time Graaff, Gray Hughes and the repentant

Waterson were bombarding Lawrence with imploring requests to resist progressive seduction. But although his replies exhibited sympathy with the progressives, he made it clear that he was not going to commit himself for the time being.

While the progressives and the United Party leadership tensely awaited Lawrence's decision, Graaff called a public meeting at the Cape Town City Hall and made a long statement about the split to an audience of 2000 people. He explained that the United Party would always stand for enlightened white leadership, whose task, he explained, was

to deal justly with the problems of our day, not arrogantly seeking to entail the future but steering its course, always guided by the highest principles and tenets of Western civilization.

Some of our former colleagues find our plans for the implementation of these principles inadequate for their political purposes and contrary to their consciences . . . Though I differ from them I respect their views and part with them, grateful for their past support and hoping that our differences will never deteriorate into rancour and bitterness.[48]

Free at last to reply on behalf of what was now called the 'Progressive Group', Steytler once again explained their attitude to the Mitchell resolution:

What concerns us and what should have concerned Congress is the question of how the Native people of South Africa will react to this decision of Congress. We believe that the time has come when white people should stop taking important decisions affecting non-white people without proper regard as to how the latter think and feel.

. . . so much for the land purchase issue. Important as this is, there are also other considerations that have weighed with us. For a long time now we have been made to feel more and more unwelcome in the Party and although we have gone out of our way not to show our resentment nor to embarrass the Party in other ways, we found at Bloemfontein a spirit of hostility towards us that amounted at times to political intimidation . . . We have come to the conclusion that the temper of the . . . Congress showed a complete unwillingness on the part of most delegates to face up to the challenge of contemporary events here and in the rest of Africa.

The impression we have is of a party reluctant to move with the times, unwilling even to interpret its own principles in a forward-looking manner. We also have the strongest suspicion that many delegates want to fight the Nationalists with the weapons of race fear and race hatred. The despicable slogans of *swart gevaar* and *Kafferboetie* will be used against the Nationalists by people who should have known better.

For our part we shall try to develop United Party principles in a dynamic and realistic way, offering to South Africa and its different race groups real hopes of security, mutual trust and the boundless progress which is our natural heritage.[49]

A crucial moral decision now confronted the four progressive Transvaal MPs. Helen, Cope, Wilson and Fourie had all signed the 'Borkum pledge' promising to resign their seats should they resign from the Party. The same onus did not rest upon the Natal and Cape rebels. On 23 August the entire group met at the Suzmans' house in Johannesburg and the Transvaal members decided that they would retain their seats until they were forced to fight for them at the next general election, due in 1963. Helen was most unhappy about this decision, which had indeed to a large extent been forced upon her by the non-Transvaal majority of the group. Cope, too, had serious scruples, but after a night spent in prayer with the Anglican Bishop of Johannesburg, Ambrose Reeves, accepted the view of the majority. It was, of course, expecting a great deal of the Cape and Natal members to resign when they were under no obligation to do so, and at the same time the group had to act as a united body. The reasons given in the minutes of the meeting speak for themselves:

It was agreed that it is essential that Members of Parliament should not resign their seats, as that would leave the people who hold and support our views voiceless in the supreme legislature. It is the duty of the MPs concerned to represent progressive thought in South Africa and to voice it in Parliament. The policies advocated by our MPs are the policies which they were elected to represent and advocate. As far as any undertaking to the United Party is concerned, the Members of Parliament giving these undertakings are entitled to assume that the Party to which the undertaking is given will not deviate substantially from the policy it proclaimed at the time the undertaking was given.[50]

In the event, the decision not to resign seems to have been fully justified on practical, if not moral grounds, even though, ironically, only Helen retained her seat in the general election two years later. During those years South Africa was exposed for the first time to a parliamentary group expressing in the most vocal manner truly progressive principles. It is probable that, had the entire group fought by-elections on a progressive ticket in 1959, only Helen and Cope would have retained their seats.

When an angry constituent wrote to Helen: 'In view of the undertaking which you personally gave to the UP it was completely immoral for you to take such a decision, which, instead, was one for *me* and my *fellow voters* in the Houghton constituency to take', she replied:

May I remind you that although I was elected to Parliament when I was a member of the United Party, I was primarily sent to Parliament to fight the Nationalist government. Can you or any other voter in Houghton claim with justification that I have not fulfilled my obligations in this regard?

As for 'guarantee', I can give you none except that I shall continue to fight racial discrimination and injustice. In the words of Edmund Burke, on being elected MP for the City of Bristol, 'It ought to be the happiness and glory of a representative to live in the strictest union, the closest correspondence, and the most unreserved communication with his constituents. But his unbiased opinion, his mature judgement, his enlightened conscience, he ought not to sacrifice to you, to any man or to any set of men living.'[51]

Chapter Seven 1959-61

'We have made the break not to split the opposition but indeed to become the only opposition,'[1] wrote Helen early in 1960. And the task that now lay before the Progressive Group, in the six months at its disposal before Parliament reopened, was to form a party and to produce a policy acceptable to the electorate. At the Group's first meeting, held at the Suzmans' house in Johannesburg on 23 and 24 August 1959, the two major policy questions propounded by Steytler were: firstly, whether or not the Group should participate in the provincial elections that were to be held the following month; and secondly, whether it was in fact wise to establish a new political party at that particular juncture.[2]

The second question was quickly resolved with the decision to announce the Group's intention of forming itself into the nucleus of a progressive political party, whose intended direction would be indicated broadly in a policy statement to be issued only after full and wide consultation, research and study. Various sub-committees[3] were appointed to establish points of detail and to consult with experts on differing aspects of policy: they were to submit their reports to a steering committee which would be meeting on 21 September in Durban.

It was, however, less easy to decide whether or not the provincial elections should be fought. Supported by Leo Boyd and Lester Hall, who were anxious to retain their Natal seats, Helen argued that failure to fight would dissipate whatever support the Group could rely on in those early days. People who, for lack of choice, had been no more than apathetic United Party supporters, were now ready and willing to work for the Progressive Group. In several constituencies, notably Houghton and Parktown in Johannesburg and Musgrave in Durban, the Group had already skimmed off the cream of United Party workers, and an election campaign would, it was thought, bring in many more. But the real importance of the provincial elections was the platform they provided for the Group from which its members could state their case and explain the events that had taken place at and immediately after the Bloemfontein Congress. Helen's arguments were carried a step further by Boyd and Hall. Natal, they said, was in a special position. Douglas Mitchell had challenged the Progressives in that politically insular province, to put up provincial candidates against the United Party: failure to accept this challenge might bring the Group into discredit and drive many sympathizers back into the United Party fold.

But Steytler, the leader-elect, backed by Eglin and de Beer, came out against fighting the provincial elections, declaring that the electorate would only vote for the Progressive Group if it fully understood the issues involved, and such understanding, in his view, needed both time and intensive conversion work. As yet, the Group had no policy to put before the voters and would be unable fully to formulate one before consulting with the leaders of the various racial groups, which it had not yet had the chance to do. Additionally, he said, it possessed no political organization capable of competing with the United Party machine and was therefore unable to field candidates who might stand a reasonable chance of success. If the United Party fared badly at the elections, which was expected, the Progressives would undoubtedly be accused of stabbing in the back the only recognized opposition party in its fight against the Nationalists while achieving nothing for themselves. And, as Eglin pointed out, there was already a widespread feeling that the Group's Bloemfontein statement had done precisely this, and he felt it imperative that no further occasion for accusations of attacking the United Party while it had an election fight on its hands should be given.[4] Eventually Boyd and Hall contested their seats as independents[5] while the Transvaal and Natal Progressives held public meetings in their major cities, and the Cape Peninsula members of the Group limited themselves to house-meetings.

In the short term, this decision not to embarrass the United Party threw doubt on the credibility of the Group and had in the long term (and most particularly in the 1961 general election) serious consequences for the Progressives, especially in the Cape Peninsula, where confrontation with the United Party had been so carefully avoided. And, as Helen had feared, during the actual provincial election campaign the United Party used every platform available to it to denigrate Progressive motives, either ignoring or damning with faint praise the Group's call to every non-Nationalist voter to vote against the Government on election day. Moreover, once the elections were over and Boyd, Hall and another Progressive-Independent, Dr W. G. McConkey, had all lost their seats by small margins, Graaff, in a post-election message, behaved precisely as she had predicted, seizing the chance given him to point out that the Progressives had been defeated at a time when their opportunity for success was at its highest. He said:

Two of their candidates in Natal were well-known personalities, who had public prestige acquired as a result of the offices which the United Party made it possible for them to hold in the Natal Provincial Administration. They will never again enter a contest in such favourable circumstances. One must expect that they will continue to gnaw at the United Party in our safe areas, but the election has proved that they will be biting on good South African steel.[6]

While the Group was thus flexing its muscles at the provincial elections, its morale was given a much-needed boost by the resignations of both Harry Oppenheimer and Harry Lawrence from the United Party, Oppenheimer specifying in his resignation speech that he found himself in broad sympathy with the Progressives. In early September, Lawrence, while still in Italy, had made a preliminary statement in which he had expressed disapproval of the second paragraph of Mitchell's land resolution, but said he intended before saying anything further to wait for a move from Graaff. Oppenheimer, however, cabled him, urging him to make a public statement in order not to cause damage to the United Party's chances in its coming provincial election contest with the Nationalists. This concern for a party which Oppenheimer had just himself left, seems in retrospect, a little odd, but many Progressive supporters had yet to shake off all their old loyalties.

On 11 September Lawrence announced from London his decision to resign. 'It is a decision not lightly made, and I part from Sir de Villiers Graaff and my friends in the United Party with very genuine regret and without rancour or bitterness,' he said. But the second paragraph of Mitchell's resolution, which he saw as a breach rather than as a suspension of Hertzog's pledge, had been for him the last straw.

The more conservative elements . . . have chosen to make what at the very least can only be regarded as a backward step on a deliberate issue and have thus left me no alternative but to leave the Party . . . It is perhaps best that the decks have been cleared and that at last an opportunity has been created for a compact group to give shape and form and meaning to the sincere belief that the interests of the various people in a multi-racial South Africa can best be served and the Western way of life maintained not on the basis of the permanent domination of any one racial group over the other, but by the co-operative effort of all the racial groups forming the South African people.[7]

The month before the Durban meeting had been spent by Helen, as a member of the Group's sub-committee for consultation with Africans, in establishing contact with leading Blacks. Among others she had seen representatives of the African National Congress who, she later told the meeting, had made it clear that they were unwilling to accept anything less than universal franchise and a Common Roll. And every African she had talked to, including ex-Chief Luthuli, wanted the abolition of the industrial colour bar, the pass laws and all influx control measures. However, she felt that, although the ANC publicly demanded universal franchise, it might be willing to accept less if it could be truly convinced of the sincerity and good faith of the Whites.[8] This belief was borne out when subsequently the ANC issued a statement in which it applauded the bold stand taken by the Progressive Party, acknowledging that the Progressives' philosophy differed fundamentally from that of the United Party and taking this to be a clear indication that the birth of the Progressives was of great significance to South Africa.[9] She reported to the steering committee that there was only one group with whom she had been unable to find common ground. The Pan African Congress flatly dismissed the new party as being twenty years behind the times; there was no question of its coming to terms with them. But the Group was consulting Africans to get their views on the Progressives' proposed policies rather than in order to obtain African endorsement of them, a cautious attitude, bound, as an

African commentator remarked, to have an inhibiting effect on the development of truly non-racial policies. Groups like the Progressives, said this writer, although they had freed themselves from the mire of racial prejudice, still had to outlive its psychological effects on their political thinking. In their attempts to attract white support, they were forced to conjure up visions of *swart gevaar* if the white electorate failed to change in time. This projection of the 'frightful prospect' of ultimate black domination only succeeded in exposing the Progressives to the criticism that they were unwilling even to contemplate a majority of Black voters.[10]

The qualified approval of Progressive thinking shown by the ANC was not echoed either by the Indian or the Coloured leaders. Both of these groups, believing that the Progressives intended merely to champion white leadership in some new form, were considerably more sceptical. It now became apparent to all the members of the steering committee that the major obstacle facing the new party was to win the white electorate's acceptance of their policies and, at the same time, with these policies, to retain the confidence and trust of the Blacks whose leaders had already indicated that, for the most part, they stood for universal adult suffrage. It was this obstacle in particular that led the sub-committee on the constitution and franchise to advocate that it was neither possible nor advisable to set out a detailed constitution before the electorate at that exact moment; and Zach de Beer, who headed the committee, proposed that the Group, shortly before the Party's inaugural Congress, scheduled for 15 November, should put its suggestions for constitutional reform before the public, and at the same time, appoint a top-level commission, headed by Donald Molteno[11] and composed of leading lawyers and jurists, to frame a new constitution for the Union.

The Group held its next meeting in Cape Town on 17 October, devoting most of its time and effort to composing the Party's draft constitution and principles to be presented to the Congress. Progress was reported by Molteno, still busy building up his team, and it was decided that the inaugural Congress should only concern itself with the essential comprehensive structuring of the new party: its constitution, its attitudes towards the constitution and franchise of South Africa, its economic and labour policy, the position of urban Africans, the pass laws and the questions of social and residential segregation.

On 13 November 1959 the Congress opened at the Cranbrooke Hotel in Johannesburg. The conference room, draped rather sombrely in black and red, was packed with delegates and diplomatic observers, and a journalist commented that 'youth, beauty, a quick wit, an agile brain and an unusual political candour seem to be the composition of the newest South African political party'.[12] The Congress's business was conducted in a somewhat exhilarated atmosphere not unlike, recalled one diplomatic observer,

... that of the 'New Frontier' in the United States. President Kennedy had come to office representing, as he used to say, 'a new generation' of Americans. Similarly, the Progressive Party, with its young attractive and dynamic leadership, seemed to herald the arrival on the South African political scene of leaders who were capable of dissociating themselves from traditional views.[13]

Another delegate, Ellen Hellmann, remembers that

it was like a honeymoon is supposed to be . . . the excitement of going to the Party's first Congress and meeting there all the people one had associated with from all over the country. Suddenly, there we were, all of us together, with a political platform which was acceptable to all of us. There was a hopefulness that was wonderful.[14]

Steytler opened the Congress on an emotional note:

In future colour and colour alone should not be the yardstick by which people are judged. We consider that all South Africans should be given the opportunity to render a contribution to the political and economic life of our country . . . we want to face the future not with fear but with confidence that we can live together in harmony in a multi-racial country.

He then asked the delegates to elect a leader for the Party. Harry Lawrence, in terms of seniority and political stature, was the obvious choice, but before the Congress opened, he had told de Beer and Eglin that while his physical disabilities* and his virtual unilingualism prevented his accepting the position, he felt that it would be in the interests of the Party that his stature and

*Lawrence had been badly beaten up by Nationalists at a political meeting during the war, and had suffered a ruptured spleen which caused him continuous pain for the rest of his life. His eye-sight was also failing.

experience should receive due recognition.[15] Consequently, Steytler was elected leader and Lawrence chairman.

With De Beer in the chair for the greater part of the time, the 300 delegates thrashed out the Party's constitution and policy. In spite of what one delegate described as 'the diverse, independently-minded people there', and largely because of De Beer's competent chairmanship, there was very little disagreement of any kind. The steering committee had seen to it that the Congress concentrated on the broader principles of policy. Details would be discussed eighteen months later when the Molteno Commission had completed and delivered its first report. The Commission's mandate from Congress was to investigate a complete reform of the South African constitution so that it should 'contain adequate safeguards for each of our racial communities and will accord to each a share in the Government'. The Commission, which apart from Molteno, had still not been formally nominated, was to draft the proposed new constitution around six principles which had been adopted by the Congress[16] to establish constitutional safeguards to prevent any one group from dominating another group; to reduce the central Government's power over the provinces; to provide the framework of a Bill of Rights entrenching fundamental human freedoms; and to provide for the maintenance of the Rule of Law and of an independent judiciary.

The Congress also produced a far-reaching programme of political and constitutional reforms (at least when set against usual South African terms of reference), calling for the abolition of the pass laws and of influx control, the creation of a stable labour force through the discouragement of the migratory labour system, the restoration of the freedom of trade unions, and the right of unskilled African workers to form unions. But paralleling these proposals was the strong emphasis placed by many of the delegates on the importance of not upsetting the existing structure of South African society, reflecting the deeply held views of Lawrence and Eglin on the necessity for gradualism in the Party's policies. Helen was later to admit that she and a great number of her fellow-delegates had wanted policy outlines to go considerably further than they actually did.

In spite of the timidity shown by this insistence on gradualism, the Party emerged from the Congress firmly committed to the principles of a multi-racial society, a concept which, since it had been accepted by the Liberal Party when it was formed six years earlier, could not really be considered a spectacular innovation. But where the Progressives differed essentially from the Liberals was in the size and content of their support. Instead of the Liberals' tiny handful of idealists, the Progressives could count on the votes of a sizable minority of white South Africans, many of them firmly established as leading figures in public affairs. The make-up of the Progressive Party was also essentially different from that of the Liberal Party, which had several thousand black members and a policy of universal adult franchise which placed it far to the left of the National and United Parties: the Progressives represented a far more moderate and centrist group. The majority of them had to shake off a lifetime of United Party affiliation and some of them, particularly the older members and some of the Natalians, found this formidably difficult to achieve.

The one discordant note at the Congress had been sounded on the republic issue by 'Sakkies' Fourie, who found himself unable to accept the Congress's attempt to remove this burning question from the emotional to a more pragmatic sphere when it resolved to campaign against a republic as envisaged by the National Party on the grounds that such a constitutional change would severely endanger both internal peace and external security.[17] Two days after the Congress, Fourie announced that he would return to Parliament as an Independent, since the Progressives had failed to offer the country a sensible compromise between Afrikaner and English interests by promoting the concept of a democratic republic within the Commonwealth. His defection saddened more than it upset the Progressives. Their first meeting as a political party had just been held in Johannesburg and had been attended by over 2500 people: the ranks of their supporters were swelling daily; and on 8 December, the Natives' Representative Walter Stanford resigned from the Liberal Party to join the Progressives, having been unhappy for some time with the Liberal policy of universal franchise. In his resignation statement he said that he believed that the struggle for better government '. . . must take place in the parliamentary political field, convincing the present white electorate that fundamental changes are vitally necessary'.[18]

The Progressives were being assailed with some violence by the United Party establishment as being dangerously left wing, but with more circumspection by the Nationalists. After the break at Bloemfontein, the Nationalist Press had put forward the unfounded theory, reportedly sanctioned by Verwoerd himself, that the Progressives were simply the United Party wearing a mask of liberalism in order to impress a section of the electorate as well as the outside world. At an opportune moment, claimed certain Nationalist editors, the mask would be dropped and the two faces of anti-Nationalism again would become one. But the divergence of opinion within the Opposition was clearly so deep that even professional Nationalists soon found themselves unable to maintain this interesting viewpoint, and a second contention emerged to the effect that the Progressive movement was an outraged revolt of idealists against the political dishonesty and immorality of the United Party: the Progressives were subtly damned for refusing to stomach this duplicity and for exposing it to the electorate. However, once the inaugural Congress was over, the Nationalist Press seems to have accepted the new party as an emergent and independent political factor worthy of serious attention. *Die Transvaler*, Verwoerd's official mouthpiece, attacked the Party's acceptance of a multi-racial society as highly dangerous, claiming that its franchise qualifications, no matter how stringent, would give the 'non-White a free passport to plough the Whites under in a foreseeable future'.

The end of 1959 saw widespread sporadic violence in rural areas of South Africa from Sekukuniland in the Northern Transvaal to Eastern Pondoland in the Transkei. Opposition was building up against unpopular Government-sponsored chiefs and headmen and against other manifestations of the policies of the Department of Bantu Affairs, such as misunderstood soil conservation schemes and increased taxation. In Windhoek, in South West Africa, in early December, after nearly a week of boycotts of beer halls and African transport services, a thousand Africans rioted in protest against the intended forced removal in terms of the Group Areas Act of residents of one of the locations. Attacked by stone-throwers and frightened of being overwhelmed, the police opened fire, killing eleven Africans and wounding forty-four others.[19]

In other urban areas the violence which had been latent for so long began to erupt. Just outside Durban, in the crowded slum township of Cato Manor, a police raid for illicit liquor one Sunday afternoon sparked off a riot which resulted in the deaths of nine policemen. Fuel was added to the fire at the ANC's Annual Congress when, to commemorate the pass law demonstrations of 1919, it proclaimed 31 March 1960 as 'Anti Pass Day'.

Parliament reassembled on 15 January 1960. On the day before she was to leave for Cape Town to begin the new session to which she and her fellow-rebels had so greatly looked forward, Helen went down with jaundice. 'When I was packing', she recalls, 'I kept falling into my suitcase.' Her younger daughter, Patricia, then a medical student, came into her bedroom and said to her:

'Ma, you look ghastly. What on earth's the matter?'

'I feel as if I'm dying,' said her mother.

'You look as if you're dying.'

'I've got to get to Parliament,' said Helen desperately. But she spent the first six weeks of that important session in bed in Johannesburg.

So Helen lay fretting in bed, longing to be in her place in Parliament, while the new Governor-General, C. R. Swart,* a former Minister of Justice, gave no indication in his speech from the Throne that the Government was aware of any political tensions bedevilling the country: nor did he indicate that any matters of importance would be placed before Parliament during that particular session. But Verwoerd, with his usual skill, first shrewdly played off Graaff's performance in the No Confidence debate against Steytler's.

I differ radically from [Steytler's] point of view . . . but at least I want to admit this: he and his party have the courage to say: This is the road we choose – down the precipice . . . I feel sorry for the Leader of the Opposition [whose speech] consisted of petty points, general attacks of a minor nature and debating points but who had nothing to say about major policy. From the United Party neither [Steytler] nor I expect much. They will remain swinging between us.[20]

The Prime Minister now dropped a long-awaited bombshell by announcing the Government's intention of holding a referendum

*Jansen had died on 25 November 1959.

on the republic issue. He assured the House that the envisaged republic would be a democratic one, and that no dramatic changes would be made in the country's political institutions or constitutional practices. 'Our aspirations', he concluded, 'are inspired only by the hope that eventually we will at least see the end of the dispute in regard to our constitutional future between the two language groups, so that we can become one united nation.'[21]

The non-Nationalist section of the electorate responded to Verwoerd's announcement with shocked amazement. Despite all the years of Nationalist propaganda, nobody, it seemed, (outside the National Party) had really ever believed that the Government would, one day, actually force the republican issue, particularly in this Jubilee year of Union.

While the effects of the referendum announcement were still being digested, Harold Macmillan, the British Prime Minister, who had been making a 'grand progress' through Africa, concluded his tour by delivering on 3 February an unexpectedly outspoken speech to the South African Parliament. He spoke of the growing policy differences between Britain and South Africa and stressed that African nationalism must be accepted as a political fact.

The winds of change are blowing through Africa. We may be tempted to say to each other 'mind your own business'. But in these days I would myself expand the old saying so that it means 'mind your own business, but mind how it affects my business too!' . . . Some aspects of your policies make it impossible for us to do this without being false to our own deep convictions about the political destinies of free men.[22]

The assembled politicians, in their varying ways, were stunned. For the Progressive Party, Macmillan's statement that '. . . individual merit, and individual merit alone, is the criterion for a man's advancement, whether political or economic' was a heartening endorsement of its own policies and principles; but the Nationalists saw in the speech only the final evidence that everywhere in Africa the West was abandoning the white man for its own selfish interests. *Die Transvaler* seized on the opportunity provided by Macmillan's speech to warn the Government that it must erect barriers against the outside pressures which it could soon expect.

Only by translating into practice as soon as possible the theory of segregation (segregation in every possible field) born on this continent, can the outside world and the sceptical non-Whites in Africa themselves, be convinced of the efficacy and absolute fairness of the segregation idea. Hastening the tempo of apartheid will assuredly demand sacrifices from the White man but for him it is a choice between temporary sacrifice and permanent eclipse.[23]

But beneath the surface of such intransigent white South African attitudes the simmering resentment of the black peoples was coming to the boil. Even so percipient a politician as Helen told her constituents later that she and the other Progressive MPs had all thought that the 1960 session would be quick and painless with the minimum amount of legislation necessary to keep the country ticking over financially and with no contentious legislation whatsoever. 'Our business over', she said, '[we thought] . . . we could then repair to Bloemfontein in a spirit of racial amity to celebrate the fiftieth anniversary of Union. Our hopes, however, were soon dashed to the ground, rather like the symbolic dove of peace and prosperity that refused to fly at the Bloemfontein celebrations.'[24]*

The cynical dove, it would appear, had rather more political nous than the sanguine politicians. The 1960 session had seen Verwoerd's announcement of the republic referendum and the intense reaction to Macmillan's speech. And now, ten days before the ANC's 31 March Day of Commemoration, the Pan African Congress declared an Anti Pass Day, calling upon all Africans to leave their passes at home and, on 21 March, to surrender themselves to the police. 'Africans', commented one black nationalist, 'smell freedom in the air.' The demonstration was to be non-violent, but those taking part were urged to accept no bail, offer no defence and pay no fine. The widespread and bitter opposition to the pass laws produced a huge response to the PAC call. In a super-charged atmosphere of tension and hostility, thousands of Africans, many of whom were neither PAC nor ANC supporters, joined in the demonstration. Large crowds converged upon police stations in a number of urban areas. At

*At the culmination of the Jubilee celebrations in Bloemfontein on 31 May 1960 Verwoerd launched into the air a dove which, dazed by the arc-lights and the noise, fell to the ground and refused to fly.

Evaton in the Transvaal, 10000 people, assembled outside the police station, were 'buzzed' by Air Force planes, and at Vander-bijlpark (the site of one of the country's major steel works), a crowd of three to four thousand dispersed only after two of their leaders were shot dead by the police. But it was at nearby Sharpeville, an African township outside Vereeniging, that the most serious trouble occurred. A crowd of some 20000 Africans, congregated at the township police station to hand in their passes, refused to disperse when ordered to by the police. Their behaviour grew menacing and when they smashed the gates in the security fence round the police station and seemed about to overwhelm the cordon inside it, the police opened fire into the mass of people, who fled, panic-stricken, while the riflemen continued shooting at their retreating backs. Sixty-nine dead were left behind and 180 were more or less seriously wounded.

That afternoon, when the news of the rioting and shooting broke into an atmosphere already tense with the bitterness and hostility aroused by the imminent republic referendum and by Verwoerd's recent provocative threats as to the Government's possible actions should the vote go against it, the House was debating the Prime Minister's vote. Graaff rose to ask if the Prime Minister had any information on the 'reported riots at Vanderbijlpark'. But, although the member for that constituency, Carel de Wet,* admitted to knowledge of some trouble, his only comment was: 'The one thing that I am concerned about is that when there are riots, whether on the part of Whites or Blacks, if it is necessary to shoot, only one person is shot dead.'[25] Later in the afternoon, the Prime Minister gave the Assembly further details. He admitted that there had indeed been rioting at Sharpeville and Vanderbijlpark, as well as at Wynberg (in Cape Town) but claimed that the situation was under control and, in one of his typical strokes of debating skill, shifted the onus for the responsibility on to the Opposition, by deploring the fact that 'the effect of the propaganda made to throw doubt on the Government's handling of the Natives, which necessarily has an inciting effect on the Bantu, has encouraged a certain organization [the PAC] to attempt the impossible, namely to defy the State'.[26] The debate on the refer-endum then continued in an acrimonious although somewhat

*Later twice South African Ambassador to the Court of St James.

desultory fashion. But outside the House, in spite of Verwoerd's claim, the riots, in fact were far from being under control and, early in the evening, Harry Lawrence forced the House's attention back to the disturbances:

I cannot help feeling how unrealistic this debate is at the present time. While we are speaking in this House tonight, there is firing going on within five miles of the Houses of Parliament. The latest information I have is that the police at Langa . . . have opened fire. Information is that they have done so with Sten guns and that there are several dead. Huts are set on fire, cars set on fire and no communication is available with the police station at the moment . . .[27]

In the face of this attempt to inject an unwelcome sense of reality into the insulated atmosphere of the Assembly, Verwoerd maintained his front of unmoved calm, but shortly before the House rose he said that, while he still did not have a clear picture on the situation at Langa, the death toll at Sharpeville had risen to fifty-three and the wounded to 156.[28]

For the next nine days the frightened country trembled on what appeared to be the brink of a major uprising. The ANC, which had originally refused to participate in the PAC's campaign, called for a 'stay-at-home' Day of Mourning on 28 March and several prominent Africans, including ex-Chief Luthuli, defiantly burnt their passes.

On 26 March the Commissioner of Police gave notice through the Press that reference books would not be demanded from Africans by the police until further notice. (This concession was in fact withdrawn after two weeks, on 10 April.) The Minister of Justice subsequently explained to the House that this had been done 'to avoid a congregation of people at police stations and possible bloodshed, and so as not to tie the hands of the police in combating riots, as well as giving protection to the public at those places where it is most essential'.[29] He also announced that the Government would ask Parliament to pass an Unlawful Organizations Bill[30] '. . . to call a halt to the reign of terror which the Pan Africanist Congress and the African National Congress have been conducting recently among the Bantu people of South Africa; to call a halt to the activities of the terrorists, White and non-White, who act as instigators behind the scenes without taking an active part themselves.'[31]

The passage of this legislation produced the clearest divergence to date between the United and the Progressive Parties. Initially, the United Party, while critical of a Bill which would destroy channels of African political expression, declared that it would oppose its introduction, giving as its reasons the absence of any time limit to the powers permitted the Government, which were wider than had ever before been granted and were, at the same time, completely outside parliamentary control. At the second reading, when the Minister agreed to limit to twelve months the duration of any ban imposed under the proposed legislation, the official Opposition abruptly changed course. Graaff said: 'I believe it is the duty of any responsible Opposition to assist in the maintenance of law and order, but once law and order has been restored, then I am in a position to tell the Government what I think of it . . .'[32] For the Progressives, this was the moment when the official Opposition finally abdicated any claim to being a party concerned with the maintenance of civil rights: this struggle was now to be carried on only by the handful of Progressives and by the Natives' Representatives.

On 30 March a young African university student named Phillip Kgosana led a march of some 30 000 Africans from Langa to the Caledon Square Police Station near the Parliament buildings in Cape Town. The marchers, being without reference books, planned to offer themselves for arrest. Looking out of the window of the basement offices to which the Progressive members of Parliament had been relegated, Helen watched, at eye-level, a pair of trembling boots belonging to a terrified young policeman, a member of the protective cordon awaiting the oncoming marchers. The constable could, had he known, have stood his ground less shakily. The police promised Kgosana indemnity from arrest and an interview with the Minister of Justice if he dispersed the mob: he asked the marchers to return home, which they did, in the belief that he would put their grievances to the Minister. But Kgosana was immediately arrested and, while awaiting trial, managed to escape and flee the country.

The effect of this march and of the Day of Mourning that had preceded it and which, in Cape Town and Johannesburg, had been 90 per cent successful, forced the Government to declare a State of Emergency under the Public Safety Act of 1953, with its effective clause suspending *habeas corpus*. In order to prevent any further demonstrations that might be set off by the declaration of the State of Emergency and by the arrest of Kgosana and other prominent African leaders, a *cordon sanitaire* of troops, sailors and police was thrown around the three Cape Town trouble-spots of Langa, Nyanga East and Nyanga West. For eight days the townships were sealed off and deprived of all provisions and services until the militant mood of the Africans cracked and they returned to work. Meetings were banned throughout South Africa and over 1900 political suspects, including some members of the Liberal Party, were arrested. Nightly raids into black town-ships all over the country were made by the police and 18000 individuals, officially described as 'idlers', were rounded up for pass offences under the Emergency Regulations. Special courts were set up to try them and strict Press censorship was enforced, effectively blacking out news on the disturbances throughout South Africa.

It was during this grim period that any doubts that Helen and the other Progressives might have felt about breaking with the United Party, or any moral reservations that still lingered in the matter of resigning their seats, were completely dispelled. If ever this small group of 'rebels' was needed, it was then. The mantle of opposition lay on them and them alone. Without the relentless performance of the Progressive members in forcing the Govern-ment to answer questions about the emergency, South Africa might have remained in total ignorance of the seriousness of the situation. Because of the clampdown on the Press, information could only be supplied to parliamentary questioners in parliamen-tary speeches. Helen was later to tell her constituents that at this time the Assembly was 'to all intents and purposes the last forum of free speech in the country . . . whose privileged proceedings could be reported in the Press'.

The attitude of the official Opposition during these weeks of emergency was inexplicable. For the first three weeks not one question on the order paper was put by the United Party. Of eighteen questions, sixteen came from the Progressives and two from the Natives' Representatives. Helen and her fellow-Progres-sives asked questions about the beatings-up, the raids, the Kgosana incident, the methods used by the police to control crowds, the arrests of the black so-called 'idle' persons, how long the State of Emergency would endure and under what conditions people were being detained, and what consultations with Africans were taking place. The official Opposition, said Helen, 'remained vigilant – and silent'.[33]

Helen herself opposed the Unlawful Organizations Bill with all the force of her vehement personality, fighting particularly for what she described as a 'relaxation of tension'.

I am pleading for members to realize that banning and force and ever greater disabilities are not going to solve the difficulties in South Africa ... [The] lesson this country should learn [is] that greater force, greater banning and greater disabilities lead to greater revolutions and greater counter-measures. Putting down a movement which is devoted to non-violent measures simply means that organizations which are devoted to violent measures will arise. Banning people does not mean ... that ideas disappear; it simply means that people go underground, that things are more difficult to control and you do not stop the rebellion that goes on in people's hearts against genuine grievances and genuine disabilities.[34]

Her impassioned pleas had not the slightest impact on the Government benches. Blaar Coetzee interrupted her speech once to say: 'I forgive you; you are very naïve; you are a woman.' With the other Progressive MPs, Helen found the Government's blandness and unwillingness to admit that African unrest was a direct consequence of its apartheid policy like a nightmare in which she and the others waded as through glue. In despair she decided to try practical action instead of desperate speech. 'I don't know how it happened,' she now says, 'but I suddenly thought: My God, I wonder what's happening to the detainees. So I upped and asked Erasmus [the Minister of Justice] for permission to visit them. And, to my utter astonishment my request was granted.'

With Kathleen Mitchell, Helen drove to Pretoria Central Gaol where the male detainees arrested after the declaration of the State of Emergency following Sharpeville were being held. It was her first prison visit and as the doors clanged behind her she said, half-jokingly, to her companion: 'If I'm not out in an hour, start screaming!' As she walked into the prison recreation yard accompanied by the colonel in charge of the prisoners, it seemed to her as though a smile rippled down the line of assembled detainees.

The colonel stopped in front of one of them, Ernest Wentzel, a young Johannesburg advocate and a leading member of the Liberal Party, with whom she had frequently disagreed before she had left the UP, saying, 'Wentzel! Your member of Parliament, Mrs Suzman, has come here to talk to you. You're allowed to talk to her but you're not allowed to tell her nothing [sic] about your detention. You can just talk about other things, not your conditions.'

'You mean I can't tell Mrs Suzman we haven't any books?'

'No, you can't tell her that.'

'You mean I can't tell her we only get out for an hour in the morning?'

'No, you mustn't tell her that.'

This conversation continued for some time while Helen, restraining her laughter with difficulty, learnt most of what she had come to learn from Wentzel's obliquities. She then visited the women detainees in their section of the prison. Immediately on her return to Parliament, she informed the Minister of Justice from the floor of the House that the detainees had been on hunger strike for four days, and gave their causes for complaint. 'You make me laugh,' replied Erasmus. But the detainees reported that conditions improved markedly after her visit.

Nineteen days after the Sharpeville shootings, on Easter Monday, 9 April 1960, a Transvaal farmer, David Pratt, walked up to Verwoerd during the opening ceremony of the Rand Easter Show in Johannesburg and with a .22 pistol shot him twice through the mouth.[35] The bullets miraculously missed the Prime Minister's brain and within two months, with none of his faculties impaired, he had made a full recovery. Verwoerd was convinced that the incident proved him to be under divine protection. If his faith in apartheid needed strengthening, Pratt's attempt on his life achieved it.

With the Prime Minister in hospital, the emergency dragged on, the Government showing no signs of a change of heart, though in a speech in his constituency of Humansdorp, made ten days after the attempted assassination, Paul Sauer, the leader of the House of Assembly, seemed to indicate a more moderate trend in Nationalist thinking. Sharpeville, he said, had closed an old book of South African history and the country now faced the need to consider, in earnest and in honesty, her whole approach to the 'Native' question. A new spirit must be created to restore faith in South Africa overseas in both white and black countries. There would have to be important changes in the practical application of government policy, and, although this would not mean any deviation from the policy of apartheid, the pinpricks which had made Africans susceptible to ANC and PAC propaganda must be removed. As a start, he suggested several minor amendments to the application of the pass laws, revision of the liquor laws to reduce the frequency of police raids, and the creation of representative bodies of Africans in the urban townships through which a better rapport between the authorities and the Africans could be achieved.[36]

Leading businessmen and mine-owners, appalled by the collapse of overseas confidence in the country's economy resulting from the disorders, and most apparent in a severe depression of share prices on the Johannesburg Stock Exchange, echoed the sense that Sauer seemed to be making. But any hopes entertained by moderate South Africans that a change might take place in government thinking died on 20 May when a long and carefully prepared speech, drawn up by Verwoerd, was read by the Minister of Finance to the assembled members of Parliament.

The recent disturbances in certain urban areas and the state of emergency which followed have given cause for general reflection. Certain authorities have submitted ideas and proposals to the Government. However good their intentions, those who made proposals often did not have sufficient facts at their disposal to test the effect of these proposals, and it remains the task of the Government, with full knowledge of affairs and after consultation with its experts to make the necessary decisions . . . The Government sees no reason to depart from the policy of separate development as a result of the disturbances. On the contrary the events have more than ever emphasized that peace and good order and friendly relations between the races, can best be achieved through this policy.[37]

The *kragdadige* Prime Minister, protected by Providence, was strengthened in his beliefs. But Sauer's words had not fallen on entirely barren ground; having issued this edict, Verwoerd followed it up with two palliatives, confirming the recommendations in Sauer's speech to give urban Bantu authorities a measure of executive and judicial powers; and a relaxation of the liquor laws to allow Africans legally to buy wines and spirits. But these minor indulgences granted, he made it fully clear that he was prepared neither to admit nor to tackle the major African grievances. The pass laws and influx control were to remain. And, maintaining that it was not government policy to exert compulsion on employers to pay higher wages, he offered no hope of increases in the abysmally low black wages.

What had moderate South Africans, and in particular the handful of Progressives, hoped for? Helen commented with great bitterness that the tragic truth was that the Government had obstinately refused to recognize the need for any change in the direction of its policy, that it would concede no genuine grievance among non-Whites, and that it ascribed all the recent happenings to the work of agitators. She spoke of the moderate and practical suggestions that had been made by leaders in commerce, industry and mining to ease the situation, particularly with regard to urban Africans, and of the fact that the Government proposed no significant changes and no modification of the policies that were causing racial friction. There was no new direction of policy. 'I can think', she said, 'of no other country in the Western world where the greatest employers of labour, and indeed, by far the biggest taxpayers and contributors to the State coffers, would be treated by their Government in the contemptuous and arrogant manner used by the Nationalist Government.'[38] She called for the emergency to be terminated. The United Party, which could still have redeemed itself by supporting the practical and eminently reasonable suggestions advanced by the Progressives, did no more than ask that Parliament should continue sitting as long as the emergency persisted. The pleas of both opposition groups fell on deaf ears. Parliament rose, though the State of Emergency was prolonged for another three months, coming to an end only at the end of August.

Verwoerd made his first public appearance after leaving hospital at the Union Jubilee celebrations held in Bloemfontein on 31 May.

He used the occasion to announce to a crowd of over 100000 people the date of the republican referendum: 5 October 1960. The Opposition-supporting section of the electorate seems to have assumed that the rioting and civil unrest of March and April would inevitably force a delay in this radical advance of Nation-alist policy. They were deeply shocked that the Prime Minister was so insensitive to push ahead with so potentially divisive a course of action. But, as Helen told her constituents, 'From the Nationalist point of view, the timing could not be better. It will create a most welcome diversion to whip up the old mystique of Afrikaner Nationalism and so distract thinking Nationalists from the palpable failure of the apartheid policy.'[39]

She had judged correctly. Verwoerd declared that with the republic he hoped to achieve a government that would be repre-sentative of both [sic] sections of the population. (For the Nation-alists, it must be remembered, the republic was an issue that concerned only white South Africans.) With its successful attain-ment, he said, the artificial divisions between White and White would vanish and together they would be able to tackle problems which would enable black South Africa to develop freely without oppression.[40]

A directive was now issued by Steytler to all Progressive Party members: the Party's opposition to a republic was total and no Progressive was free to vote for it. Zach de Beer wrote that the Party's task was that of stripping away the irrelevant arguments and persuading South Africans to think realistically about the central issue.

It is the chief aim of Progressive policy to reform the South African constitution so as to protect fundamental human rights and the dignity of the individual. We realize that this could be done under a republican form of government. But we do say that it is most unlikely to come about under the Nationalists and therefore we oppose Nationalist proposals for a republic which would have their sort of constitution and not ours . . . the Progressive Party is firmly pro-Commonwealth; and though a Nationalist republic might not involve immediate seces-sion there is little doubt that it would have the effect of a move in that direction . . . Our policy is therefore that the status quo should be maintained in present circumstances; that the constitution must be reformed according to Progressive ideals; that when this has been done and when a Progressive government can ensure membership of the Commonwealth, then, if republicanism is still an issue, a referendum of all registered voters [which will of course include a substantial number of non-Europeans] should be held to decide the matter.[41]

Ironically the Progressives' attitude towards the coming referendum forced its members into a close alliance with the United Party in mobilizing anti-republican votes.[42] But however hard the opposition parties worked, there was little doubt in most South Africans' minds that the National Party, with its consummate skill in electioneering tactics, would not have held a referendum had it not been certain of victory. In the event, 91 per cent of the electorate voted and in a total poll of 1 625 336 voters Verwoerd achieved his republic by a mere 73 380 votes.[43]

Once again the National Party had reason to exult. All its racial and historical goals had now been achieved. After the referendum Verwoerd said: 'Seen both numerically and geographically, the decision is clearly final.' And, faced with this irreversible situation, the opposition parties seemed indeed impotent. Both leaders did what they could. Steytler called on Verwoerd to summon a national convention representing all races and political groups to discuss the Union's future constitution, and Graaff appealed to the Government not to establish a republic until it was certain that South Africa could stay in the Commonwealth.

But as was to be expected, Verwoerd ignored them both. Six weeks after the referendum, he announced that the republic would be proclaimed on 31 May 1961, and early in the new parliamentary session, in an emotional bilingual speech, 'to symbolize', as he said, 'that we shall carry into the republic our treasured possession: the two official languages' – introduced the Republic of South Africa Constitution Bill.[44] The worst fears of many English-speaking South Africans were allayed by the contents of the new Bill which, as the Prime Minister had promised the previous January, bore no resemblance to the 1940 Draft Constitution, but closely followed the existing constitutional structure, retaining the entrenched language clauses and replacing the Governor-General by a President elected by the senators and members of the House of Assembly.

Shortly afterwards, Verwoerd flew to England to attend the

Commonwealth Prime Ministers' Conference, where he made formal application for the new South African republic to remain in the Commonwealth. But it was, by then, clear that the majority of Commonwealth Prime Ministers, implacably opposed to apartheid, would reject his application. Verwoerd, who in January had warned his electorate that he was not prepared to allow as a *quid pro quo* for continued membership of the Commonwealth the interference of other member governments in the domestic policies of South Africa, nor to sacrifice 'principles on which her Government has been elected repeatedly since 1948, [nor] of submitting to any reflection on her sovereignty or national honour', withdrew the application and returned home. Macmillan, commenting at the time in the House of Commons, said that 'Verwoerd made it clear beyond all doubt that he would not think it right to relax in any form the extreme rigidity of this dogma, either now or in the future'. But once back in South Africa, any sense of failure that Verwoerd might possibly have felt in London vanished in the adulation of the enormous crowds gathered to meet him in Johannesburg and Cape Town airports. 'What has happened', he announced to them, 'is nothing less than a miracle. So many nations have had to get their complete freedom by armed struggle . . . but here we have reached something we never expected.' It was typical of Verwoerd's complex logic that he was able to turn a humiliating rejection into a national triumph, and equally typical that his charisma enabled him, in a few words, to convince his followers that his thinking and his actions were beyond doubt or question.

From that moment the Prime Minister was determined to let nothing delay the final establishment of the republic. As black solidarity grew stronger with an all-party African conference held in Pietermaritzburg and a mass rally of Coloureds and Africans in Cape Town, when all Blacks were called upon to support another three-day stay-at-home strike, scheduled to last from 29 to 31 of May, the Government rushed a wide extension of the security legislation through Parliament and the police carried out mass raids throughout the country, concentrating on black and white radical political leaders. All gatherings in South Africa and South West Africa were banned from 19 May till 26 June; the Active Citizen Force (the army reserve) was mobilized; and all army leave was cancelled. These measures achieved their purpose. On 31 May the republic was proclaimed without one sign of outward protest. The Union, which had lasted for fifty-one years, was dead, and South Africa, no longer a monarchy and with its last ties with Britain cut, set off on the lonely road its leaders had chosen for it.

For Helen the 1960 and 1961 sessions had been the 'tensest and most bitter' in her years as Houghton's representative. And yet, ironically, she was still able to describe these two sessions in which the twelve[45] Progressives took part as the happiest of her parliamentary career. 'We had', she later said, 'two very good years when we put up some very good debates and some very good teamwork . . . I had friends who thought exactly the same way as I did on all the major colour issues [so] I wasn't in constant conflict with my own party.' The new party had already earned a reputation for itself as a first-rate parliamentary team. In its first session, its members had asked more questions than the whole of the official Opposition, especially on aspects of the emergency. It was the Progressives who had led the opposition to the Unlawful Organizations Bill, and so forced the United Party to vote with the Government at every division. During two other debates[46] in the 1961 session the expediency of the United Party's policy caused its members to cross the floor; and the Progressives and their supporters were well satisfied that they at least had been able to present a consistently solid opposing front.

During 1960 the Molteno Commission[47] had been working under pressure to present the first volume of its proposed new constitution to the Party's first National Congress to be held on 15 and 16 November that year. Because the members of the Commission were scattered throughout South Africa, the information to be studied was condensed by Molteno into the form of memoranda and circulated to members for their comment. The Commission held three full meetings at which all the members were present – a preliminary meeting on 20 February and two further ones in July and October in Cape Town and Durban respectively. At the October meeting its interim report was presented to the Party's National Executive. Some Commission members maintain that there was inadequate time for proper discussion of the report, or for a proper consensus of opinion to be obtained. But the interim report was lucid and sound: the South African electorate was at last presented with a practicable alternative to apartheid. The difficulties of steering a middle course between the Liberal Party philosophy of universal adult franchise and the Nationalist and United Party alternatives had been considerable, but the qualified franchise system which was finally recommended in the majority report seemed to offer a genuinely workable plan much in advance of the vague 'federation' ideas propounded by the United Party.

The Congress (rudely described as the 'Asphyxiation Congress' by many of the delegates crammed into the tiny assembly room adjoining the Johannesburg City Hall) spent most of its two-day session in debating the report, before announcing in detail the Party's official policy which, with one exception, followed closely the majority recommendations. The franchise policy proposed to demolish all barriers of race and colour and to give the vote to all South African citizens over the age of twenty-one provided they met certain specified qualifications.* A minority recommendation by Harry Oppenheimer and Zach de Beer to establish a 'B' roll for those citizens who did not qualify for the ordinary roll but who could pass a literacy test in one of the official languages was also adopted by Congress. Voters on the 'B' roll would, through specially delimitated constituencies, elect not more than 10 per cent of the members of the House of Assembly.

The Party further fully accepted the Commission's plan for a Senate so constituted and empowered as to provide an effective check on any racial majority that might emerge in the House of Assembly, so that the rights of any racial group which might find itself threatened by the advancement of another group's interests at its expense would be safeguarded.

The contents of the Commission's proposed Bill of Rights were also accepted. Entrenched in a reformed constitution, this Bill was fundamental to the Progressive philosophy, guaranteeing personal liberty, the freedoms of speech, assembly and association, equality before the law for any citizen. The Commission listed eighteen classes of rights and freedoms which were commonly

*See Appendix E.

guaranteed in the constitution of modern democratic states, pointing out that not only were there no guarantees of these rights in the South African constitution but that in many instances they were flagrantly denied by the laws on the Statute Book. But even these proposals were to be subject ultimately to the over-riding principle that any future constitution would have to be drafted by a new National Convention representative of all the major ethnic groups.

The Progressive Party now at least had a straightforward and unambiguous policy that the electorate should have been able clearly to comprehend. Its moderation as well as the Party's attempts to bring South African political ideas into line with changing conditions and a slow but sure evolution of public opinion, were based on a reversion to the historical Cape liberal concept of equal rights for all civilized men and demonstrated unequivocally its rejection both of apartheid and of the United Party's latest policy of communal representation, based on race and with white leadership as a prerequisite.

Its concept of gradualism, however, made it anathema to the Liberal Party and to the black political movements and was rejected by all of them on the grounds that, as long as the Progressives opposed the principle of immediate universal suffrage, they stood little chance of acceptance by any representative organization of Blacks. But even these groupings of the left grudgingly admitted that the Progressive proposals represented an essential first step. The United Party preferred to describe the new policy as unrealistic and inappropriate to the multi-racial problems of South Africa. 'Individuals', it said firmly, 'cannot by arbitrary political division be separated from their racial origin and background.'[48] The Nationalists, surprisingly, took a softer line. *Die Burger*, the Cape Nationalist newspaper, in a thoughtful editorial, considered that the Progressives were going too far ahead for the Whites without reaching the 'Natives', but concluded by stating that nevertheless '[the policy was] important as a line of thought which is asserting itself to an increasing degree in South Africa.'[49] Verwoerd was not in disagreement with the second of *Die Burger*'s conclusions: and he was not a man to sit idly by while such a movement was gathering force in the land his party ruled.

Once Parliament had risen, the *Groot Induna* showed his hand by calling a general election, two years before it was necessary. He had several reasons for so doing. Firstly, he wanted to gain the support of those members of the electorate who did not normally vote for his party but who might be pushed in a rightward direction by their uneasy preoccupation with the recent events in the Congo, where anarchy and bloodshed had filled the vacuum left by the sudden departure of the Belgian colonial administration (and given the lie to Helen's optimistic forecast on her foray into the north six years earlier). Secondly, he wished to bring into line any National Party supporters whose concern with the uncertain security position might be causing them to waver, and he saw that it would be wise to act before the economic effects consequent upon the country's resignation from the Commonwealth became too apparent. 'It is', he said, 'in the interest of the republic that all concerned, here and overseas, should know that a stable and strong government will once again be in power for the next five years.' And lastly he desired to eliminate the Progressives from Parliament, where they were making their presence increasingly felt. He found little to enjoy and much to dislike in their speeches, particularly in ones such as Helen's, when she had described South Africa as 'fast becoming little different from an occupied country'. She had said:

The average African cannot move about in the country in which he was born, he cannot move without passes, without permits, and without being accosted at every turn to prove his legal right to be in whichever area he happens to be. His political organizations are banned. He has absolutely no voice through the normal political channels, through constitutional channels, to voice his grievances. His leaders are banished without trial. The economic grievances of the African cannot be voiced through the normal channels. Their trade unions are not legally recognized . . . what sort of freedom is it that these people enjoy?[50]

Verwoerd was rapidly coming to the conclusion, as he listened to such unpalatable truths as these that were continually being expressed by all ten of their members, that the Progressives' impact in Parliament and on the electorate was out of all proportion to the size of this small party which hung grimly, bull-terrier-like, upon every major issue, in spite of all the efforts of the Government and of the official Opposition to steer debates into less embarrassing channels. B. J. Vorster, the member for Nigel, and Minister of Justice in Verwoerd's reconstituted republican cabinet, stood firmly behind his Prime Minister on this issue. 'The Progressive Party', he said in Brakpan on 6 September, 'should be wiped out in the election because it is a dangerous party undermining the foundations of our existence in South Africa . . . The annihilation of the Progressives [is] one of the reasons why a general election has become necessary.' And on the following day, in his own constituency, he went even further. 'The Progressive Party', he said this time, 'has no right to exist in South Africa. They are people with the most dangerous policy ever chosen by a political party.'[51]

The omens in the coming election were far from propitious for the Progressives. The Congo crisis, South Africa's exodus from the Commonwealth, with its implications of future political and economic isolation, boycott threats, widespread disturbances in Pondoland (where yet another State of Emergency had been declared) and an alarming outflow of capital investment had all had the effect of uniting a great number of white South Africans of varying shades of political opinion and of thrusting them into a laager. Between February and May of 1961 the Party had contested four by-elections but had won none of them, even that of Hospital (Johannesburg) previously held by Boris Wilson, who had resigned in January 1961. The praise they had earned from their supporters had given them high hopes, and although they had done well for such a fledgling movement, these defeats were bitterly disappointing.

'The distinctive feature of this general election', wrote Lawrence Gandar, Editor of the *Rand Daily Mail*, 'is the virtual certainty about the outcome coupled with a profound sense of *ennui*.'[52] And indeed out of 150 parliamentary seats, 67 were uncontested.[53]

Many well-wishers urged the Progressives to fight on a broad front in order to spread the Party's gospel as widely as possible. Though at first there had been talk of contesting forty seats, in the end the Party fought only twenty-three: two against National Party candidates; eighteen against the United Party; and three in seats being fought by both major parties. Within the Party hierarchy there had been a repetition of the 1959 dispute as to

G

whether or not there should be involvement in three-cornered battles. Helen saw no reason why the United Party should claim a monopoly of opposition, since neither its past record nor its future prospects gave it such entitlement. '[It] offers', she said, 'nothing but a half-hearted display of shadow-boxing on vital issues. [The] electorate must cut its losses, chop away the dead wood that is the United Party and allow the strong new growth of a real opposition to the Nationalists.' The official Opposition now underlined its total rejection of the Progressives by forming an electoral pact with J. du P. Basson's newly formed National Union party.[54] J. L. Horak, the General Secretary of the United Party, was heard to say: 'We want nothing to do with the Progressives. They were not invited to take part in the political discussions in Cape Town [with the National Union] and they will not be invited to do so in the future.'

Despite the implacable hostility displayed towards it by the United Party and Graaff's attacks accusing it of 'hindering the Party in its fight against the Government through its assault in the rear'[55] the Progressives decided not to fight three-cornered election contests where a split Opposition vote might result in a National Party victory. Steytler himself withdrew his candidature in Queenstown, where a Nationalist and a United Party candidate had been nominated, to fight a United Party candidate in Port Elizabeth South, and Ray Swart withdrew from the Zululand contest after a last-minute nomination by the National Party. De Beer fought and lost Maitland against a United Party and an Independent candidate. This failure to grasp the nettle continued to dog the Party in every subsequent election, and as late as 1974 the leadership was avoiding three-cornered fights as far as possible, and was still, in the few constituencies where it undertook them, being accused of impeding the United Party in the anti-Nationalist struggle.

Helen was fighting her recurrent unwillingness to stand for re-election. Perhaps because of speculation on her reluctance in the Nationalist Press and in *Die Weekblad*, the United Party's official mouthpiece, or perhaps due to the fact that the English-language Press (whose editors, with the exception of Gandar of the *Rand Daily Mail*, were exclusively United Party supporters) seemed to have made up its mind that by fighting constituencies throughout the republic the Progressives had lost any hope of retaining even one parliamentary seat, but most probably because she was reluctant to abandon the Party as it was fighting its first general election, she again accepted the Houghton nomination. To the voters of her constituency she wrote:

I have been asked – why create a splinter party, why split the forces of opposition. My answer is that the United Party has failed as an opposition. Millions of non-Whites in South Africa are anxiously hoping that this election will show signs of a change of heart in the white electorate.[56]

After so many years of unopposed nominations, the Houghton electorate was now to be given a chance to exercise its right to choose between two parliamentary candidates of opposing parties. Helen said at the report-back meeting before the election:

We believe that thousands of people throughout this country recognize the need for a thorough reappraisal of our racial policies. We will give them this opportunity and we will go all out to retain our parliamentary seats. And whatever the outcome we will at least have had the enormous satisfaction of fighting for what we believe in and for what is morally right and economically sound and wholly in step with the thinking of the civilized world. No crusader could have asked for a better cause – I am proud to have been part of it all.[57]

The boundaries of the Houghton constituency had remained relatively unchanged over the years by delimitation. Its voters were much as they had been when Helen first went to Parliament eight years earlier. Professor Lever has noted that the constituency overall displayed a higher level of education than the South African average and it is interesting to note that more of the voters were university graduates than in any other constituency in the country.[58]

It was not only because of the atypical nature of her constituency that, of all the Progressive Party candidates, Helen started her 1961 election campaign with the greatest advantages. Although no election had ever been fought in Houghton and the United Party there had no organization as such, most of the party workers had often assisted in campaigns in other constituencies, and when Helen had resigned from the United Party, she had taken the majority of her committee and office workers with her. Max

Borkum, who up to 1959 had headed the United Party's Action Committee and who was a highly experienced campaign manager, became her election agent,* and what her workers may have lacked in election experience they made up for in enthusiasm. For this, Helen, because of the conscientious years of service she had given to her constituents, was chiefly responsible. From the moment she had entered Parliament in 1953, she had kept in constant contact with them, both through a monthly news sheet to committee members and through her annual report-back meetings. She was known to take her parliamentary duties extremely seriously: but above all, she was respected by her electorate for her uncompromising attitudes. During the 1961 session a government member had angrily asked her: 'Have you never changed your policy?' She was able to reply: 'No, I never have. I am enunciating the principles I have always enunciated.' And her constancy was underlined in the opening speech of her campaign on 9 August when she said:

If the English-speaking people want white *baasskap* they should go into the Nationalist laager and fight black Nationalism . . . You have no idea what a pleasure it is for me, after so many years in the United Party, to be able to put an unequivocal policy to the electorate in the name of the Progressive Party . . . [Now] it is over to you to decide whether what we have been saying in Parliament was worth saying and whether it will weaken or strengthen the Nationalists to have us there, voicing sentiments that the timid United Party will never dare to voice and fighting issues that the United Party will never dare to fight.

The Progressive Party's Houghton office had been operational for seven months when Verwoerd announced the election, and a considerable proportion of the constituency had already been canvassed. Helen now threw herself into two months of unrelenting sixteen-hour working days. Before breakfast she was daily subjected to a stream of telephone calls from voters and party helpers. She would then drive to the constituency office where she would help collate the mass of information gathered in the previous evening's canvass, often taking home a large pile of canvass cards

*Despite being the author of the undertaking signed by Transvaal United Party candidates to resign their seats should they leave the Party, Borkum himself left the Party after the 1959 Bloemfontein Congress and became a founder member of the Progressive Party.

headed 'Doubtful Voters' and those of people she wanted personally to canvass. At midday a meeting with party officials to discuss
the campaign was usually held, to be followed by an afternoon of
canvassing. On most evenings there would be house-meetings
attended by twenty or thirty 'floating' voters to whom Helen
would endeavour to explain party policy for an hour or so before
answering questions. She quickly acquired the reputation of being
the hardest-working candidate in the Party.

Towards the end of the campaign, Oppenheimer came out in
open support for the Progressives: 'My judgement', he said, 'for
what it is worth, is that if you are lucky enough to have the choice
between a Progressive and a United Party candidate – and if you
have the honour, safety and prosperity of South Africa at heart –
the best thing you can do is vote Progressive.'[59] Where Oppenheimer led, many voters were prepared to follow: there can be no
doubt that his speech brought many waverers over to Helen's cause.

Shortly before election day, her opponent, Hymie Miller,
United Party MP for Florida and ex-mayor of Johannesburg, who
had left his 'safe' constituency to fight Helen in Houghton,
informed Graaff and the Press that he was confident of winning
Houghton by at least 2000 votes. Miller was clearly blessed with
a vast confidence both in his own reputation and in the power of his
party: Helen, in spite of years spent representing Houghton, was
less confident, although the canvassing figures gathered by her
workers had indicated a much closer result.

Polling took place on 18 October. In Houghton the atmosphere
was particularly tense. Voting was brisk at the four polling
stations where crowds of United and Progressive Party supporters
milled round the tables among the green and gold and the blue
and white posters and slogans of their respective parties. Helen
spent most of the day travelling backwards and forwards between
the four stations. She still recalls with amusement that at one of
them a woman she knew well and who had promised faithfully
to vote for her, was scrutineering* for the United Party. Helen

*In South African elections, party workers are permitted to assist electoral
officers in checking the *bona fides* of voters, and although party colours may not
be displayed inside the actual polling booth, it is customary for the representative scrutineers of each party to sit in pairs behind the electoral officers. Helen
must have seen the renegade sitting beside a scrutineer she knew to be a Progressive.

went up to her and asked: 'Do I believe my eyes – or my ears?' The embarrassed scrutineer replied that although she was helping the United Party, she was, of course, voting for Helen. This dichotomy of loyalties often occurred in those early years of the Progressive struggle, and indeed, was still to be found in isolated cases in the Johannesburg constituencies as late as the 1974 campaign.

At the end of the day, a beaming Hymie Miller, surrounded by cheerful supporters, was still confidently predicting a 2000-vote win. The Progressives were moderately hopeful of victory, though by a much smaller margin. (In the event, it was found that Max Borkum had calculated the result to within twenty-six votes.) From eight o'clock in the evening until two o'clock the following morning Helen's workers and supporters sat in one of the classrooms at the King Edward VIII School in Upper Houghton waiting for the results, and hearing with growing depression the wireless report the defeat of candidate after candidate in Progressive-contested seats all over the country.[60] Shortly after two o'clock, when the returning officer flung open the doors of the school hall where the count had been taking place and declared that Helen had won by 564 votes,[61] the cheering crowd of Progressive supporters went wild more with relief than with triumph.

Helen herself was both elated and sad. At Ellen Hellmann's house, where she had gone after the Houghton result had come through, she heard of the final Progressive defeat in the adjacent constituency of Parktown. There had been three recounts before it was finally declared that John Cope had been beaten by no more than eighty-five votes by the United Party candidate S. Emdin.* Helen broke down and wept into the glass of whisky she was holding. '*I* was the only one who really wanted to get out,' she recalled later. 'Politics made me sick. I saw no hope for the future but I thought I might as well go down with flags flying. And now – one tiny little flag fluttered on by some 500 votes – and it was *me*!'

---

*Cope's defeat is attributable in part to a smear campaign by the United Party. His name was reported to be on a petition against the construction of a synagogue in Greenside, part of the Parktown constituency. Although untrue, the rumour lost him a large proportion of Greenside's Jewish vote. Emdin held Parktown until he was defeated by R. de Villiers (PP) in 1974.

Chapter Eight 1962-70

A less committed person than Helen on that election night that was to make her, for thirteen years, the Progressive Party's sole representative in Parliament, realizing what a fearful burden the events of each successive session were to put upon her, might well have opted for the easier choice of extra-parliamentary resistance and let the United Party continue with their half-hearted opposition alone. She was, at that time, only beginning to be the extraordinary personality she was later to become. She had always had courage and intellectual force; she had always been a fighter. But looking back it is possible to see that it was the battle she had to fight that gave her the ability to survive; that it was those thirteen hard and lonely years in Parliament, ostracized by the United Party, hammered and hated by the Nationalists, that brought to full maturity her latent powers. She was later to write that each session became to her a long dark tunnel through which somehow she had to make her way. 'It is not the tremendous amount of work ahead but the fear that I won't come up to expectations. So many people depend on my acquitting myself well.'[1] It was because she was the lone voice of dissent in a con-formist Parliament, the sole focus of the unenfranchised millions, that she was now to become known as more than just an opposition MP in an unrepresentative Parliament. The harsh spotlight of world censure fell ever more strongly upon South Africa; and in a society where most of the leaders of dissent were in exile or in gaol, Helen was to be heard more and more as the authentic voice of meaningful opposition. She could certainly not rely on the official Opposition for any kind of moral support. Once, at the beginning of the 1962 session, Higgerty, the United Party Chief Whip, asked her if she wished to sit on any parliamentary Select Committees, but she replied that she would not have the time. No other approach was ever made: the United Party could not forgive the events of Bloemfontein.

Accepting that she represented far more than the electors of Houghton alone, she decided to concentrate on those issues which most affected the South Africans unrepresented in Parliament. Her strategy had been mapped out as early as November 1961: she would ask questions on all subjects of importance to the various peoples she represented; she would keep a watchful eye on all legislation affecting their interests; wherever possible she would publicize Progressive ideas on the franchise and otherwise concentrate on economic, constitutional and labour issues. Donald Molteno and those former Progressive MPs who lived in Cape Town – Walter Stanford, Zach de Beer, Harry Lawrence, Clive van Ryneveld and Colin Eglin – offered to form themselves into an unofficial caucus with the idea that they would then meet with Helen weekly throughout the session to evaluate Bills coming before the House, to discuss policy and to outline the path she should follow. They would also do some 'devilling' and gather facts for her. The intention was excellent but the plan failed to work. Most of the ex-MPs had their livings to earn and times for meetings, suitable to them all, were hard to find. Although some of them were able to advise her on specific subjects – from Donald Molteno and Clive van Ryneveld in particular she received valuable help with the 'Sabotage Bill' in 1962 – the weekly meetings dwindled, diminished and finally ceased. To cope with the volume of work confronting her, Helen had to enforce a strict discipline upon herself, organizing her life rigorously. Each morning was spent in her office writing speeches which, if the subject was unfamiliar, would take three or more hours; if she could possibly help it, she never spoke extempore. Her 'back-up' research was done by a small parliamentary secretariat – Jacqueline Beck, who not only helped with research but also formulated a steady barrage of questions to keep Ministers and their deputies, as Helen put it, 'on their toes', and Barbara Mouat, her secretary, who helped her dispose of the astonishing volume of mail she daily received – much of it from those thousands of Blacks who were relying so urgently and desperately upon her. For the first time in ten years of parliamentary experience, Helen was discovering that it was necessary to master the details of procedure – 'the sort of things

I had always happily left to Party Whips to arrange I now [have] to do for myself. And if I say it myself, experts like Kilpin[2] will have nothing on me regarding parliamentary procedure . . .'

The new year had begun uneasily in the country. Signs of renewed unrest manifested themselves in sporadic outbreaks of violence and sabotage in rural areas, and there were scattered acts of sabotage in the towns, while a new organization called Umkonto We Sizwe (Spear of the Nation) threatened more sophisticated varieties of destruction for the future. Faced with these rumblings, and with the demands from the Transkeian Territorial Authority* for self-government, Verwoerd, with his unfailing gift of opportunism, seized on a chance offered him by the United Party when on 26 January 1962 it placed before the House a motion censuring the Government for 'failing to take the country into its confidence' in the matter of independent Bantustans. The wording of the motion played straight into the Prime Minister's hands. 'Without further ado', wrote Helen, 'he climbed into the debate and took us into his confidence. After some two and a half hours of this exposé, I could only think of the final line of a rather rude American joke which ends as follows: "That's telling 'em ain't it, fat lady?" '

Verwoerd's marathon speech dealt with plans already well advanced for the accelerated granting of a constitution to the Transkei. A sessional committee had accepted the Government's proposals, money was to be voted for development purposes and certain local functions would be taken over by the Bantu authorities.[3] Verwoerd claimed that these plans demonstrated the Government's belief in 'common justice . . . for the solution of the problems facing us in this country, to bring about good relations and friendship and co-operation between Black and White . . . in doing this, the international struggle against South Africa will be deprived of whatever background there is to it.'[4] The official Opposition, having invited the Prime Minister to reveal his proposals for the Transkei, found no counter-argument but a revival of its old 1959 outcry against the 'balkanization' of South Africa; but Helen had no difficulty in giving battle.

---

*A body of chiefs and councillors which had in 1957 replaced the partly elected Bunga (an advisory council).

I am in the lucky position of being the only person in this House who won't be called upon to define any boundary, racial or territorial. I am also the only person in this House, apparently, who belongs to a party that does not have to indulge in *swart gevaar* tactics . . . It seems to me that my party is the only [one] in this country, apart from one other small party [the Liberals], which does not shake with fear at the implications of accepting South Africa as what it is and that is a multi-racial country.[5]

It was pointless, as she saw it, for Verwoerd to boast of his advances in grand apartheid, since the world wanted to see apartheid abandoned, not implemented. She pointed out, not for the first nor the last time, that two-thirds of South African Africans lived outside the Reserves. 'Strangely enough, people like to enjoy rights where they live not where they do not live. To two-thirds of the Bantu population, therefore, the bitter fruits of racial discrimination are unchanged by the creation of independent Bantustans.'[6]

Helen had expressed the feelings of many thinking people in the country, but no arguments, no matter how valid or just, had ever been able to change or move Verwoerd's mind, once it was made up. His speech was an advance notice of the Transkei Constitution Bill[7] which came before the House in the following year and was made law on 29 May 1963. This important piece of legislation, as Helen was quick to point out, had two faces – one for South Africa and the other for the benefit of overseas observers, to which latter end a great deal of time had been spent on glossy pamphlets and on advertisements in overseas newspapers and magazines which purported to demonstrate the ethical background to apartheid. She told her constituents:

The Transkei [has been] depicted [in this publicity] as a thriving little independent territory run by its own people under the temporary tutelage of a benevolent Nationalist Government . . . [But] all existing laws remain in force in the Transkei unless repealed by the republican Government . . . If the Bantustans were a true form of partition with viable economic areas set aside for Africans there might be something to be said for them from the ethical angle. But it is no such thing.[8]

While Verwoerd with one hand bestowed severely limited self-government upon the Transkei, his other was engaged in developing a policy designed to unite the two white groups in a *laager* against black Africa and the outside world. Solemnly the government Press began to delineate the sacrifices the Whites would have to make for the sake of apartheid. 'Our country and our people,' wrote *Die Volksblad*, 'face a time of emergency, and we are sure they will not be found wanting if additional demands are made on them. Let us be thankful if these demands are no more than material sacrifice.'[9] Justifying a record defence budget of R120 million, an increase of 150 per cent over that of the previous year, the Minister of Defence, J. J. Fouche, explained that military action against South Africa was being openly advocated and secretly planned by 'some Afro-Asian states'. Veiled warnings as to the consequences to white South Africans who failed to co-operate with government plans began to be heard, successfully panicking the official Opposition into expressing overt support for the Nationalists, voiced by Graaff in Parliament and loyally defended by a United Party back-bencher, O. Newton-Thompson, in a magazine article.

As patriotic South Africans, our attitudes could not have been otherwise. There are all too many countries in the world who would dearly like to compel us to introduce 'one man, one vote' by force of arms, if necessary. The United Party, just as the Nationalists, will not bow to this. Hence we must keep our armour bright.

It was inevitable that increasing alarm at the sporadic outbursts of sabotage continually being perpetrated by agents of the banned ANC and PAC should manifest itself among the voters, and upon these fears both the Nationalists and the United Party played with some success. Most white South Africans could not, apparently, distinguish between acts of sabotage in which only pylons, empty government offices and letter-boxes were involved and acts of true terrorism committed against people. The first intimation of this came in the results of two provincial by-elections in Johannesburg constituencies where Progressive candidates lost to United Party opponents by small margins.[10] Immediately, sections of the English-language Press appealed to the two parties to sink their differences: but the Progressives were encouraged to 'go it alone' (which they had every intention of doing) by Lawrence Gandar of the *Rand Daily Mail* who took the pleas of his less committed colleagues severely to task. He wrote:

[They are] typical of the confused thinking which handicaps our politics. The fact of the matter is that the choice is not so much between the Government's Bantustan policy and the United Party's race federation but between policies of race domination and the policies of complete non-discrimination in race and colour. This is the only choice that matters and it is the one demanded of us by the rest of mankind. So fight on, Jan Steytler – and to hell with expediency.[11]

The struggle for the control of the electorate continued to go badly for both Opposition parties. In the Johannesburg municipal elections of 1962 all fifteen Progressive candidates were defeated and three United Party seats fell to the Nationalists. There were political observers who saw the trend to the right as the beginning of the end for the Progressive Party (although B. J. Vorster went on record at this time as saying that he thought the Progressives would supersede the United Party within fifteen years). In the event, Steytler's forecast at the time of the formation of the Party – that it was entering a wilderness where it would remain for the next decade – was the one that proved correct.

Helen's stand in Parliament, though at that time failing to win general support for the Progressive Party, added to her own reputation every time she spoke. On 23 February 1962 she introduced the first of what became an annual series of private members' motions to amend apartheid legislation. Formally seconded by C. Barnett, the Coloureds' Representative for the Boland, she appealed to the Government to repeal those sections of the Immorality Act that made sexual relations across the colour line a criminal offence. The Act was, and is, one of the grimmest of South Africa's laws, whose implementation has resulted over the years all too often in blackmail, suicide and even murder. There was nothing, she said, that to her mind could outweigh the misery and degradation that this law had brought in its wake.

Thousands of people have been publicly humiliated, have had their careers ruined and their community lives rendered non-existent . . . and for a crime which is only a crime where colour is involved . . . What social conventions, moral, religious and ethical considerations cannot control, I do not believe the law can control . . . miscegenation goes on whether there is a law or not.[12]

The United Party, which agreed with her criticisms of the Act but refused to commit themselves to voting against it, asked for a Select Committee before the Second Reading of Helen's motion and Vorster, as Minister of Justice, now took the offensive. He did not attempt to defend the immorality laws but chose instead to launch an attack on liberalism in general and Helen in particular.

Every argument used by the honourable member is in my opinion a further reason as to why this Act should remain unchanged . . . in taking this stand she is simply faithful to the philosophy which underlines her views. In the nature of things one is not liberal in respect of one matter only. Liberalism is a philosophy which permeates the whole of one's life and determines one's attitudes in all spheres of life.[13]

He followed this up with a personal onslaught based on an accusation that Helen condoned immoral relations across the colour line, apparently feeling that this was such a damning statement that he need say no more. His assessment of white thinking in general on this emotive topic was not incorrect: colour prejudice in South Africa, as elsewhere, seems to be deeply rooted in sexual fears. Nevertheless, Helen, disregarding the strong prejudices of many otherwise quite liberal voters, never disguised her deep dislike of the dogma of sexual apartheid: her consistency in this, as in all other issues, helped win the Party, over the years, the votes it needed, but in the short term, attacks of the nature of Vorster's struck home as he intended.

In 1961 the General Laws Amendment Bill[14] which had, with other new security measures, been passed to ensure the uneventful birth of the new republic, had given the Minister of Justice wide powers which he could exercise without the interference of the courts, among them the right to detain suspects for twelve days without trial. When, after the 1961 election, the Nationalists were for the first time returned to power with more votes than the official Opposition,[15] the Government, despite the disturbances and unrest among the black population, clearly felt confident that growing numbers of the electorate were beginning to look with favour on the course it was pursuing. Certainly it had less fear than it had had in the past of adverse reaction to harsh security legislation. The continuing black unrest gave the Minister an ostensible reason for the introduction of a second General Laws Amendment Bill.[16] Popularly known as the Sabotage Bill, it was described by Vorster as being intended to 'preserve rather than to kill democracy'. 'It will only take away the freedom of the saboteur to destroy . . . it will only take away the Communists' rights to sabotage,' announced that former *Ossewabrandwag* activist. Under its provisions, sabotage became an act of treason (and consequently a capital crime) and the concept of 'house arrest' without trial was introduced. It contained, said the *Sunday Times*, 'the most fantastic powers ever sought by a Minister in peace-time', and even the government-supporting *Sondagblad* commented that 'its contents made the country catch its breath'.[17] For a week after the publication of the Bill, the United Party remained silent. But after the English-language newspapers, including the Party's strongest supporters, the *Sunday Times* and the *Cape Argus*, had expressed unanimous disapproval, and after protest meetings and marches, organized by the Progressives in Johannesburg, Cape Town and Durban, had shown the strength of public reaction, the Opposition broke its silence with a qualified condemnation of Vorster's proposals. 'We are', said Graaff, 'against sabotage and Communism . . . [but] we are not prepared to see unreasonable powers given to the executive which cannot be controlled by the courts or by this House.'[18]

By contrast with Graaff's half-hearted disagreement, Helen's opposition again brought her unflinching integrity into sharp focus. She described the Bill as an 'Intimidation Bill' (because 'the idea is to frighten the life out of anybody who disagrees with the Government, on colour issues particularly') and likened it to Hitler's 'Protection of the People Decree' which had also given wide powers to the State to detain alleged Communists and saboteurs and which had also been described at the time by the Nazi Government as a defensive measure against Communist acts of violence. 'If in order to defend South Africa against Communism, it is necessary to introduce the most abhorrent features of totalitarianism into our system of government, we can no longer pretend to be a democracy,' she told her constituents . . . 'William Pitt said long ago, "Necessity is the plea for every infringement of human freedom. It is the argument of tyrants. It is the creed of slaves." ' She moved that the Bill be read 'this day six months' but found no seconder, and was forced to resort to the introduction of seventeen amendments, including – in response to a government challenge – the Progressive Party's definition of sabotage.*

Outside Parliament, some bizarre side-effects were produced by Helen's attack on the Bill, one of which was a telegram sent to her by Robey Leibbrandt, a former Nazi condemned to life imprisonment during the war for treasonable activities but freed when the Nationalists came to power. Leibbrandt's telegram contained the interesting message that 'Mordecai, alias Karl Marx, the father of modern Communism, was a Jew'. Helen, by now inured to obscene and abusive postcards, letters and telegrams – a postcard addressed simply to 'The Yiddisher Know-all from Houghton' had once found its way safely into her parliamentary post-box – was unperturbed, although the Postmaster-General felt it incumbent upon him to apologize to her, and, rather to her amazement, the United Party asked Vorster to institute an inquiry into the incident. This was met with a flat refusal on the grounds that the telegram 'quite correctly' attacked Karl Marx but not the Jews!

When the session ended, Helen was met at Jan Smuts airport in Johannesburg by a crowd of cheering Progressives. 'We must keep fighting for the things in which we believe . . . we must not allow ourselves to be intimidated,' she told them, and later said to a reporter, 'It's so wonderful not to have a committed day ahead.' Her first session on her own had been a feat of remarkable physical and mental stamina. In the one hundred and four days that the session lasted, she had made a total of sixty-six speeches, moved twenty-seven amendments and asked a hundred and thirty-seven questions. During the committee stages of the General Laws Amendment Bill debate she was in the House for twelve hours a day for three successive days. She had made more than

---

*Anyone will be guilty of sabotage who commits any violent and unlawful act with the intent to: cause or promote general dislocation, disturbance or disorder; cripple or seriously prejudice any industry or undertaking . . . or the production or distribution of commodities or foodstuffs at any place; cause or encourage or further an insurrection or forcible resistance to the Government; cause serious damage to State property; seriously interrupt the supply or distribution at any place of light, power, fuel or water, or of any sanitary, medical or fire-extinguishing services. Saboteurs convicted of any of these crimes should be liable to any gaol sentence or fine the Court may 'deem fit'. The death penalty was excluded but if any act of sabotage amounted to murder or treason, the offender could be hanged under existing law.[19]

twenty speeches in moving amendments to sixteen clauses of the
Bill, and in many cases had led the Opposition attacks. 'My
daughters', she would say to anyone who expressed amazement at
her formidable stamina 'have always said I have the constitution
of a Basuto pony.'

Shortly after her return to Johannesburg, Helen went to
America to take up a United States Foreign Leadership grant and
spent two months there studying racial problems and the federal
system of the country, returning home just in time for the Progressive Party's annual Congress in Durban, where the second Molteno
report was presented. The commissioners had concentrated in
their report on constitutional proposals, advising the subordi-
nation of the central government to a rigid constitution protected
by a special bill of rights; had advocated the granting of wider
powers to the provincial administrators, with entrenchments
against possible interference by the central government: and had
enunciated for the first time the Progressive belief that with the
plural nature of its society, South Africa would operate more
effectively under a federal system of government than under the
existing unitary system.*

This Congress was marred by a serious disagreement on the
question of residential segregation. Many of the delegates felt
in spite of their 'liberal' views on other aspects of the problem,
that the present all-white suburbs should be protected by law
against non-white infiltration, while the more idealistic held firm
to the belief that restrictive clauses in title deeds represented a
form of racial discrimination contrary to the Party's basic principles. In the brotherhood of man, as in Heaven, there are many
mansions, but the white South African tends to be more preoccupied with who occupies the mansion next to his. After a
prolonged, acrimonious and heated debate, a compromise formula
unsatisfactory to many, was agreed on, official party policy now
stating that Blacks should be allowed to live in white areas provided
a majority of existing residents agreed. This decision remained
an unofficial policy until the National Congress of 1974, when the
prejudices of the many otherwise tolerant Whites who had
initiated it were finally overcome.

*See Appendix E.

Helen's chief parliamentary antagonist between 1963 and 1972, was Balthazar Johannes Vorster, Minister of Justice when she first took her lonely seat, and later Prime Minister. He had been born in 1915, the thirteenth son of a farmer at Jamestown in the Eastern Cape and had become involved with Nationalist politics while studying law at Stellenbosch University in the 1930s. In 1940 he left Malan's purified party to join the *Ossewabrandwag*, in which he quickly rose to the rank of 'commandant'. In 1942, he was arrested on charges of high treason, but like so many other anti-war Afrikaners was not brought before the courts. Instead he spent two years in the Orange Free State internment camp at Koffiefontein, and a short time under house arrest after his release in 1944. In 1948, Havenga put Vorster's name forward as an Afrikaner Party candidate for the parliamentary elections. His nomination – subject in terms of the electoral pact between the two parties to Nationalist approval – infuriated Malan who declared that he wanted no truck with ex-*Ossewabrandwag* members, but Vorster nevertheless stood as the Afrikaner Party candidate in Brakpan and, though receiving no support from the local National Party organization, lost the seat to the United Party by only two votes. When the Afrikaner Party merged with the National Party in 1949 the prodigal returned to the fold, and in 1953, under official National Party auspices, he contested and won the Transvaal constituency of Nigel.[20] As a protégé of Verwoerd, his rise through the ranks of the Party hierarchy was remarkably rapid. In early 1960, he became Deputy Minister of Education, Arts and Science, and of Social Welfare, and in October 1961 Verwoerd gave him the key portfolio of Justice. The 1962 General Laws Amendment Act established his calibre in the minds of all South Africans, whether they were for or against him. At a mass protest meeting against the Bill in Johannesburg, Helen told a tense, subdued audience of over 2000 people that in her view Vorster, who appeared to understand neither the meaning of democracy nor the Rule of Law, was a most dangerous man to hold the portfolio of Minister of Justice:

And why should one expect him to [understand]. He says himself he has not changed since he was a leading member of an organization whose pronounced aim was to found a one-party authoritarian and disciplinarian state, whose political thinking is so warped that he cannot distinguish between liberalism and Communism; who has the impertinence to say that the Sabotage Act has nothing to do with the freedom of speech, and who describes the house arrest clause as benign.[21]

The year closed badly for Progressives and liberals on the African continent. In Southern Rhodesia the crushing defeat of Sir Edgar Whitehead's United Federal Party by Winston Field's apartheid-orientated Rhodesian Front sounded the death-knell of the Central African Federation and its half-hearted experiment in 'race partnership'. Helen said prophetically:

The members of this Government are taking comfort in the thought that white Rhodesians have joined them in the laager. They gloat about the fact that black Rhodesians have turned their backs on the concept of partnership . . . Are people so foolish in this country to believe that the recent elections mark a closing chapter in the history of Rhodesia? . . . If there is anything that we should learn from the lesson of Rhodesia, it is that it is no good offering concessions too late, [no good offering] . . . them when the black man has lost all confidence in the assurances and promises of the white man.[22]

In South Africa, African Nationalist leaders who had either fled their country or gone underground, proclaimed 1963 as 'the year of destiny' and stated that their long-standing policy of non-violence was finally at an end. Riots fostered by a new African organization called Poqo (a Xhosa word meaning 'pure') broke out in the Cape Province towns of Paarl and Beaufort West as well as in the Transkei, and Judge Snyman was appointed as a one-man judicial commission to investigate the causes.

Verwoerd, meanwhile, was beginning to elevate himself above the hurly-burly of daily political infighting and had become engaged in fostering an image of himself as the champion of white rather than of specifically Afrikaner nationalism, a champion whose main task was to protect white civilization in South Africa against the tide of pan-Africanism spreading from the north. Commenting on the change in the Prime Minister's attitudes, Helen said (in reporting on the 1963 session):

We received the benefit of his wordy wisdom on very few occasions – the No Confidence debate, the Bantustan debate, and on his own vote.

For the remainder of the session, until the final debate on the Appropriation Bill, the Prime Minister sat in lofty silence while his henchmen
did their stuff vigorously on a number of far-reaching measures. It was
almost as if the father-figure was giving his offspring the opportunity
of demonstrating how well they had learned their lesson at his knee –
or maybe over it.[23]

Shortly after the beginning of the 1963 session a family of six
Whites, camping beside the road at Bashee Bridge in the Transkei,
were savagely murdered in an attack attributed to Poqo, whose
activities cast a shadow over the proceedings of the parliamentary
session. These murders and the Paarl riots provided unlimited
ammunition for parliamentary speakers of all persuasions. Graaff,
in his traditional motion of no confidence, had attacked the
Government on a broad front, speaking of its failure to maintain
good relations with the West, to come to grips with the country's
racial problems, or to implement apartheid and reverse the ever-
increasing flow of Africans to the towns. Helen aimed her shots
chiefly at the target of black civil rights: that most of them went
home was evidenced by the hostility of the House. The ever-
increasing acts of violence all over the country came, she said, as
no surprise to her at all.

As long as there are people who are denied rights of political expression,
who are denied equal opportunities in the economic field, who live
the barracklike sort of life that the Africans live in this country, who
are denied normal family life, so long will individuals and groups of
individuals find some means of expressing their frustration. The
Government has left such people with few measures other than violent
means [of such expression]. It refuses to understand that if non-
violent protests are not allowed then [they] will be replaced by violent
protests. If moderate leaders are silenced, they will be replaced by
extremist ones.

Nelson Mandela, the leader of the ANC, had recently been sentenced to life imprisonment on Robben Island for his political activities,
and she quoted his words after the passing of his sentence.

We have warned repeatedly that the Government, by resorting continually to violence, will breed in this country counter-violence among
the people, until ultimately if there is no dawning of sanity on the part
of the Government the dispute between the Government and my people
will finish up by being settled in violence and force.[24]

The Government's response consisted largely of heavily ironic congratulations on her defence of what they called her new 'leader' (Mandela). As the session progressed it was obvious that Nationalist members were taking full advantage of Helen's stand to emphasize her isolation from the rest of the Opposition and also that they were using the continuing sabotage and unrest in the country to put the United Party on the defensive with accusations of 'softness' and 'liberalism'. The object of these carefully planned tactics was to reduce whatever United Party opposition there might be to Vorster's next dose of Draconian security laws, which he was in the process of preparing and of which he made no secret. It was his intention, he told a passing-out parade of policemen in March 1962, to give them (the police) full powers 'to check the forces of destruction', even if such powers might be regarded as deviating from established practices and 'time-honoured conceptions' and he had added that the Government would not hesitate to put the 'technicalities of the ordinary administration of justice below the safety of the country and the citizens'.

In the same month Judge Snyman became so alarmed by his findings on the activities of Poqo that he tabled an interim report recommending that the State take swift action against that organization. Poqo, he found, was the PAC gone underground: its salute, aims and speakers were the same, and it planned to overthrow the Government by revolutionary means during 1963 and to create an African socialist state in which only Africans would have any voice. It was his contention that as the law presently (and unfortunately, in his view) stood, the State would have to prove a link between each individual Poqo member and the banned PAC and, in order to overcome this difficulty, he recommended retrospective legislation. He also suggested that the procedure of preparatory examinations of suspects be eliminated where Poqo was thought to be involved, and that suspected members of the organization be tried before special courts. His report was tabled shortly before the Budget debate, which immediately, as is the manner of South African parliamentary debates at such moments, changed its nature and became a discussion on national security. Fierce attacks were launched from the Government benches on the United Party, now rather unfairly stigmatized as being 'the father of Poqo' and accused of failing to assist the Government in taking steps to combat this dangerous organization. Helen was convinced that this assault was deliberately planned to 'scare the United Party out of its wits' and finally to intimidate it into supporting the drastic Vorster legislation which was about to be placed before the House. It certainly had, at that particular moment, the effect of virtually silencing any Opposition criticism of a further enormous increase in the Defence budget, from R120 million to R157 million, plus an additional sum of R5 million voted for the police.

On 24 April 1963 Vorster duly introduced the second reading of his third General Laws Amendment Bill[25] which, he said, was designed to 'exterminate this cancer [of Poqo] in our national life'. The Bill laid down that any organization or group of persons that had been in existence since 7 April 1960,[26] could be declared retrospectively unlawful, thus enabling the Government to equate Poqo with the banned PAC, and the 'Spear of the Nation' with the banned ANC. Persons convicted of certain offences of a political nature could be held in continued detention after the completion of their prison sentences, should the Minister of Justice consider that they were, if released, likely to further the achievement of any of the statutory aims of Communism.* The system of ninety-day arrests was introduced, empowering commissioned police officers to arrest without warrant, and detain for up to ninety days on any particular occasion, persons suspected of committing or intending to commit, or of having information about, specified types of political offences. On the expiration of the ninety days such persons could be re-arrested under the same clause and this process could be repeated indefinitely.

The Bill's flouting of the authority of the courts and of the hallowed precedents of the South African system of Roman-Dutch and English law with regard to the rights of accused persons, gives a strong case to the many critics of the official Opposition. The United Party had opposed the 1961 and 1962 Bills because (as Graaff had said) 'they deprived citizens of the protection of the Courts and put them at the mercy of arbitrary ministerial decisions in such a way as to threaten the freedom of

---

*This clause became known as the 'Sobukwe clause' since Robert Sobukwe, former leader of the PAC, was the only person detained under it.

law-abiding people'. But now, confronted with a third, and infinitely more dangerous Bill, Graaff saw fit to announce that while his party was opposed in principle to such clauses as 17,[27] it would support the legislation *in toto* 'because we are a responsible Opposition and because we want to see law and order maintained as much as they [the Government] do . . .'[28] 'The United Party lay down like curs,' gloated one Nationalist newspaper, and Helen was later to write: 'If ever I felt sick at heart it was on the day I witnessed the tragic capitulation of the official Opposition the day they supported the second reading of that monstrous Bill.'[29] Although during the past two sessions she had watched the United Party jackal spending much time in each of its convenient earths, she had never believed that at such a serious and important moment it could behave in so craven a manner. She herself had made a quick study of the Bill, had collected a fair amount of historical background material, and had had a brief consultation on its legal aspects with Donald Molteno. Nevertheless when Graaff so unexpectedly announced the support of the United Party in principle for the Bill, she was ill-prepared for a solitary battle. As the leader of the Opposition sat down, the Speaker put the question to the Government benches and no one rose to speak. He looked at the Opposition and repeated: 'I put the question.' Again, no one stood up, and Helen suddenly realized that unless she spoke the second reading would be over and the Bill would go straight to committee without further debate. Springing to her feet, she made a rare because virtually extempore speech. Against a barrage of Nationalist interjections, she opposed the Bill as

. . . undermining the fundamental principles of the Rule of Law . . . which is synonymous with civil liberty as far as I am concerned, synonomous with the ordinary freedoms of the individual, of which one of the most important is that he should not be held by the State unless he has been duly charged before a proper court of law, unless he has been properly tried openly, publicly and objectively by an impartial court of law.

Vehemently she reiterated a theme she had never abandoned during her parliamentary career:

If the honourable members would suffer one day the indignities that are suffered in the ordinary everyday life by the black citizens . . . they would perhaps have their eyes opened . . . [This Bill] will undermine the Rule of Law, it will build up tensions outside against this country and it will go on increasing the tensions inside South Africa . . . the . . . Minister . . . should learn perhaps that it is the very failure of moderate African leaders to achieve any improvements in the everyday lives of Africans that has led to the rise of extremist leaders in South Africa . . .[30]

Angrily Vorster retorted with the well-tried 'red smear' technique. Envisaging the remote possibility of his visiting, at some future time, what he called a 'Communist camp', he was convinced, he said, that he would see a lady there, 'and if I did not know the . . . member for Houghton so well, I would be prepared to say that she is the one I see [here]'. Undeterred by so puerile a reply, Helen called for a division. The United Party, as they were to do so frequently in the future, trudged over to the Government side of the House and Helen was left alone in a sea of empty green benches.[31]

From that time on, she became an ever more constant target for government attacks. 'I can't say I'm blameless', she wrote, 'since I'm provocative. Most of the questions I put were embarrassing, many of the speeches I made were on awkward subjects.' Whether or not Verwoerd was behind the attacks now launched on her with unprecedented ferocity is uncertain. But during one particularly heated debate, he descended from his Olympian heights to shout at her as she was speaking, 'You are of no account', an unusual incident which excited a volley of accusations from Nationalist back-benchers, who described her variously as a Communist and a traitress, and warned her that her days in Parliament were numbered. All she could reply was: 'Why? Are you going to put me under house arrest, or send me to Robben Island and coop me up there or something?' When bombarded with nursery insults (and the South African House is notorious for its low standard of parliamentary wit), it is occasionally difficult not to reply in kind.

The Prime Minister, whether or not he was the instigator, certainly did nothing to stop what Helen called the 'lunatic fringe' of the Party from continuing with their tirade of abuse as the session went on. She gave the members on the opposite side of the House all the opportunity they needed, as each Tuesday and Friday at question time she made a point of asking Vorster whether anyone was being kept for a ninety-day incommunicado interrogation, and, if so, who they were, where they were being held and whether their next-of-kin had been informed. By the end of the 1963 session, she had asked over 180 questions. Helen's armour had grown tougher with each successive session; the intimidatory barracking of the 'fringe' failed to disturb her unduly, for their tactics were too obvious to make much impression. She also saw, behind the sneers and insults, a healthy fear of her Party. Had not the Nationalist Chief Whip, J. C. Potgieter, said: 'The United Party is a farce. They will disappear from the political scene. The people we fear are the Progressives, because they are going in a dangerous direction'? The dangerous direction, Helen replied, was multi-racialism, a course followed by the entire civilized world.

The task of all who believe in multi-racialism in South Africa is to survive. Quite inevitably time is on our side. I am one of those who think that great changes are around the corner . . . I am absolutely certain that we cannot maintain our isolation indefinitely and that sooner or later a settlement will have to be reached between moderate Whites and moderate non-Whites.[32]

The Afrikaans Press was less certain than Potgieter that the Progressives, in the shape of Helen, had a future in Parliament. *Dagbreek* said:

The nature of much of the information . . . she collects and her behaviour during the Sabotage Bill gives rise to suspicions about the political motives of some of the PP's new friends. It also confirms the prediction that the Progressive Party, as its hopes of white support diminish, is already far on the path which began as anti-Government and ends as anti-White . . . Mrs Suzman's last year in the House will be accompanied by increasing bitterness and provocation which will try the patience of the House more and more.[33]

The two years that preceded the next general election emphasized the growing unrealities of South African political life. Externally, the country was subject to increasing pressures from the United Nations, from the members of the Afro-Asian bloc and even from its Western allies. Internally, it was experiencing a wave of economic prosperity and, due to the efficient enforcement of the security laws, presented an appearance of superficial tranquillity. By the end of the 1965 session Helen was convinced that fifteen years of legislation had completed what she called the 'jigsaw puzzle of apartheid'. Verwoerd was a master planner: there was a very careful pattern in the measures he had succeeded in placing on the Statute Book during his years of power. Every facet of every South African's life was covered by his laws: the Population Registration Act which had defined the racial group to which each individual belonged; the Group Areas Act which established the geographical areas in which each group could live and earn its livelihood; job reservation and trade union limitations determining the work an individual could do according to his colour; separate racial education ensuring that each child would grow up to fit the role the Government intended he should play in adult life; the separate amenities laws which had further reduced what little social contact there was between the races; and the Mixed Marriages and Immorality Acts for the preservation of racial purity. These measures, coupled with the Government's unceasing onslaughts on the few civil rights still enjoyed by Blacks, left no doubt in any perspicacious observer that all participation in the country's power structure was to be reserved exclusively for Whites.

As the apartheid pattern of life was thus forced upon South Africa, the Rule of Law was slowly but surely eroded. Practically every speech made by Helen at this time contained a reference to yet another curtailment of civil rights in the country and her chief target was the vital role of B. J. Vorster, whose security legislation had enabled Verwoerd to turn the grand dream of apartheid into a kind of reality.

Each new security measure produced less and less reaction from a punch-drunk and complacent general public and still less from the official Opposition: the South African threshold of tolerance to the assaults on civil rights had become unimaginably high. In the fifties, citizens had been prepared to demonstrate publicly at the mere idea of imprisonment without trial or of a man being kept in prison indefinitely after completion of his sentence; now they were either too intimidated to protest or else had developed a tendency to shrug such matters off on the assumption that the

Government knew things of which the general public was innocently unaware.

Helen, however, went on fighting although as the decade advanced the Progressive cause began to seem almost hopeless. Referring to the 'Sobukwe clause' in her private member's motion, she moved, in an impassioned speech, that any statute which deprived citizens of their liberty without recourse to the courts of law be repealed. The Government benches met her with a blank wall of indifference; the United Party sat in a stony and embarrassed silence. At their refusal of support, she rounded on the official Opposition, crying: 'Why do you not get up? Are you not going to support the Rule of Law?' Even the Government newspaper, *Die Burger*, like the ranks of Tuscany, could scarce forbear to cheer. 'She is putting up a parliamentary performance', said its editor with a rare generosity, 'which is impressing even her enemies. For one person alone to state her party's viewpoint on every major item of legislation is crippling work . . . and she is doing it well.'[34] But the highest, although unwitting, compliment she had ever received from a Nationalist MP came from the member for Rustenberg, L. J. C. Bootha, who said:

When she gets up in this House she reminds me of a cricket in a thorn tree when it is very dry in the bushveld. His chirping makes you deaf but the tune remains the same year in and year out. In her fight for the Bantu, the honourable member also sings the same tune for year after year. One must admire her for the fight she is putting up.[35]

Helen needed all the moral support – expected and unexpected – that she could get. The Progressive Party fortunes were approaching their nadir. On 24 July 1964 a Liberal Party member, John Harris, exploded a time-bomb in the White concourse of the Johannesburg railway station, killing one woman and wounding and maiming several others, a unique act of South African political terrorism in that it was perpetrated by a White and directed against other Whites. The Progressive Party officially condemned the bombing in the strongest terms, but Helen's own qualified condemnation, dispassionate though it was, undoubtedly did her party serious damage. 'I don't think', she said, 'that we should be stampeded into losing our sense of balance and use ugly incidents like the bomb outrage as a justification for the ninety-day detention. Surely a properly run democratic country should be able to enforce law and order without such measures.'[36] The mood of both sections of the white population was, however, very far from dispassionate and there was little resistance to government thinking when the Nationalists used Harris's trial and the exposure of the group to which he belonged, the African Resistance Movement (ARM), to attack the Liberals (and by association the Progressives) as 'offering a home to people whose activities in practice cannot be distinguished from those of Communists'.[37] Liberal Party leaders, too, had hastened to express their abhorrence of both terrorism and sabotage, but Harris and ARM had destroyed, once and for all, their chances of ever becoming a political force in the land and came very near to doing the same for the Progressives.

Harris's crime and trial and the subsequent rounding up of the ARM members, closely followed as it was by the arrest of the leader of the South African Communist Party, Abram Fischer,* greatly eased the passing of the last major security legislation of the Verwoerd administration. This was the Criminal Procedures Amendment Bill[38] which introduced the 180-day detention clause, enabling the Government to detain potential State witnesses during criminal cases of a serious nature and providing prison penalties for refusal by such witnesses to give evidence.

A speech by T. Gray Hughes, a United Party front-bencher, during the second reading, made it obvious that the official Opposition had failed to agree on a common approach to the Bill:

We realize that there are some forces at work which the Government cannot control but the Government must realize that all these drastic measures are not curing the evil . . . We will oppose the second reading of this Bill, we will move certain amendments in the committee stage . . . and depending how the Bill comes out from the committee stage we will decide on our attitude towards the third reading.[39]

The United Party's egg-dance excited a great deal of derision from the Nationalists, and Helen remarked that the United Party would have fought the Bill '. . . in those days when it had teeth and nails

*Fischer was arrested in September 1964. In January 1965 while on trial under the Suppression of Communism legislation, he estreated bail and was only re-arrested in November 1965. He was sentenced to life imprisonment.

with which to fight, but if this is a tooth-and-nail fight, I have yet
to see the sign of a tooth or the sign of a nail'.[40] She moved that
the Bill be read 'this day six months'.

The provincial elections, held four months earlier, had given
fresh indications of the electorate's continuing swing to the right,
except in one small area. Disregarding government warnings that
Progressive 'interference' in the election of Coloured provincial
representatives might lead to curtailment of the Party's activities,
two Progressives stood as candidates in the Cape provincial
Council elections, the Party having, as Steytler said, little enough
to fight with but its principles. The Coloured representatives'
election was held two weeks before the national contest for white
provincial councillors: both Progressives were successful, one
getting in with a very slim majority.[41] This choice by the Coloured
voters, Helen said, vindicated all the Progressive Party had stood
for and fought for over five years. The white electorate, however,
had different views: the current backlash was accentuated even
at the expense of the United Party despite its desperate attempts
to woo the reactionary vote by beating the drum of 'red peril' –
which they supposed might subvert the independent Bantustans
– while at the same time calling for white leadership over the
whole country, with Blacks being allotted an undefined share in
the government. With gloom Graaff and the Party leadership saw
their attempts to outflank the Nationalists on the right completely
rejected, particularly in the English-speaking heartland of Natal,
where a strong swing to the Nationalists was apparent.[42] Natal's
desertion of its imperialist past and its concerted rush into the
common white laager enabled Verwoerd to claim, with some
justification, that

the English-speaking vote is, in ever increasing strength, and more and
more openly, aligning itself with the Government policies . . . [This]
means growing political as well as national unity. More than anything
else this has been caused by attacks on and threats to South Africa and
the white man's future from outside. Together we wish to, can and
will solve our own problems – economic and racial – in our own way.[43]

The disastrous results of the provincial elections, apart from
its Coloured victories, made the Progressive Party depressingly

vulnerable to the accusations now being hurled at it by the Government, of which the most effective was that it was a party for Blacks controlled by a handful of Whites. Many of its original supporters began to believe that the party was no longer in a position to compete seriously for seats in white elections, and the English Press muttered that it should consider adjusting its role to be less that of a political party and more that of an educative force or pressure group. As the year closed and speculation grew that an early general election was in the wind, these journalistic pundits openly began advocating either the disbanding of the Party or some form of pact with the United Party. The *Cape Times* wrote: 'The Progressives must realize that the main brunt of the battle to keep democracy alive will be borne overwhelmingly by the United Party. If the United Party were to be reduced to a tiny handful in the House, that same trend would sweep the Progressives out of existence. The Progressives have no hope of winning any of their seats and are only impeding the opposition effort.[44]

The Government added to the gloom of the English editors. Surprisingly alarmed, in view of its sweeping success in the white provincial elections, by the minor success of the Progressives in securing their two Coloured Cape provincial seats, it now rushed through the Separate Representation of Voters Amendment Act, fixing the period of office for the Coloured parliamentary representatives to five years, regardless of the dates of future general elections.[45]

The time bought by the passing of this Bill was used to work out an effective means of preventing the Progressive Party from winning the four Coloured parliamentary representatives' seats.

Sure enough, the Separate Representation of Voters Amendment Act was closely followed by a curious and unique piece of legislation, entitled the Prohibition of Improper Interference Bill and supposedly designed 'to prevent the exploitation by one population group of the political rights of another population group' but in fact abolishing multi-racial political parties. Helen said

I picture some cynical official . . . cackling to himself as he comes up with yet another symptom of our sick obsession with race and colour. The title of the Bill [has] been appropriately described . . . as a euphemism for rape . . . Anyway this extraordinary Bill . . . unintelligible in either language and unspeakable in both [is] an intricate device with a simple objective – to prevent the Progressives from winning the four Coloured seats.[46]

The Bill was not passed immediately: it was opposed by both the United Party and Helen, and after reference to a Select Committee (later converted into a commission) it was introduced in a revised form two years later with substantially the same provisions and was duly passed under the name of the Prohibition of Political Interference Act.[47]

The main result of the revised legislation was the disbanding of the Liberal Party, which refused to compromise its principles of multi-racial membership: the Progressives, however, decided 'under protest and compulsion' to abide by the requirements of the new Act and to confine their party membership to Whites. Helen said:

I have not the slightest doubt that we are absolutely right to continue. This is what the non-White members wanted us to do and definitely what the Government did not want us to do. It is essential that we continue to exercise whatever influence we have on the political structure in South Africa. . . There is a great need for our party . . . greater perhaps than ever before.[48]

Of this need, the electorate seemed to be unaware. The stock-market slump that had followed the events of Sharpeville and Langa, had become, as the economy moved back into top gear, a matter of distant memory. The boom had not benefited Blacks to any extent but the Whites were living in a state of euphoria brought on by full employment, rising wages and an, as yet, insignificant inflation. Against this background of prosperity, the Rhodesian crisis erupted in November 1965. Feelings ran high among white South Africans in the months following Ian Smith's unilateral declaration of independence, and voluntary donations of money and petrol poured north across the Limpopo. Verwoerd called his 1966 general election six months earlier than had been intended, wishing to take full advantage of the economic boom and the emotional mood of the country – engendered this time not by domestic disturbances, by now largely crushed, but by a new phenomenon: trouble in what had for sixty years or more been a peaceful white sphere of influence south of the

Zambezi. In August 1966 Helen had predicted that the 'next election will be a patriotic election, an election wherein the theme will be "I stand back for no man in my loyalty to South Africa". Drums will beat and flags will fly . . .' This time there was no need for the politicians to beat the drums: the bemused, euphoric electorate were more than willing to bang out the music for themselves. Well aware of the value of his Rhodesian cards, the wily Verwoerd played them close to his chest, upholding in theory, if not in practice, his well-known dictum that no country should meddle in the internal affairs of another. His voters by now on a fine chauvinistic rampage took Harold Wilson's punitive measures against the rebel government to mean that Britain had gone over into the 'enemy's camp', and this, coupled with the advent of the republic and the consequent loosening of ties with 'Home', made large numbers of them conscious, for the first time, of a South African identity. The election results were to show an extraordinary desire to emphasize this new-found identification.

The National Party election manifesto remained essentially unchanged. In it, Verwoerd expressed his belief that South Africa's golden age lay ahead of it – if it could only gain the understanding of the world and be given time to solve its racial problems. 'To those who cannot accept South Africa as it is and as it grows, but seek to change it into something wholly new with the resulting chaos as elsewhere in Africa, I have nothing to say.' He might as well have begun the sentence with 'To Helen Suzman and the Progressive Party', since, at this particular moment, there was almost no other area of the electorate to whom he could have been referring. The United Party, for election purposes, had taken up its stand somewhere to the right of Verwoerd himself and was busily engaged in advocating permanent and total white control over the entire country. Only the Progressives 'refusing as always', as the *Rand Daily Mail* put it, 'to bow to expediency or compromise their principles', wearily trod their lonely road.

Helen addressed her constituents in her Houghton election campaign:

My main strength is the knowledge that I was voted into Parliament to represent a point of view that exists in South Africa – despite intimidation, despite the unfavourable climate, despite the bullying of the Government and the toadying of the one-time anti-Government forces – a point of view still exists in South Africa that wants to be expressed, unequivocally, on a hundred and one issues. And it has been my job in Parliament to express that point of view – unpopular though it may be in Government or United Party circles. It is not to indulge a passion for opposing, as has been suggested: it is to provide an outlet, a means of expression for those thousands of people who are not prepared to conform to the strange practices that are becoming more and more accepted as the 'South African way of life', as if this very phrase is in itself a justification for the most shameless discrimination, the most inhuman attitudes . . . If mine is the voice of dissent, it is so because conditions in South Africa call out for such a voice and because I know that so many people want it to be heard.

In the reigning emotional climate, however, this reiterated commitment to her principles had, throughout the country, an adverse effect on the Party's vote. At its last Congress in November 1965 it had been decided somewhat rashly, to fight forty-one seats, some in the Nationalist-dominated Orange Free State: in particular the Party had pledged itself to oppose the three United Party leaders, Graaff, Douglas Mitchell and Steyn. Lack of finance and organization eventually limited its contests to only twenty-six constituencies, but in almost all of them it lost badly, chiefly on the emotive Rhodesian issue, which was used as a theme with monotonous but effective insistence by Graaff. 'South Africa will never forgive you if you sit by and let civilization be destroyed in Rhodesia,' he told Verwoerd, who cannily refused to be drawn into debate on this delicate subject. Support for Smith had become the most popular Opposition platform: it was one on which the Progressives, disapproving of the blatant racism of the Rhodesian Front, could not hope to compete with the old imperialists of Natal and the deep-rooted prejudices of the *bloedsappe* and of so many of the urban English-speaking voters. In vain Steytler begged the Government and all responsible political leaders 'whatever the future may bring, and however close the kinship between many white South Africans and Rhodesians, not to say or do anything that indicates even indirect support of the unlawful Rhodesian regime';[49] and Helen, speaking in Durban (where she observed, with the usual amazement of a Johannesburg liberal entering that outpost of British colonialism, 'There were more "I hate Harold" stickers floating around than in Salisbury'), caused dismay to her supporters and joy to her enemies when she ventured to criticize the Smith regime.

With the tide of feeling running so strongly against them, it became the first priority of the now beleaguered Party to achieve the re-election of Helen in the Progressive heartland of Houghton. Her opponent was Dr A. D. Bensusan, a reactionary of no uncertain order with some claim to a local public reputation (he later spent a year as Mayor of Johannesburg). The English-speaking Press gave Helen overwhelming support. Even the leading United Party newspaper, the Johannesburg *Sunday Times* devoted an editorial to her on the Sunday before the election. 'If', advised its editor, 'anyone does choose to vote for Mrs Suzman, he will do no hurt to his conscience; he will inflict no injury on political justice; and he will help to ensure that a familiar voice continues to be heard in Parliament.'[50] The *Post* (a Black newspaper) wrote:

It is not our job to tell the Whites whom to vote for. We make an exception in the case of Helen Suzman. Surely white South Africa, entrenched in its strength, can afford this one solitary voice. [It is in the Houghton electorate's] power to do a positive act for South Africa by returning this doughty fighter, this most respected opponent of the Government. The good wishes of millions of our people are with you, Helen . . .[51]

In the early stages of the campaign it was believed that the outcome would be a very close-run thing. Indeed, for the first weeks, even hardened optimists thought that Helen might lose her seat. But some three weeks before the election a sudden, strong and sustained swing away from the United Party manifested itself in this one constituency. It was due in some part to the support Helen had received in the public print (Bensusan later complained that the Press had let him down),[52] and in some to Harry Oppenheimer, who appeared at one of her meetings and told the voters that a vote for her would be a blow struck for all that was best in South Africa. But what had actually happened was that a personality cult had been born (at its lowest expressed in the words of a Houghton worker – 'suddenly it became fashionable to vote for Helen'), a cult that centred on the woman rather than the Party ('We noticed the feeling of importance felt by the voters as they spoke to Mrs Suzman and also how this feeling was

H

enhanced if they could call her by her first name,'[53] said an observer), and which prevailed in Houghton till the municipal election of 1972 when Selma Browde, on her own recognizances and her party's platform, was elected as Progressive City Councillor for a ward comprising a large area of the parliamentary constituency. The United and Nationalist parties found useful propaganda in it, sneering that without Helen her party would collapse, and thought this is a distortion of the truth, it must nevertheless be seen as having a basis of fact.[54] This cult, by preserving her presence in Parliament, kept the Party alive during its years of otherwise total eclipse in the late sixties and early seventies. Without Helen Suzman as a focus for the minority who saw Progressives as the only political hope in an otherwise hopeless situation, without what she and Houghton did to ensure that in Parliament a Progressive voice would continue to be heard, it is most unlikely that the Progressives in 1974 would have been capable of returning six other members to Parliament. Without the 1966 Houghton result, the Party, voiceless and unrepresented, must have gone the way of all the other splinter groups whose bones litter the byways of South African political history. After the election, Helen had retained her seat with a slightly increased majority[55] but every other candidate had been defeated, with a noticeable decline in its numbers of votes.

Helen was more than a little bitter at the thought of another five years alone in Parliament: but the years since 1961 had built up her resilience and the prospect was no longer as frightening as it had been when she had first found herself so unexpectedly alone. 'I suppose I have my uses,' she said. 'I'm more use in improving South Africa's image than the whole of Frankie Waring's office [The Department of Information] and I cost the taxpayer considerably less.' She both disliked and vigorously denied the opinion of the public that the mantle of the Party's *de facto* leadership had fallen on her shoulders by virtue of her second victory: but it was obvious that Jan Steytler's crushing defeat (he had lost his deposit in East London North) had taken the heart out of him. He withdrew to his farm at Queenstown and, in the ensuing years, appeared to become more and more removed from reality. Party officials waited for days and sometimes weeks for replies from him to urgent telegrams and such public utterances as he made grew increasingly repetitive. It is unusual and difficult for a political leader to run his party without a parliamentary seat and almost impossible for him to do so from a remote rural area hundreds of miles from the scene of main political activity. Steytler asserted less and less control over this struggling party in the years that followed the 1966 election and in the public mind Helen, who held no position in it other than that of member for Houghton, came to exemplify the Progressive Party.

On her return to Parliament, she found herself, for the first time, a front-bencher. 'This is an honour,' she wrote. 'It is also a sombre thought. Fourteen years is a long time. I find there are only ten MPs on the Opposition side who are senior to me.' The election had given the Government two-thirds of the seats in Parliament; they now occupied not only their own side of the House but all the cross-benches and two and a half rows on the Opposition side. 'I am', Helen told her constituents, 'not only faced with Nats and flanked by Nats but I have them sitting behind me too – it is considerably unnerving to turn round and find myself confronted with several sets of beady eyes fixed on me with unblinking hostility.'[56]

The short session, which it was supposed would offer little of greater interest than the formalities of passing the Budget, began in unpleasantness and ended in high drama. Verwoerd began it with what was, even for that past master of the art, a performance of unprecedented arrogance by totally ignoring Graaff's customary motion of censure, which he left to be answered by the Minister of Mines and Planning. The election results had raised the Prime Minister to new heights on his private Olympus: what god-like schemes he was formulating will never be known, for he was never again to address the Assembly. On 6 September, a month after the session had opened, he was scheduled to make his first speech in the debate on the Prime Minister's vote, which, it was believed, would contain a major policy statement on foreign affairs. The bells were still ringing, summoning members to the Chamber, when a parliamentary messenger, Demetrio Tsafendas,[57] approached the Prime Minister where he sat on the Government bench, pulled out a dagger and stabbled Verwoerd three times in the throat and chest. Helen, sitting opposite, reading a letter, heard the sudden uproar and looked up to see Nationalist members clustered in front of the Prime Minister's seat, some attacking Tsafendas, some trying to give what assistance they could to Verwoerd, who lay dying in his seat. She has never been able to forget the shock of the assassination, made for her, personally, particularly dreadful by the loathing in the voice of a Nationalist Minister who shouted at her that it was she who was responsible for the act.

Verwoerd was buried seven days later, on 13 September. His mantle fell on the shoulders of B. J. Vorster, chosen unanimously by the Nationalist caucus to be the country's seventh Prime Minister. The former Minister of Justice seemed to be an apt successor. 'I believe', he said to the cheering crowd who greeted him outside Parliament after the news of his choice was made known, 'in the policy of separate development not only as a philosophy but also as the only practical solution in the interests of everyone, to eliminate friction and to do justice to every population group as well as every member thereof.' To her constituents, Helen commented:

Whether or not the new Prime Minister is one of the convinced adherents of the independent Bantustan concept is yet to be seen. He is not a philosopher as his predecessor was. My own impression of him over the years is that he is a pragmatist, dedicated to the maintenance of the *status quo* for white domination – more at home with *baasskap* than with the Bantustan ideal. He knows full well that the security of the State depends on the maintenance of a strong army and a strong police force in a country where unpopular laws are passed that bear hard on the majority of the population – to whom the democratic procedures of voicing their objections are denied and who have not been consulted about the laws that govern their lives.[58]

South Africa had moved too far along the apartheid path for Verwoerd's death to signal any significant change in overall policy. All the major legislation of 'separate development', masterminded and planned in its smallest and to its most final detail by the Party's dead leader, was already on the Statute Book, enforced by Vorster's security legislation. Helen thought it likely that the new Prime Minister would govern more on a basis of the old Malan–Strijdom style of *baasskap*, using the laws intended for the maintenance of the vision of Verwoerd. However, Vorster continued to pursue the distant dream of independent Bantustans (albeit more circumspectly than his predecessor), and there was certainly no slackening, but rather an intensifying of the security legislation.

The next four years in Parliament were a period of 'sheer slog' for Helen. In retrospect, session after session merged for her into a continual repetition of her chosen task – to persuade the electorate

that the only logical course for South Africa is to follow a policy that is based on reality, not myth; the reality of a multi-racial country inextricably bound together; and a policy that will end hostility against us by giving all the races a fair chance to participate in our country's development – to work, in other words, towards a just society.[59]

It was an almost impossibly difficult task and must often have seemed hopeless. She described it at one stage as

a frantic scramble to keep up with all the different subjects appearing on an order paper. I have a batch of votes coming all together – Justice, Prisons, Police, Bantu Administration, Bantu Education, Coloured Affairs, Indian Affairs, etc., etc., and the miracle is that I manage to deliver the appropriate speech on each vote.[60]

There were too many issues, too many cases of individual hardship brought to her attention for her to deal effectively with them all. An idea of the dependence of the voteless Blacks on her can be found in a quotation (from a letter received from a banned African) used by her in the Assembly:

I cordially and sincerely beg and beseech you to exercise even your personal parental sympathy that I may receive assistance in my present predicament. I am still restricted as one in gaol. At present I am without income. I am faced with accounts, family, clothing and taxes, and I have to report to the police station once every month.[61]

And to cap her unremitting and mountainous task she presented each session a private member's motion on issues ranging from migratory labour to the abolition of the death penalty.

This was the era when Vorster's obsession with security legislation seemed, now that he was Prime Minister, to have become almost an end in itself. Each session a whole new series of laws were passed, each fresh one imposing yet another restraint on what little remained of the individual liberty of those actively opposed to the Government. The Suppression of Communism Amendment Act of 1967[62] placed further restrictions on members of banned organizations and in the same year the Terrorism Act[63] produced an extraordinarily wide definition of the word 'terrorism' and allowed indefinite detention without trial.[64] This Act was supposedly justified by an infiltration of guerrilla bands from Zambia into the Caprivi Strip of South West Africa, although it was employed, in the event, primarily against urban dissidents; its provisions buried the concept of *habeas corpus* once and for all in the republic. The Nationalist Press greeted the Act with cries of glee ('the police will now have a free hand to act without legal restraint'), the United Party, with their invariable reservations, voted for it, and finally it was passed with Helen's usual solitary vote against.

In 1969, the Public Services Amendment Act[65] set up a Bureau for State Security, popularly known as BOSS, with General H. van den Bergh, the former Head of the Security Police, as its head. This organization was presented to Parliament as being the South African version of the CIA or MI5 and its functions were, said the Minister of the Interior, to co-ordinate the security sections of the police and the Defence Force. Some weeks after its inception, a further General Laws Amendment Act[66] was passed, containing two clauses (2 and 10) which greatly extended the scope of the Official Secrets Acts, enabling a Minister or a delegated subordinate to declare that it was not in the public interest to have a particular piece of evidence produced in court, even if it was essential for the defence of an accused. Additionally it became an offence to publish or disseminate any matter concerning the Bureau and, as Helen observed: 'What does concern BOSS nobody knows; it could be anything.'

Outside debates, much of Helen's time in Parliament was taken up with the tabling of a continuous barrage of questions to Ministers, causing these harassed gentlemen to hurl at her wrathful accusations of 'time-wasting' and 'Suzman-inquisitiveness'. Dirk Richard wrote in the Nationalist organ *Dagbreek*:

So many of Mrs Suzman's questions are connected with prosecutions under the anti-Communist Act, the anti-Sabotage Act [*sic*], the Immorality Act [with] detainees and restricted persons, [with] apartheid and other colour questions. These are questions related to legislation connected, *inter alia*, with subversion, sabotage, maintenance of segregation and our fight for existence. More than once a Minister has had to reply that the furnishing of the desired information is not in the public interest. Last year, Mr Vorster wanted to know why she asked this sort of question. What value does it have for the South African public, members are wondering more and more . . . Mrs Suzman is more than the member for Houghton. She is the representative of internationalism,* the sole flame who has to keep the light of this liberalism glowing in Parliament.[67]

To Richard's innuendoes Helen replied:

Our Statute Book is crammed with legislation that gives the Ministers vast powers, such as detention without trial, banning and house arrest. The victims have no recourse to the courts. Other laws like pass laws and group areas bear harshly on those who have no vote. At least the Ministers wielding these powers know that their actions are subject to inquiry in Parliament.[68] I am not the instrument of any extra-Parliamentary body, organization, movement or ideology, whether local or overseas . . . I attempt to do my duty as an MP, as I see it . . . and I try to the best of my ability to preach and promote the principles and views of my Party [and no other].[69]

The ceaseless demands of her exhausting task were beginning to tell. In a letter to her daughter Frances, she wrote: 'There is no time to read during the day and I am too damned tired at night. I long for the end of this parliamentary life so I can just laze around and read and read and do what I damn well please all day long.'

Another long period was to pass before Helen's dream of an end to her solitary and overworked parliamentary days was to be realized. Somehow, in spite of her very occasional and always private moments of desperation, she kept going. 'To be a progressive', she explained, 'you have to be an optimist, and optimists are happier than pessimists.' There was still very little, if any, cause for optimism, although by 1967 the Nationalist Party had begun to show the first signs of internal division since the resig-

*The use of the word 'internationalism' in Nationalist jargon parallels in some ways the Nazi propaganda usage of 'cosmopolitanism' in the 1930s.

nation of Malan and the election of Strijdom. The charisma of
Verwoerd had been able to hold his party together, mesmerizing
its members with the inexorable arguments of his grand apartheid
vision. But before his death the great leader had begun to lay
realistic rather than visionary foundations for a future South
Africa based on an apartheid which did not, indeed could not,
correspond with the dreams of Afrikaner domination and race
purity that possessed the hearts of so many Nationalists, corrupted
in their impressionable youth by the heady propaganda of the
New Order and the simplistic fascism of the *Ossewabrandwag*. It
was one thing to classify the population groups and force them into
separate railway carriages and post-office entrances, but quite
another to contemplate the reality of self-governing Bantustans
occupying large areas of national territory. The bogy of white
displacement by Blacks, so assiduously nurtured for years by the
right wing of the United Party (who had achieved nothing by the
exercise) now raised its head in the Nationalist ranks, and those
alarmed by its existence looked for and found other areas of
government policy – originated indeed by Verwoerd but developed by Vorster – equally little to their taste. The wooing of the
English-speaking section of the population, long an important
plank in Nationalist platforms, seemed to the disciples of Strijdom
and Pirow a betrayal of the *volk*, for whom the English, as well as
the Blacks, must always be a traditional enemy. Large-scale
immigration from Europe, encouraged by both Prime Ministers
for the sake of economic growth, was bringing in relatively fewer
'acceptable' nordic Dutch and Germans and more of the less
privileged, vividly described by Albert Hertzog – the son of the
old General and Vorster's Minister of Posts and Telegraphs – as
'the scum of Southern Europe', Greeks, Italians and Portuguese.
And, bringing all these resentments and fears to a head, Verwoerd
in 1965 and 1966 had begun the establishment of what was called
an 'outward foreign policy', especially where black Africa was
concerned. The hard-core Nationalists were unable to regard with
equanimity such heretical activities as South African Foreign
Ministers shaking hands with black leaders and, yet more dis-
turbingly, the setting-up of a Malawian embassy in Pretoria,
headed by a black ambassador whose daughter, by special edict,
was permitted to attend a white school.

Even before Verwoerd was dead, these developments were beginning to sow dissension in the ranks of the Nationalist Party, and Vorster's faithful continuation of his predecessor's set pattern led inevitably to explosion. The ultra-conservative English-language newspaper, the *SA Observer*, had for some time been indulging in a polemic war with *Die Burger* and *Die Beeld* against the 'liberals' within Afrikanerdom, but it was the Professor of Logics and Ethics at the Afrikaans University of Potchefstoom, Professor W. J. de Klerk, who at a SABRA Youth Congress in October 1966, first openly revealed the rift among his people. In his address to the Congress he defined two types of Afrikaner – the *verligtes* and the *verkramptes*. By definition, he said a *verligte* was a forward-looking Afrikaner, one who retained the traditional values while taking a positive attitude towards future development. Unfortunately, *verligtes* were, the cautious Professor qualified, liable to promote dangerous 'liberalist' tendencies in Afrikanerdom. *Verkramptes*, on the other hand, he defined as ultra-conservatives who opposed all change *per se*. With Professor de Klerk's crystallization of the latent dissension within the Nationalist Party, the opposing groups could be clearly seen in their battle stations. For the next two years a violent dispute raged through every interlocking facet of Afrikanerdom – its newspapers, its churches, its cultural organizations and its political arm – until, by 1968, the *verkrampte* movement was clearly identified with Hertzog as its leader. The authors of an anonymous 'smear' letter attacking Vorster which had been circulated throughout the Party, were, in that year, unmasked by the Security Police and Hertzog, who in February had lost the portfolio of Posts and Telegraphs but retained that of Health, was summarily dismissed from the Cabinet. On 14 April 1969 he openly attacked the 'outward policy' for its erosion of the true values of the Afrikaner *volk*. Afrikaners, he said, were still anchored by their church and religion, their whole being permeated by a 'great complex of principles called Calvinism, that code of moral, ethical and religious principles. 'They form', he said, 'part of our pattern of life. They form part of our being, of our upbringing. We cannot be anything else.' Liberalism, to this arch-apostle of reaction, was the essence of English-speaking South Africans who could no more divorce themselves from it than the Afrikaner could from his Calvinism. Nor could they ever identify themselves with the measures which were necessary to maintain Afrikaner domination in South Africa, and Afrikaners who co-operated with the English were infecting themselves with liberalism and would be incapable of defending white civilization against the *swart gevaar*.[70]

In September 1969 Hertzog and two other MPs were formally expelled from the National Party. Between them they formed the '*Herstigte Nasionale Party*'* committed to an unashamedly pro-Afrikaner policy in which the English would be relegated to the status of a second-class language group, apartheid even more strictly applied, and immigration severely restricted.

Before the expulsion of the Herstigtes, Vorster had announced an early general election. 'I wish', he said, 'to place myself at stake.'[71] His tactics were identical to those of Verwoerd when he called the 1961 election with a view to the destruction of the left: but this time the target lay at the other end of the political spectrum. Helen had no illusions about Nationalist *verligtheid* but saw the power struggle as an internecine battle between *verkramptes* and super-*verkramptes*. 'I do not believe', she said, 'that there is such an animal as a *verligte* Nat.' In a speech in Durban in August 1969, she dismissed out of hand the belief that the Vorster premiership had heralded a new and enlightened era. Vorster she saw as little more than a first-class public relations officer. 'In no time at all', she observed sceptically, 'he has transformed the image of himself as a stern-faced policeman wielding a truncheon into that of a genial golfer carrying nothing more lethal than a putter.'

This was an odd time in South African politics, chiefly for the United Party who were suffering an onset of optimism and seemed to believe that the Nationalists were about to move in a more liberal direction whose effects would in some mysterious way enable the official Opposition to sweep into power. Helen, remembering that some of the most repressive legislation on the Statute Book had been introduced *after* Vorster became Prime Minister, was unable to understand the trance into which the United Party had fallen. It was perfectly clear to her that the influence of Hertzogism must, in the future, make the ruling National Party show more caution and circumspection in the

*Restructured or Reinforced National Party.

tentative implementation of their 'outward policy' and that, even more importantly, the Hertzog appeal to rooted Afrikaner instincts would act as a brake on any possible re-thinking of economic or migratory labour policy.

The election campaign was short and bitter, the National Party concentrating its attacks on the Herstigtes, and claiming, somewhat vaguely, that the Government would guarantee security, create more white employment opportunities, improve educational facilities, solve the housing shortage and eliminate tension, resentment and hate. The United Party devoted itself to promoting its latest policy (white leadership with limited representation (by Whites) in one Parliament for all races) and such attacks as it made on the Government were largely based on accusations of administrative incompetence.

The Progressive Party had just celebrated its tenth anniversary. Helen told the Tenth Birthday Congress that 'the Party's survival was nothing short of miraculous and that only exceptional determination could have saved it from extinction during or after the post-Sharpeville period. 'In the following years', she recalled, 'intimidation, "passport snatching" from vocal opponents of apartheid and propaganda consistently linking liberalism with Communism and opposition to racial discrimination with lack of patriotism had stunted its growth.'[72] *Die Vaderland* found her utterance too modest. 'If the Progressive Party was to be congratulated on its tenth anniversary, it was actually a matter of congratulating one woman, Helen Suzman, without whose capability and acute bellicosity [*sic*] the Party would have long withered in the political wilderness.'[73]

The Progressive approach to the 1970 election was more realistic than it had been four years earlier. The Chairman of the National Executive, Colin Eglin, declared that the Party aimed at getting at least six members into Parliament in 1971 and, in order not to over-extend its forces, would only nominate nineteen candidates.[74] The Party's campaign was based almost exclusively on the issue of civil liberties, and attacked not only the Government's disregard for human values and its consequent abuse of powers, but also the United Party's dubious and inconsistent record in this area. Helen pointed out that the official Opposition had supported the 90-Day Act in 1963, opposed the 180-Day Act in 1965, supported the Terrorism Act in 1967 and opposed the General Laws Amendment Act in 1969. 'Unlike them, I do not take fright just because a Bill is entitled the Terrorism Bill. I look at its contents and when it is obvious that such a measure can lead to the grossest abuse, I have no hesitation in opposing it.'[75]

Once again, a country somewhat weary of elections went, on 22 April 1970, to the polls. The HNP were altogether wiped out, although achieving marginally more votes than the Progressives. The split in the National Party ranks lost it a significant number of votes (chiefly English-speaking) to the United Party, which regained some seats, mostly in Natal, which it had lost in 1966, though conceding ground in the more affluent urban areas to the Progressives.[76] Helen herself increased her majority from 711 to 2049[77] despite the distribution throughout her constituency of a United Party pamphlet entitled 'Are these the deeds of a South African?' which attacked her with traditionally Nationalist accusations of lack of patriotism and support of terrorism. When the Houghton result was announced, it was said that 'the silent majority danced in the streets of the townships'.[78] But the swing to the Progressives benefited only Helen and failed to defeat the United Party organization in the other eighteen contested constituencies. Yet again, at the end of an election day, the member for Houghton wept – this time when she heard that Colin Eglin had come within 231 votes of victory in Sea Point. As her supporters, with their unfailing, almost desperate optimism sang 'We shall overcome', she could only cry out, in total despair, 'Here I go, for another five years, with that bloody mob.'*

*This remark quoted by *Life* magazine resulted in Helen having to apologize to the House.

Chapter Nine 1970-4

Now, for the first time since the National Party victory of 1948, a trend away from the right was seen. This reversal showed itself again in the provincial elections in October 1970,[1] when the National Party once more lost ground to the United Party. The Progressives, however, did not appear to be benefiting. Their failure to win the Houghton and Sea Point provincial seats enabled Graaff to reiterate the claim that there was no Progressive Party, only a Helen Suzman, and that when she went there would be nothing at all. In the same speech he announced a five-point plan for the achievement of what he called a 'compassionate society' based on sanity and justice. Helen, who over the years had listened to the United Party evolving policy after policy and goal after goal, none of which ever came to fruition, was profoundly unimpressed. 'I do not believe', she said, 'that our people need compassion: they need opportunity, and only the Progressive Party proposes to give it to them, irrespective of race or colour. South Africa does not so much need compassion as civilized values.'[2] But, although believing that too much was being made of the small swing to the United Party, since the Nationalists still controlled two-thirds of the seats in the Assembly, she was uneasily aware that the Progressive Party needed a major shake-up if it was to survive. She, personally, had a very high regard for Steytler, but it was impossible not to face the fact that he had abdicated responsibility to a deplorable degree. The Party clearly needed a new leader to improve both its extra-parliamentary image and its electoral performance. It was a great relief when in December, at a National Executive meeting in Johannesburg, Steytler unexpectedly (and to the consternation of some of the Executive) announced that he would not be standing again for the leadership. There was some speculation as to whether Helen herself would stand, which she brought to an end by making it quite clear that she had more than enough work in the Assembly without the daily problems of party administration. As a temporary measure, Harry Lawrence was made acting leader but it soon became evident that the man for the job was Colin Eglin.

The former member for Pinelands was in some ways cast in a similar mould to J. H. Hofmeyr. Sent from Cape Town at his mother's insistence to be educated at an Afrikaans-medium primary school in the tiny Orange Free State town of Hobhouse, he matriculated at the unusually early age of fourteen from the De Villiers Graaff High School in Villiersdorp, in the Cape Province. His studies at the University of Cape Town were interrupted by the war, in which he spent two and a half years on active service in North Africa and Italy, before returning to complete a degree in quantity surveying. In 1954 he became a United Party MPC, and an MP in 1958. A big man, with soft eyes and a puppy plumpness, he had an open manner and an infectious and unfailing cheerfulness. 'When he smiles', an admirer once said, 'which is often, his whole face radiates benign good-will. With a false beard he would make a wonderful Father Christmas.'[3] The *bonhomie* of his exterior, however, concealed an uncompromising interior toughness combined with a pragmatic sense of political realism. He was forty-five when an enthusiastic National Congress in Cape Town in February 1971 unanimously elected him as the first English-speaking leader of the Progressive Party. Until this moment it had been an accepted tradition in South African politics that party leaders (other than in the periodic formations of Natal separatists) must invariably be Afrikaners. A political opponent commented: 'Eglin . . . is a wide-awake young man who makes a good impression and apparently can blow new life into the Progressive Party.'[4]

In his acceptance speech the new leader sounded an optimistic note, expressing his belief that the Party, having battled for eleven years to keep alive, would, with the new fluidity in South African politics, now begin to grow much faster. Alone among the other parties, he claimed, it was flexible and modern enough to take advantage of the inevitable socio-economic changes that must occur in the country, and he added that it was interesting to remember that every change of government since Union had taken place with three parties in the field and that each time the third party had been the key factor in the change. It was the Progressive Party's task to articulate changing attitudes while keeping alive a set of values that would include the Party's concept of individual human dignity, the Rule of Law, parliamentary democracy and natural human justice and also to deal effectively with current issues such as manpower problems, deteriorating standards of education, the destruction of African family life and the social and physical problems arising from proliferating urban development. He concluded with his most important announcement – the structuring of what was to become the Progressives' new strategy. The Party, from this time, would increase its dialogue with Afrikaners, particularly those urban-dwellers whom he believed to be the section of the white South African public most likely to bring about political change in the future.

It was at this Congress that the Progressives became the first opposition party to accept the existence of the Bantustans as an irreversible *fait accompli*. The policy of the Party allowed for the maximum decentralization of political and administrative power, and independent Bantustans as a concept fitted without undue difficulty into its vision of a federal South Africa.[5] This decision opened up the way for discussions between Party officials and Bantu homeland leaders, many of whom were openly expressing their growing disenchantment with separate development. The concept of autonomous black states with provincial status in a progressive South Africa was seen as a good starting point towards a more tolerant society by both the homeland leaders and the Progressive politicians.

Helen was content with Eglin's election to the leadership. She thought him both able and sincere and believed that if anyone could lift the Party out of its current doldrums he was the man to do it. Unlike Steytler, far away on his Queenstown farm, and resentful of his anomalous role as leader without a parliamentary seat while Helen took the limelight, Eglin found no difficulty in working closely with his party's solitary MP. Living in Cape Town, he was available at all times for consultation during sessions, and indeed, from now on Helen made a point of asking for his advice and opinion on controversial legislation. They did not always agree. ('Helen and I', he admitted in 1973, 'can get bloody aggressive towards each other.') The occasions for aggression were usually those when the leader's tendency towards pragmatism and practical politicking clashed with Helen's increasingly uncompromising stand on current matters of principle. A case in point was the stand she took up against the harsh anti-drug laws introduced by the Government in 1971, which found her at variance both with her new leader and, it must be admitted, with much of the party rank-and-file.

On 4 May of that year the Minister of Social Welfare and Pensions, Dr C. P. Mulder, introduced the Abuse of Dependence Producing Substances and Rehabilitation Centres Bill[6] to the House. He proudly described the legislation as '. . . the toughest anti-drug laws in the Western world . . . [to prove] . . . we are truly in earnest about stamping out with might and main this diabolical underminer and destroyer of Western man and his morals here in our country.'[7]

The Bill's methods of dealing with drug abuse, which in South Africa related chiefly to the traditional smoking of marijuana (or '*dagga*' as it had locally been known from time immemorial) by Blacks, and also to a large extent, by Whites, were Draconian and provided for savage minimum sentences whose imposition was no longer to be at the discretion of the courts. The onus of proof of innocence in such cases lay largely upon the accused, and powers to detain suspects without trial were granted to the police. The Bill was rushed through all its stages in three days, supported by the United Party, whose 'compassionate society' did not, apparently, include *dagga* smokers. It fell to Helen, once again, to stand alone in opposition, this time against a veritable hurricane of self-righteous condemnation from both the other parties. Although she was against drug abuse, she was allergic, she said, 'to all laws in terms of which people may be locked up without trial'. The United Party spokesman for Justice, Michael Mitchell, accused her, in what must have been an unguarded moment, of '*having nothing but a lot of principles** she waffles about . . . merely for the purpose of making political capital out of [them]'. But both United and National Party speeches in the debate were only the forerunners of a new attack of great ferocity upon what was now portrayed as Progressive sympathy for drug pedlars, saboteurs and, by definition, terrorists; for it was a short step from selling

*Author's italics.

a 'zoll' of *dagga* for a few rands in a back street to mounting a large-scale armed insurrection (at least, it seemed, in the minds of many members of Parliament).

However much they may have differed on the drug legislation, before the year ended Helen and her new leader achieved a major breakthrough for their party's attempt to establish its credibility as a third force in South African politics. In late September and early October they made a 'whistle-stop' tour of a number of West and East African states and became the first white South African politicians to make contact with any political leaders in Black Africa outside the immediate South African sphere of influence, which extended no further than Malawi. Helen's international stature gained the two Progressives immediate recognition in the countries they visited, and they met Leopold Senghor, President of Senegal, President Diawara of the Gambia and Dr Kofie Busia, successor to the Nkrumah dictatorship in Ghana. Taking the lead in the discussions, Helen stressed to these leaders that the situation in South Africa was not as rigid as it was portrayed in the OAU's propaganda, and that she and Eglin represented thousands of enlightened white South Africans who were totally opposed to any form of race discrimination. She believed, she told them, that three elements for change were present in South Africa: the gradual integration of Blacks into the economic infra-structure, the rise of black politicians such as the Bantustan leaders, who were advocates of radical change while working within the apartheid structure, and a marked liberalization in the attitudes of a large majority of English-speaking white youth. If the two Progressives had received sympathetic hearings from the West African leaders their reception in East Africa delighted them. Commenting on their arrival in Nairobi, the *East African Standard*'s editor said:

A lone, persistent voice, Mrs Suzman is more than welcome . . . it is to be hoped that even so small a voice in South Africa can persuade more white people [there] that the vast continent of Black Africa can manage its affairs very well in peace and prosperity, without an ugly atmosphere of colour prejudice . . .[8]

'Nairobi was especially open-hearted in its welcome', Helen wrote to the young South African, Gary Ralfe, who had acted as their interpreter in Senegal, 'and Colin and I were given a rousing cheer in the Kenyan House when the Speaker announced we were present.'[9] It was, she commented wryly, an infinitely warmer response than any she had received from the Assembly of which she was an elected member. But it was in Tanzania that they made their most important breakthrough. Neither of them expected even to be allowed to enter the country, and they had been warned that, even in this unlikely event, they would almost certainly face demonstrations from members of the exiled ANC and PAC, whose headquarters were in Dar-es-Salaam and in whose eyes Progressive political thinking was as undesirable, for different reasons, as that of the Nationalists. However, once Nyerere had decided to meet them, the only hostile manifestation was a newspaper description of them by a PAC spokesman as '. . . the grinning friends in the enemy camp and the apostles of merchant democracy' and of Helen personally as 'an economic baroness', who with Oppenheimer really ruled South Africa (Helen commented on her return she wished she did, for if it were so, things in South Africa would change fast). Of all the leaders she met, Helen found Nyerere the most intelligent and forthright. But in contrast with Senghor's expressed view that a mere indication by the South African Government of an ultimate intention to abandon apartheid would be sufficient to create a major shift in the attitude of many OAU states, Nyerere unequivocally supported force as a means of effecting change in South Africa. Helen understood the emotional background of the Tanzanian President's approach, since for years she had been fully aware of the frustrations of Africans living under a far harsher system than Britain had ever imposed on Tanganyika or any other of her colonial possessions, but could not agree with Nyerere's revolutionary solutions and said so. Nevertheless, as she was leaving Dar-es-Salaam, she was deeply moved when Nyerere took her by the hand and said: 'When all this is over, your role will be remembered.'

Returning to South Africa, she said she would not have missed the trip for the world, heat and exhaustion notwithstanding. The comments of the Nationalist Press were, said Helen, 'as mean as catfish', and described the expedition as a 'journey to nowhere by nobodies'. One of their newspapers, essaying wit, described the two Progressives as 'Walter Mitty Eglin and Mrs Kaunda-dialogue Suzman'.[10] The Government, it said, was well aware that South Africa had 'just to abdicate, and then the whole of Africa will embrace us. We have long known this. But it is not our task to win a cheap and fatal popularity competition. We must create a stable and fair order from South Africa's variety. And for this Mrs Suzman's instant solutions will not do.'[11] Any euphoria which might have been generated for the Progressives in the north was swiftly diffused by the harsh political realities of South Africa. In October a young Indian, Ahmed Timol, arrested under the Terrorism Act in a mass sweep by the Security Police, fell to his death from the tenth floor of the police headquarters in Johannesburg while under interrogation.* In the public outcry that ensued, the United Party called upon the Minister to appoint a special judicial inquiry, and complained about treatment meted out to detainees held under Section 6 of the Act. The Shadow Minister of Justice, Michael Mitchell, objected with righteous indignation that Section 6 had been specifically designed and passed in 1967 to allow the police guarding South Africa's remote borders to hold suspected persons for as long as they needed where access to a magistrate was impracticable, while the recent wave of detentions had not taken place in the bush, but in urban areas where magistrates and judges were easily available. It was ironical that Helen's own prognostications of the obvious abuses to which this section was open were now being voiced by the official Opposition, who had shouted her down when, alone, she had voted against the Act: at a protest meeting at the University of the Witwatersrand she reminded the audience of the naïvety of the United Party in accepting such assurances from the Minister of Police, and the consequent futility of their complaints when their co-operation was thus abused. 'When the crunch is on', she said, 'when the powers are being implemented, no one gives two hoots about the possible intentions behind the law – all that matters is what the law in fact contains, and the law makes no mention of the bush.'[12]

*In June 1972, at Timol's inquest, the presiding magistrate announced that Timol had committed suicide and no one was to blame for his death. The police claimed (but never proved) that, judging by documents found in Timol's possession, he was a member of the banned Communist Party, and, as such, had preferred to commit suicide rather than betray the Party.

The new rash of dawn raids, the arrest and trial of the Dean of Johannesburg, the Very Reverend G. A. ffrench-Beytagh, for alleged contraventions of the Terrorism Act were well-staged preludes to an accusation by the Prime Minister that South Africa's enemies were attempting to undermine the country 'with greater venom and hatred than ever before'. The Government, as usual, had spectacular plans for the next parliamentary session.

While the Press wrote off the 1972 session as 'boring and dull', and although it did indeed not pass much contentious legislation, Helen described it as the nastiest in which she had ever participated. The Government's strategy of reassuring those waverers on the Nationalist right who might be thinking of moving into the HNP camp became apparent in the Prime Minister's reply to the United Party's No Confidence motion. At the end of a long speech notable for its quotations of Winston Churchill on the subject of Communism, Vorster recommended that Parliament keep a watchful eye on all organizations and trends which could possibly give rise to Communist subversion and that it should take 'cognizance of four organizations with widespread subsidiaries and ramifications . . . [and] . . . as the chief guardian of our liberties, should acquaint itself with the objectives and activities of these organizations.' He named the four organizations as the National Union of South African Students, the South African Institute of Race Relations, the University Christian Movement and the Christian Institute.[13] Vorster continued that he considered that *prima facie* cases existed for investigation of these groups and that he intended appointing a Select Committee to do just this. 'I am not putting them in the dock . . . if they are innocent, this Parliament will give them that certificate of innocence.' The trap was ingenious: the United Party fell into it with scarcely a backward glance. Graaff, indeed, at first asked for a Judicial Commission of Inquiry instead of a parliamentary Select Committee, which, he correctly maintained, could not be objective (both National and United Party members had for years been publicly claiming that NUSAS, in particular, was a subversive organization whose actions were inimical to South Africa) but concluded his speech by saying that his party was in fact prepared to serve on the Select Committee[14] as a part of its parliamentary duty. Helen now made an unequivocal stand that was to be more important for

her party than any that she had made before. She believed, she
said, that the Prime Minister's reasons for investigating the four
bodies were simply that they were all outspokenly critical of the
Government's racial policies; that they were all multi-racial and
that they received financial support from abroad; that the Government was indulging in one of its favourite pastimes – the smear
tactic designed to frighten off potential supporters from the
organizations under investigation. She, for one, would have no
part at all in the Select Committee. She condemned the United
Party out of hand for giving the pseudo-judicial inquiry a false
aura of respectability. 'It would have been far better', she declared,
'to leave the Nationalists to sit communing with themselves, like
yogis contemplating their navels.' Nevertheless the Committee
was formed, and during the recess became a Select Commission
known by the name of its chairman, the Nationalist MP, A. L.
Schlebusch. The activities of the Schlebusch Commission were
to dominate South African politics until the next election.

But the Nationalists had their own never-ending row to hoe.
Having shown their supporters that they meant business in their
dealings with the students, clerics and liberal do-gooders, they
now set about retrieving their electoral image, dented by the cut
in their majority which they had suffered at a by-election in
Brakpan in February. Another by-election was due to be held in
the Cape *platteland* town of Oudtshoorn in April and the governing
party was soon to be seen trotting out some very ancient shibboleths, many of them concerned with British atrocities inflicted on
the Boers seventy years before, and all of them designed to bring
the Afrikaner faithful back, at the double, into the Nationalist
fold. This well-tried technique, popularly known as *boerehaat*,*
was highly successful in its effect upon the United Party, which
was at once side-tracked from the major issues at stake and
involved in futile arguments about its attitudes to the Afrikaner
volk. The campaign was begun during the Budget debate by the
Minister of Labour, Marais Viljoen, and carried on by the Minister
of Defence, P. W. Botha, who, while attacking United Party
members for their alleged inadequacy in the Afrikaans language,
took some vicious sideswipes at the Progressive Party, denouncing
it as the '. . . forerunner of anarchy and eventual communistic

*Hatred of the Afrikaner.

dictatorship . . . the intercessors for all the people who commit sabotage. They are the intercessors for all the enemies of law and order and of democracy.'[15]

It was left to the Minister of Mines and Health, Carel de Wet, to bring the campaign to its climax with an impassioned description of the 'martyrdom' of the *volk*-hero Jopie Fourie, with the interesting moral added to the effect that a clear indication of the United Party's fundamental loathing of the *volk* was the fact that its hero, General Smuts, not only had the heroic Fourie shot, but had shot him on a Sunday. A combination of treachery and sacrilege, Helen afterwards remarked, that set the Nationalist members gibbering with rage, albeit it had taken place well over fifty years previously.

This ferocious mauling directed with violent intensity upon the United Party by no means left Helen unscathed: indeed the abuse and hostility directed at her were unparalleled since the attacks of the 1966 session. It was the Prime Minister himself who unleashed the Government's artillery against the lone Progressive, apparently infuriated by three questions put to him by her on labour unrest among the Ovambos in South West Africa, the Government's vendetta against NUSAS and the progress of the 'outward' foreign policy. 'I am not talking to that member', he declared (while conveniently failing to answer any of the points she had put). 'We are talking to reasonable people. I can't include her.' P. W. Botha, delightedly joining the fray, described her as being the official mouthpiece of permissiveness and all subversive activities in South Africa (a remark the Speaker subsequently made him withdraw), but, as Helen said later, once she had recovered from her initial surprise she fought back with spirit, 'up and down like a jack-in-the-box, taking points of order. It was the only exercise I [got] during the session.' And even *Die Burger* mildly rebuked the Government. 'Why', it asked, 'has it become necessary in recent times to attack Mrs Suzman so sharply? Surely it cannot be because she gets under the skin of the Nationalists?'

Meanwhile, the campaign against the students gathered spectacular momentum when on Friday 2 June 1972, a group of students from Cape Town University peacefully demonstrating on the steps of St George's Cathedral, close to the Assembly buildings, on the issues of academic freedom and the recent expulsion of the entire student population of the showpiece of Bantu education, the black University of the North, were baton-charged by the police. Some of the demonstrators fled into the cathedral itself, whither they were pursued by the policemen, and many of them beaten up in the aisles. The student leaders sent for Helen, who hastened over from Parliament, five minutes' walk away, to find the cathedral totally encircled by a police cordon. Pushing her way through the ranks, she was able to enter the building and to negotiate a safe-conduct through the police lines for the fugitives still huddled within. She hurried back to Parliament, where she obtained an immediate interview with the Minister of Police, S. L. Muller. The Minister, professing ignorance of the dramatic events taking place so close by, promised an immediate investigation to be followed by a statement in Parliament on the following Monday. Helen was now once more called away, this time to the Caledon Square police station, where a number of students who had been arrested on the cathedral steps were being detained. At her intercession, Muller ordered their release. On the following day, however, he made a Press statement declaring that the police had acted with great tolerance, and on Monday informed the House that the student demonstrations were the work of Rhodesian and other foreign students encouraged by the British Liberal Party leader, Jeremy Thorpe (a recent visitor to the country), who, claimed the Minister, had endeavoured to discredit the existing order and to subvert the Government's authority with the students, while Helen had deliberately fanned the flames.

While he was still speaking, a crowd of 10000 people, mostly white and by no means all of them students, was gathering once again outside the cathedral to protest at the police action at the previous meeting, unaware that that very morning the Minister of Justice had banned all meetings within one-mile radius of Parliament. With Colin Eglin, Helen again hurried over to the cathedral, where a police officer was informing the crowd (somewhat inaudibly since his megaphone was not working) that the meeting was illegal and should disband. She said to the officer in charge, whose men were preparing to baton-charge, 'Keep your men back and I'll help to get as many of the crowd as possible into the cathedral.' Although she and Eglin successfully helped disperse the throng, a procession of students, unaware of the situation on the cathedral steps, was marching down from the University and came into collision with the police in the street who dispersed them with tear gas and batons. The incidents in Cape Town had immediate repercussions all over the country, with white English-speaking students taking the initiative: their demonstrations were ruthlessly crushed by charges of uniformed and plain-clothes police, the latter frequently indistinguishable from civilian enthusiasts with noticeably strong feelings about student demonstrators. After a week of intermittent clashes between the students and the police the Minister of Justice imposed a blanket ban for one month on all political demonstrations in Cape Town, Johannesburg and Pretoria. An uneasy quiet descended. Except for the spontaneous gathering in Cape Town on 5 June, few outside the student bodies of the English universities had been actively involved in the demonstrations, and the Government was disposed to shrug the incidents off as unrepresentative and insignificant. Nevertheless, in May of the following year, at the unanimous recommendation of the Assembly's Committee on Standing Rules and Orders of the House and of the corresponding Senate Sessional Committee (both of which were representative of both the Government and the United Party) all demonstrations within one square mile radius of Parliament were banned in terms of a Gatherings and Demonstrations Bill[16] which the Government introduced. Michael Mitchell expressed the United Party's full support for it. '. . . If any single individual, for instance my African messenger boy, going about his lawful business in the public places and streets, is interfered with . . . by anyone having a demonstration, then his inalienable right to move about public places is affected. Such demonstrations should therefore not take place.'[17] Helen was the only member of Parliament to oppose the Bill, moving that 'it be read this day six months' and pointing out that no demonstrations had ever affected the work of the House. She believed, she said, that '. . . to demonstrate, to assemble, to protest and to voice views which may differ from my own are the very fabric of democracy.'[18]

The latter half of 1972 was dominated by a series of events which indicated that the political flux which had imperceptibly begun with Verwoerd's death was visibly gathering momentum, the first being the resignation from the Cabinet of the Minister of the Interior, T. J. A. Gerdener. At the beginning of the 1972 session this thoughtful and unusually independently-minded Nationalist had earned the disapprobation of his colleagues by giving it as his opinion that, unless something was done to close the gap between white and black earnings, violence and murder would result, and that the white standard of living was disproportionately and unnecessarily high in comparison with that of Blacks, at whose expense it was being continually raised. Public repudiation of his views by other Ministers forced Gerdener's resignation from the Cabinet and subsequently from the National Party: but he was unable to see either of the Opposition groups as a political haven. Helen saw his resignation as proof that the Government had discarded all attempts to present itself as *verlig* and was instead trying to shrug off its 'liberal' wing in order to prevent further defections to the Herstigtes. Certainly it gave impetus to a growing feeling among many Afrikaner intellectuals and leading businessmen that the Government was following a road which must end in economic and political catastrophe. But, like Gerdener, they could not bring themselves entirely to abandon the fundamental apartheid philosophy in which their roots were so deeply embedded. The United Party and the Progressives gained few, if any, recruits from their disillusioned ranks. Instead mushroom pressure groups with names like *Verligte Action*, which by their very apolitical nature were doomed from the start, sprang up. Gerdener himself, on his resignation from the National Party, had initially formed such a group, called 'Action South and Southern Africa', intended to promote better race relations and to establish as much common ground as was practicable between the various race groups, but soon formed a political party whose self-proclaimed liberal philosophy was rendered sterile by its inability to divest itself of the underlying preconceptions of its founder with regard to racial differences. The Democratic Party, as it was called, propounded what was described as a 'twin stream' policy which simplified the complexities of Nationalist-style

apartheid by splitting the country into only two racial groups –
the Africans on the one hand, and, on the other, the Whites,
Coloureds and Indians. All the basic rights enjoyed by the Whites
would gradually be extended to the Coloureds and Indians.
Gerdener suggested that urban African areas might become
autonomous city states if they could not merge geographically
with a convenient homeland. The clumsiness and ambivalence
of his policy illustrates the difficulty experienced by many otherwise *verlig* Afrikaner Nationalists in shedding even the smallest
of the racial shibboleths of their traditional philosophies, but
Gerdener clearly hoped that, by making such limited concessions,
he would attract reasonable numbers of educated Afrikaners out
of the Nationalist fold, where the United and Progressive parties
had over the years had such small successes.

Within the United Party, too, a revolt of a more significant
nature was beginning to take place. In 1972 a 'reforming movement' (popularly known by the English-language Press as the
'Young Turks') gained control of the Party's Witwatersrand
General Council. Its aim was advertised as the revitalization of
the Party and the capture of thirty-five seats at the next general
election: its true target was the achievement from within the
Party of what the Progressive Group had failed to do in the 1950s,
if indeed this had ever been the Progressives' conscious aim:
nothing less than the overthrow of Graaff and the Party establishment and their replacement by the more 'liberally'-minded
reformists. Led by Harry Schwarz, MPC for Yeoville (Johannesburg) and the Party's deputy leader in the Transvaal, the group
numbered few, if any, members of Parliament. Nevertheless, in
a brilliantly organized campaign at the Party's 1972 Transvaal
Congress, they succeeded in ousting the veteran right-winger
S. J. Marais Steyn (once described by Graaff as 'my right hand
and my left hand') from the provincial leadership. The spectacular
early success of the Schwarz group led to speculation in the Press
of a United Party renaissance and revivals of suggestions for a
United Party–Progressive electoral pact, which were swiftly
rejected by the leadership of both parties. Helen successfully
remonstrated with those Progressives who were toying with the
idea:

Opting out of elections would result in a few more irrelevant United Party MPs, a re-elected Nationalist majority and a destroyed Progressive Party. To stay in business we have to fight elections. To me this is the crux of the issue. Either it is desirable to have a white political party in South Africa that is dedicated to the removal of race discrimination and to the promotion of equal opportunities and of a just society in our country or it is not. And if it is desirable, we have to behave like a political party and not like a discussion group or we will go out of business . . . I believe that South Africa deserves something better than second worst.[19]

Helen had few illusions as to the effectiveness of groups such as the 'Young Turks' among the gallimaufry of heterogeneous politicians who for so long had lived in de Villiers Graaff's shadow, and she saw clearly both the similarities and the disparities between the Schwarz faction and Steytler's group of MPs of thirteen years previously. Indeed the similarities were there, and the ultimate fate of the 'reformists' was to have many aspects in common with that of the Progressives. Both groups found themselves considerably to the left of the Party leadership and of official policy: both inevitably became targets for ruthless attacks from the conservatives: both were finally forced into resignation or were expelled. The differences, however, though less immediately apparent, were marked and fundamental. In the first instance, where the Progressives had reacted as individuals to developments within the caucus, the 'reformists' were from the first a cohesive and well co-ordinated group formed with the clear and definite intention of taking power in the Party. Their power base was the Witwatersrand General Council, and, subsequently, the Transvaal organization. From this they intended to infiltrate the other regions, beginning with the Western Cape, nominating their own supporters for key official positions and as provincial and parliamentary candidates and forcing out the old-guard conservatives who had been entrenched in the leadership since the days of Smuts. As their organization and efficiency was so much greater than the loose and unplanned grouping of progressive MPs had been, so their idealism and liberalism appeared proportionately less. They used the issues of urban African home-ownership, job reservation and 'petty' apartheid to rally the support of some businessmen and English-speaking voters, and they were given to the composition of 'declarations of faith' and well-publicized pronouncements of good intentions towards black leaders. But their roots were in the old United Party and its fundamental concept of white leadership: they could not accept the Progressive programme of a qualified franchise with its inevitable end (however far off) in majority rule. They also shared a firm conviction that political power in South Africa must reside with one or other of the major parties and that the Progressives were doomed never to make electoral headway among the Afrikaans-speaking majority of the voters. Thus their whole strategy was based on the use of the United Party machine as the vehicle to control the Opposition.

So the Progressives continued their battle to establish themselves as a credible third force: but in November they were to receive a sharp set-back. At the Johannesburg Municipal elections in March they had achieved what to them appeared to be a significant electoral success when Dr Selma Browde was elected as municipal councillor for Ward 22, an area comprising a part of the Houghton parliamentary constituency. It was the enthusiasm generated by this victory that inspired the Party's leadership to announce, first, its intention of fielding fifty candidates at the next general election, and, more immediately, of contesting in three-cornered fights two forthcoming by-elections in the Nationalist strongholds of Vereeniging and Johannesburg West. But the Party was not yet strong enough to fight seats where it had neither local organization nor evidence of grass-roots support. The results[20] of both by-elections were massive Nationalist victories, with the United Party coming a poor second and the Progressives losing their deposits, major set-backs for both opposition parties.

The United Party reformists, certainly, lost much of their movement's early momentum, while the damage to the Progressive morale was such as to place the whole future of the Party in seeming jeopardy. The Government, on the other hand, entered the 1973 parliamentary session reinvigorated by its success, and in no mood to play a defensive game.

Yet the events of the early months of 1973 must have given the ruling Party some cause for thought. For many years South Africa's labour laws had been held up by the Government as examples to the whole capitalist world, the key to an industrial peace unknown in Britain, and the supposed envy of Germany and the United States. This legislation, originating with Hertzog's Industrial Conciliation Act of 1924 and improved and polished by post-1948 Nationalist administrations, had indeed operated until recently with notable success. The segregated white trade unions had small cause for complaint: in a booming economy they were concerned primarily to keep their wages acceptably far ahead of those of their black inferiors, and found no problem in doing so. But the accelerating inflation of the early 1970s began to render the predicament of the underpaid black proletariat increasingly intolerable. Across-the-board percentage increases, which were a popular solution in management at this time, only worsened the situation: a 10 per cent rise for a white artisan earning R300 per month meant a rise of R30, but for his black assistant who might only be earning R40, it meant only R4; the gap between them widened continually. Helen's economic training had enabled her to give clear warnings to successive Ministers of Labour throughout the 1960s and in 1970 and 1971 of the dangers inherent in a situation where the poor were not only getting relatively poorer, but had no voice to make their plight heard. And her prophecies began to be fulfilled when in December 1971 illegal but initially uncontrollable strikes aimed at the injustices of the contract labour system swept the Ovambo work-force of South West Africa. But Windhoek and Walvis Bay were a long way off: the leading strikers were arrested and the rank-and-file repatriated to their remote homeland on the Angolan border, and the troubles were swiftly forgotten as 'a little local difficulty'.

But in January 1973 labour unrest moved uncomfortably closer. In Natal the Zulu workers in the docks, textile and other industries, reacting against their abysmally low wages in what was, in common with those of all Western countries, becoming a highly inflationary economy, came out in a series of wildcat strikes. The scale of the strikes was, as in South West Africa, too great for them to be crushed on the spot by police action and although the workers, through lack of funds, were unable to sustain their action for any length of time, they wrung some pay increases from their employers, who were under pressure from the Government to settle.

The Government, too, made concessions. It had moved a long

way from Verwoerd's intransigence and wordy visions, and, these days, was prepared to give a few inches of ground if pushed sufficiently hard. A Bantu Labour Relations Regulation Amendment Bill,[21] which, it was supposed, would provide some kind of safety-valve for the frustrations of the African worker, was passed with Helen's grudging support. It was no true solution, and the goal for which Helen had fought even before she had entered Parliament, that of collective bargaining rights for African as well as white workers, organized in non-racial unions, was as far off as ever. And Nationalist pragmatism, when it occurred, always had a reverse side, in this case taking the form of a successful red herring drawn across the public's view of the strikers by the Minister of Labour. The unrest, he explained, was, at bottom, the work of agitators, and not merely black agitators, but white students, members of NUSAS and of a recently formed body called the Students' Wage Commission, which had been particularly active at Natal University. So potentially dangerous were the activities of these radical agents among the (essentially peaceful) African workers that nothing less than the Schlebusch Commission was worthy of tackling them.

Consequently, when on 27 February the Prime Minister tabled in the Assembly the first two interim reports of the Commission,[22] it came as no surprise that although no action was recommended against NUSAS as a body, it had been decided 'in a spirit of urgency' to name eight of its leaders as members of a group which was consciously endangering the internal security of the country. These individuals, declared the Commissioners, were intensely active politically but did not support any of the country's existing political parties, while trying to bring about changes which would result in a replacement of the existing order in South Africa. The Commission's findings were sent to the Minister of Justice, who concluded that the cases of the eight student leaders named in the report[23] fell within the broad net of the provisions of the Suppression of Communism Act, and served them all with five-year restriction orders, a course of action which may well have been suggested by one of the Commissioners when he observed in Parliament that '[there is] . . . only one solution and that is to put these young men and young women somewhere in cold storage for three to five years so that they can cool down as far as their so-called student politics are concerned'.[24] Helen was the only member of the House who protested that day and earned the new soubriquet of 'Mrs Devil' from a Nationalist member for her pains. The report, she found, contained 'suppositions and deductions from suppositions and insinuations and many "probablys" and lots of "*miskiens*" [perhaps]'. There was no evidence whatsoever of any overt or covert illegal action. If there had been, she said, there was a wide selection of laws under which the students could have been charged.

I do not think that any single one of these students, if charged in a court of law, would ever be found guilty of any crime against the security of the State . . . I think this is a most appalling action of the Government and I am aghast that the official Opposition should have given *carte blanche* to the Government to take any action it sees fit against these young people who have not committed any unlawful act up until now . . .[25]

The United Party's role in this dubious affair finally aroused a significant number of its usually apathetic *stemvee* to revolt. Having first opposed the investigation on the grounds of its parliamentary rather than its judicial nature, it justified its final decision to serve on the Commission on the grounds that its representatives would act in a 'watchdog' capacity. Its early denunciations of the inquiry had been strongly worded, but later criticisms couched in similar language emanating from the Progressive Party and the English Press, particularly after the NUSAS bannings, should, Graaff suggested, be treated as contempt. It was an old jibe of the Nationalists that the United Party was two-faced; and Graaff's statement on the bannings was a vivid illustration of this. While deploring the fact that the eight students had not been brought to trial, there was he said, 'undisclosed information' constituting a strong *prima facie* case against them and he had no doubt that they would be convicted under the Suppression of Communism Act. The banned students, were however, never charged, and the United Party's credibility suffered accordingly. Even some of its most conservative supporters criticized the UP commissioners for not having composed a minority report recommending submission of the evidence obtained to the Attorney-General for action, while the more liberal wing, notably Catherine Taylor, the shadow Minister of Education, and some members of the Schwarz group, urged the Party to leave the Commission altogether. Despite these rumblings, the caucus chairman, T. Gray Hughes, announced soon after-wards that it had passed a vote of full confidence in its four members of the Commission and had requested them to remain in office. It was premature, he said, to assess or criticize the Commission's findings until the final report on NUSAS was released. The statement continued that failure by the Party to have participated in the Commission would have been failure to play a necessary part in ensuring a fair and just hearing for those whose actions were being investigated, and a grave dereliction of the Party's constitutional function as the official Opposition. Nevertheless, the caucus reaffirmed the Party's total opposition to arbitrary banning as a form of punishment, and its unshakable belief that if such action was contemplated or taken against anyone, compliance with the Rule of Law demanded that the person concerned must have access to the courts. The United Party would not tolerate any attempts to achieve political change other than by democratic procedures within the law. It would 'continue to oppose any tendencies on the part of the Government, or of any other persons or agencies, to impose totalitarian methods in the maintenance of order'.[26]

These tortuous and self-contradictory explanations were thrown into sharp relief by Helen's continuing refusal to recognize the validity of the Schlebusch Commission, a stand which was echoed outside Parliament by Colin Eglin for the Party as a whole, when he said:

We believe that . . . a permanent political inquisition [into which the Commission had proposed converting itself] which will give practising party politicians the right to pry into and interrogate citizens about their political activities will constitute a serious inroad into the Rule of Law, the rights of citizens, freedom of association – it will take South Africa one step further from parliamentary democracy.[27]

Within a week of the banning of the eight white student leaders – and (as Helen sarcastically commented) no doubt to show its lack of racial bias – the Government banned eight black students,[28] putting two of them under house arrest. Helen obtained a half-hour debate on these bannings and pointed out that the black students had not even been accorded the courtesy of an inquiry by the Schlebusch Commission. The Black Power movement they represented and which was now emerging after a decade of relative political docility by the Blacks (largely leaderless as they were since the chief figures of the old political organizations had been gaoled, banned or, in some cases, had fled the country), was directly attributable to the Government's policies. 'The Government', she said, 'can ban leaders and others will rise up in their place because the Government has itself spawned an indestructible Black Nationalism which all of us are going to regret and which, is after all, only a by-product of White Nationalism.'[29]

Many observers thought that the 1973 session was Helen's finest. The United Party's performance in relation to the Schlebusch Commission indicated that its attitudes remained essentially unchanged from those of the early 1950s when it had abdicated its moral responsibilities over the question of the Coloured franchise. Helen's unequivocal opposition provided a focal point round which the usually apathetic opposition forces at last began to rally. The United Party, whose judgement of the situation was so wide of the mark that it had actually been putting out feelers (not for the first time) to establish whether grounds for consensus existed between it and the Government, was forced to veer wildly to the left again in a desperate attempt to retrieve its image and regain lost electoral support.

But however admirable Helen's performance was during that session (as one commentator remarked, 'It takes guts to stand up there alone to tackle not only a tough and ruthless Government but a bitter and resentful Opposition'), the inability of the Progressive Party to make any significant electoral headway was beginning to induce a certain overall weariness in her. She feared that she would be alone forever in an increasingly hostile House, and admitted that what had once been her 'sunny nature' had become somewhat warped, and that Parliament for her had ceased to provide even rare moments of amusement. 'Like everybody else I long to be loved,' she said, 'but I am not prepared to make any concessions whatsoever – they can take me as they find me.'

I

The fact that over the years she had become a figure of international stature was poor compensation for the apparent hopelessness of her struggle. In the Sheldonian Theatre at Oxford in June 1973, when to thunderous applause the degree of Honorary Doctor of Civil Law was conferred upon her by Harold Macmillan as Chancellor of the University, she was described as 'standing with courage against those who declared the seamless robe of humanity to be torn by differences of colour . . . the voice of one crying in the wilderness . . .' She must have found the Public Orator's words to have an unintentional kernel of bitter truth. In Oxford she was a heroine: in her own country, for most of the electorate, she was a pariah, and only the support of the voteless masses, eloquently expressed by Gatsha Buthelezi, Chief Minister of KwaZulu, at a banquet to celebrate her twenty-first session in Parliament when he described her as '. . . the one flickering flame of liberty amidst the darkness that is such an enveloping feature of South African politics', and the devotion of her Houghton electorate, can have been of real significance to her at this time.

Towards the end of the year, rumours of an early general election became rife. The defection of Marais Steyn to the Nationalists had exposed the growing strength of the Schwarz faction within the United Party and provoked furious counterattacks and accusations from the conservatives in the caucus. In the Western Cape, reformists and conservatives plotted and counter-plotted, and the widespread publicity of the resulting disarray and near anarchy in the official Opposition, exacerbated by the continuing controversy over its participation in the Schlebusch Commission, gave Vorster an opportunity of further strengthening the Government's already entrenched position. A political tactician of the Prime Minister's calibre could scarcely ignore such an opening or fail to take advantage of his opponent's difficulties, and early in 1974 he announced the general election date as 24 April.

The Progressive Party, from its leadership down to the lowliest of its workers, was ony too aware that this election might well be the last it would contest. Repeats of the by-election fiascos of a year before and another failure to break out of the Houghton bridgehead would doom the Party irretrievably. Helen knew that she would again win Houghton, but was depressed to find that before the United Party had even nominated a candidate, over 3000 potential United Party votes in the constituency had been counted by Progressive canvassers. She thought that the Party might win two more seats, Sea Point, which Eglin was again contesting, and Parktown, which appeared to have a significant Progressive vote and consequently had been nursed with extreme care by the Party. But she was not confident of even these victories and admitted to a 'sneaking feeling' that this election could see the final demise of the Party in spite of all the efforts which were being put into the key constituencies. Publicly she appeared as optimistic and as self-confident as ever. 'I have a dream', she told country-wide meetings, 'in which I sit on my little front bench and with me are Colin Eglin, Gordon Waddell, Van Zyl Slabbert and Réné de Villiers.' (The last three were the candidates in Johannesburg North, Rondebosch and Parktown.) Privately she let it be known that there was no possibility of her facing another lone session and indeed that she would resign her seat if no other Progressive were elected, feeling that if the Party could retain only one parliamentary seat after fifteen years of struggle, its members should accept the realities of the situation, disband, and devote their energies to extra-political work such as that under-taken by the Black Sash. Without Helen as a candidate, past canvassing results indicated that the Party could not guarantee, even in Houghton, the election of another Progressive. In the light of these chilling facts, the campaign strategy was evolved with extreme care. Instead of spreading its efforts over fifty constituen-cies as it had rashly committed itself to do before the 1972 by-elections, the Party contested only twenty-one parliamentary and twenty-two provincial Council seats.[30] Some candidates were nevertheless nominated in United Party strongholds for the purpose of 'showing the flag', even though the Party failed to honour its pledge to fight all the United Party members of the Schlebusch Commission: but the main efforts, apart from Hough-ton, were directed primarily at Sea Point; at Parktown, lost by so narrow a margin in 1961; at Hofmeyr's old constituency of Johannesburg North, and finally at Orange Grove in north-eastern Johannesburg, which had been held for many years by the senior United Party front-bencher and Schlebusch Commissioner, Etienne Malan. In Houghton itself, the United Party, unable to find any candidate of calibre prepared to oppose Helen, at the last moment nominated an unknown minor party official named Senekal. Helen said she relied on the Houghton electorate to return her to Parliament to continue what she called 'our long-standing agreement of mutual trust . . . to represent their enlightened views in Parliament' and her only comment on her opponent, as she devoted herself to six weeks' campaigning not only for herself but to ensure the election of her running mate for the provincial Council, Selma Browde, was 'Where did [the United Party] find this poor innocent victim?'

As the intensive six-week campaign drew to a close, the years of bandwagon politics were beginning at last to bear the United Party a bitter fruit. The official support it had given to the Star Chamber-like activities of the Schlebusch Commission in its own strongholds roused a deep-seated revulsion among many voters who had been unmoved by the most drastic of Vorster's security laws. In and around northern Johannesburg, Schwarz himself and three of his reformist lieutenants had been nominated as United Party candidates, and the Progressives forbore to fight them, while in Orange Grove Etienne Malan was amazed to find himself fighting for his life against a Progressive who started the campaign with no organization at all. The English-language Press gave formidable support to any 'anti-Schlebusch' candidates whether reformist or Progressive, who might contribute to an improved opposition. The Progressives themselves, on the basis of their canvassing figures, discovered a visible swing towards them which indicated that they might scrape to success in some of their key seats by a handful of votes: as the results began to come in, they were amazed by the landslide victories they achieved in Orange Grove and Johannesburg North and in de Villiers Graaff's former Cape Town seat of Rondebosch where an inexperienced, albeit star-quality, candidate, F. van Zyl Slabbert, had been expected to do no more than dent the traditional United Party majority. In Houghton, moreover, the legend of the Suzman personality cult was finally broken, when Selma Browde was elected to the provincial Council with a respectable majority.[31] With six members in Parliament, and a seventh shortly to be elected in a by-election, as well as three provincial Councillors, the Party's bleak years in the wilderness were at last ended. The election had indeed for

the first time in South African political history demonstrated a
pronounced and effective swing to the left, at least among the
higher socio-economic groups of urban English-speaking voters.
Northern Johannesburg and its periphery fell entirely into the
hands of the Progressives or of the United Party reformists (all
four of whom were to leave their party before a year was up).
The Cape Town suburbs exhibited a similar trend. Even in Natal,
where the imperial past had always been traditionally strongest,
Progressive candidates did better than ever before, despite the
unsuccessful intervention of Gerdener's Democrats. The predominantly Afrikaans parts of the country were, however, unaffected, and many *platteland* constituencies even experienced a swing
to the right as the *bloedsappe* abandoned their old allegiance and
moved finally into the Nationalist camp in the wake of Marais
Steyn. The final results, in terms of seats, showed the Nationalists
in fact to be as strongly entrenched as ever, but a beginning had
been made in the formation of the kind of opposition envisaged
so long ago by the 'liberal' United Party back-benchers in 1953.
It was not a united opposition, split as it was into two distinguish-
able sections quite apart from the old United Party establishment:
the Progressives led it, but had not yet reached more than a small
percentage of the electorate, whether English or Afrikaans.
Nevertheless, the beginning was there. Whether or not it had
come twenty years too late in the South African political context
cannot be speculated upon: even Helen remarked that she could
hardly imagine the vast difference the results were going to make
to the Party as a political force to be reckoned with. For her, the
results were only a beginning. The future of South Africa was, she
said, entirely dependent upon men of goodwill getting together.

What is important is that those of us who come together shall do so
on very firm grounds: there must be agreement on the fundamental
principles on which our party was based when it was formed fifteen
years ago and on which it has stood without compromise during those
long hard years in the wilderness and for which its representatives . . .
have fought so unflinchingly for so long. We will not depart from those
principles under any circumstances. We will not sell out on any basic
issue . . . We have our firm base, our good name and our first-class
leader. All who wish to join the fight against reaction and strengthen
the opposition are more than welcome.[32]

Of her own performance, all she would say was 'Well, it's been a job worth doing.' What is certain is that without her thirteen lonely years in the House of Assembly, the Progressive renaissance could never have happened. As it was, the six newly elected members inherited from her a tradition of uncompromising integrity and stubborn opposition to injustice seldom seen in the legislatures of the world, and which had been her strongest weapon in her solitary defence of the Party's parliamentary bridgehead. But at last the reinforcements had arrived: and it was time to leave the defensive position and to move on to the attack.

EPILOGUE

It was ironical that only fifteen months after the Progressive Party had finally established itself as a force to be reckoned with in white politics, it had ceased to exist. The reformist movement in the United Party broke away in February 1975, their position made untenable by the conservative establishment. The ostensible cause of the break was a public-opinion poll conducted and published at the instigation of one of the reformist MPs, Richard Enthoven, without the authority of the Head Committee. Enthoven was forced to resign, and over the next week Schwarz and two other MPs followed him out of the United Party together with a number of Transvaal MPCs and Johannesburg municipal councillors and one member of the Senate. Although the circumstances were in many ways similar, the break lacked the high drama of the 1959 Bloemfontein split. Instead of gravitating directly to the Progressives, the dissidents formed a new party, called the Reform Party, destined to exist for only 165 days and which immediately entered into negotiations for a merger with the Progressives.

There was little room for manoeuvre by either party. When merger was first mooted a considerable body of Progressive opinion was opposed to it; on the grounds that firstly the Reformists, had they truly been men of principle, would simply have joined the Progressive Party as the authentic voice of the moderate left; and, secondly, that the Party, still flushed with its election successes and with the impressive performances put up by most of its new MPs in their first parliamentary session, had no need of mergers or alliances but could dictate its own terms to the refugees from the United Party. This group looked to Helen (who was reported to oppose merger) for leadership, but it was not forthcoming. No longer the solitary voice of the Party in Parliament, she was now once again part of a caucus: a different one from that of 1959–61, and she herself a far more dominant figure within it. But the Party was moving out into a wider political spectrum, and the tightly-knit group of idealists who had kept it alive for so many years found themselves giving way to the pragmatism of the new MPs and their supporters, to whom the promise of the electoral support claimed by the Reformists represented an opportunity which it would have been lunacy to have turned down. Helen, possibly with relief, had taken a back seat in the 1975 parliamentary session, allowing her new colleagues to assume a larger share of the burden she had become used to carrying alone. Now, in the debate that began to rage about the pros and cons of merger in the national and regional executives and councils of the Party, she maintained her low profile. Never herself ambitious for the Party leadership, she was not prepared to allow her fears as to the course the diluted Party might take and her own personal misgivings about Harry Schwarz to jeopardize her loyalty to her party, as personified by Colin Eglin. Once it was understood that neither the Party's principles nor its leadership would be affected (in the event Schwarz was given the key 'number three' position below Eglin and Swart in the new party) her apprehension lessened and the attitude of the rank-and-file to merger began to soften. Time was also running out for the Opposition. The Reformist desertion had demoralized the United Party to the extent that its right wing was beginning to look towards the Nationalists for a political home, while the remainder of the Party wavered undecidedly between the Scylla of loyalty to Graaff and the Charybdis of defection to the Reformists. The UP was no longer a force to be reckoned with: but this did not mean that the left could afford to remain fragmented. A merged Reform–Progressive party seemed to have an excellent chance of stepping into the breach left by a collapsing United Party to form a new official Opposition. Unmerged, the parties could only lose support from disillusioned voters.

The merger was concluded at a series of congresses held in Johannesburg on 25 and 26 July 1975. Both parties voted almost unanimously for the merger: both debated with acrimony the proposed name of the new party (the South African Progressive Reform Party), more as a safety valve for the feelings of many of the delegates on joining forces with people whom they had fought bitterly in numerous election battles than as a matter of genuine conviction. The final Congress of the newly merged Party, however, passed off amid acclamation, and the new group, based on principles essentially the same as those of the old Progressive Party (with certain variations of the franchise policy and some new concepts as to the federal nature of its proposed constitution), was born after only a short labour.

It symbolized a new polarization of white feeling in South Africa, the result of internal and external pressures which had only begun to be apparent since 1970: the collapse of the Portuguese colonial empire of Angola and Mozambique and the consequent isolation of Rhodesia, whose political and military situation suddenly became untenable: the increasing pragmatism of the Nationalist Government itself, as it pursued its new policy of *détente* with black Africa with a wary eye cocked over its right shoulder. The new party offered, as an alternative to the conflict threatening between the races of southern Africa, a policy which had a real chance of acceptance by the white voters of the republic. The child of the Progressive Party and the grandchild of the old liberal tradition of the Cape, almost, but never quite submerged, it owed its existence, just as much as its predecessor had done, to Helen Suzman. And in spite of its more disparate nature, it represented a continuance of that tradition whose spirit she had kept alive in those thirteen years which may yet be seen as some of the most crucial in South Africa's history.

'The Memoirs were finished today,' Moominpappa announced in a thick voice. 'At six-forty-five. And the closing sentence – it's, well, you'll hear.'

'Haven't you written anything about your wicked life with the Hattifatteners?' Snufkin asked.

'No,' replied Moominpappa. 'I want this to be an instructive book.'

TOVE JANSSON, *The Exploits of Moominpappa*

APPENDIX A – *The Entrenched Clauses and Rules for a Joint Sitting under Section 152 of the South Africa Act, 1909*

In the South Africa Act there were three sections which required a special machinery of legislation to alter them.*

Section 137 provided for the equality of the two official languages – English and Afrikaans (Dutch in the original Act) while Section 35(1) ensured that those black voters who were already, or who would become qualified to vote, under the Cape and Natal franchise laws† would continue to enjoy those rights. It also provided that no person in the Cape 'who is or may become capable of being registered as a voter' could be disqualified unless by an Act passed at its third reading by a two-thirds majority of the total membership of both Houses of Parliament sitting together. Section 35(2) further provided that no person who, at the time of the passing of any such law, was registered as a voter could be removed from the register on grounds of race or colour only.

These sections were entrenched in Section 152 which required Parliament to sit and legislate in a manner laid down in 35(1). If the two Houses of Parliament – the Senate and the House of Assembly – sat separately while amending an entrenched clause, they were not legislating in the sense which the constitution required the amendment to be made and the legislation was invalid. Thus to become law under Section 152, a Bill had to receive the assent of two-thirds of the total number of all the members of both Houses whether present at a Joint Sitting or not. This requirement applied only to the third reading of the Bill. Special rules were drawn up for each Joint Sitting. Joint Sittings under Section 152 have been held on the following issues:

*The Republic of South Africa Constitution Act (32 of 1961) with slight exceptions followed the existing constitutional structure and the clause entrenching the equal status of the official languages was retained.

†Before Union only the Cape Colony had a franchise approximating to a multi-racial one, in that a common qualification was laid down which applied to all male British subjects regardless of race or colour. In Natal the franchise qualifications were so stringent that very few Blacks qualified. Both the Transvaal and the Orange River Colony restricted their franchise to Whites only.

1918   Electoral Divisions – Redelimitation Amendment Bill.*
1929   Native Parliamentary Representation Bill.†
      Coloured Persons' Rights Bill.‡
1930   Native Parliamentary Representation Bill.§
      Coloured Persons' Rights Bill.§
1936   Representation of Natives Bills (JS1 and JS2).*
1953   South Africa Act Amendment Bill.† (2JS)
      Separate Representation of Voters Act Validation and Amendment Bill.‡ (2JS)
1954   Separate Representation of Voters Act Validation and Amendment Bill.†
1956   South Africa Act Amendment Bill.*
1963   Constitutional Amendment Bill.*
1971   Constitutional Amendment Bill.*

(2JS) = two Joint Sittings held that session.
JS1 and JS2 refer to separate Joint Sittings held for each Bill.
*Bill passed.
†Not passed by a two-thirds majority.
‡Dropped owing to prorogation.
§Withdrawn.

APPENDIX B – *Composition of the House of Assembly and the Delimitation of Constituencies*

According to the original provisions of the South Africa Act, when the House of Assembly first met it was to consist of 121 members elected by a plurality of voters of white males of 21 years and over in single-member constituencies. Membership was arbitrarily distributed among the provinces: the Cape having 51, the Transvaal 36 and Natal and the Orange Free State each 17. The Act provided that, as from 1911, a census should be taken every five years, and as the population increased so the membership of the Assembly should be expanded, subject to the proviso that no province's representation should be increased until the increase in its adult white male population entitled it to additional seats. Once the composition of the Assembly had reached a stipulated maximum of 150 seats, the allocation of seats would be strictly *pro rata* to its adult white male population* and then, and only then, could decreases occur in the representation of the smaller provinces.

In 1936 the first major change in the membership of the Assembly occurred when, with the passing of the Representation of Natives Act, three members were added to represent the Cape Africans. As the number of members had by then already reached 150, the Assembly increased its size to 153. In 1949 this number again increased to 159 when six members were added to represent the white voters of South West Africa. The Separate Representation of Voters Act Validation and Amendment Act of 1956 brought four more members into the Assembly to represent the Coloured voters of the Cape while three years later the Promotion of Bantu-Self Government Act abolished the three Natives' Representatives and a similar fate befell the Coloureds' Representatives in 1968.

In 1965 an amendment to section 42 of the Republic of South Africa Constitution Act of 1961 caused the ordinary membership of the Assembly (excluding the South West African and the Coloureds' Representatives) to be increased from 150 to 160. In 1973 the Constitution and Elections Amendment Act again increased the Assembly's

*Amended in 1930 to include white women. The voting age was lowered from twenty-one years to eighteen by the Electoral Law Amendment Act (30 of 1958).

membership to 165 for the republic (the six South West Africa Representatives remained unchanged). The distribution of seats in the republic at the present time (1976) is:

Transvaal	76
Cape	55
Natal	20
Orange Free State	14
	165

These numbers will not be altered until a period of ten years has elapsed from the date of commencement of the Amending Act.

The responsibility for the delimitation of constituencies was placed in the hands of a judicial commission known as the Delimitation Commission. Initially the distribution of seats was related to the white population, and the basis on which the Delimitation Commission has worked has been the census, which, up to 1952, was taken every five years, and, since 1952, at intervals of not less than five years and not more than ten years.

In drawing constituency boundaries the Delimitation Commission is also required to take local authority and magisterial district boundaries into consideration and the probability of the increase or decrease of the population of the various areas, as well as factors such as community or diversity of interests; means of communication; physical features; boundaries of existing electoral divisions; scarcity or density of population.

Within these parameters, the Commissioners may, whenever they deem it necessary, depart from the quota by increasing or decreasing the number of voters in a constituency, but by no more than 15 per cent of the quota. This provision therefore allows a maximum variation of 30 per cent of the quota at the time of the delimitation. This is the system generally referred to as the 'loading' and 'unloading' of seats. Since the Delimitation Commissions have always favoured rural areas, the representation of these constituencies has always been loaded at the expense of the urban areas.

Before 1965 the constituencies were delimitated by provinces according to the formula (150 times the number of white voters in the provinces concerned and divided by the total number of white voters in the republic).

From 1965 onwards, delimitation was made on a country-wide basis. The quota was arrived at by dividing the total number of voters by the number of seats (increased from 150 to 160). Taking this quota as a basis for division, constituencies were then delimitated in such a way that no electoral division would fall partly in one province and partly in another. If an electoral division had an area of 10 000 square miles (approximately 26 000 square kilometres) or more, the Delimitation Commission could reduce the number of voters to 8000 or a number equal to 70 per cent of the quota, whichever was the greater. The number of seats per province was thus altered from time to time according to the distribution of the population. In 1973 (before the Constitution and Elections Amendment Act) it was:

Transvaal	73
Cape	54
Natal	18
Orange Free State	15
	160

The amending Act of 1973 defines the average quota for the republic as the number of voters on the current lists divided by 165, provided that in the case of an electoral division with an area of 25 000 square kilometres or more, the Delimitation Commission may reduce the number of voters to a number equal to 70 per cent of the quota. (The quota for the republic was in 1974 about ± 14 000 voters per urban constituency while the rural average was ± 10 000.)

APPENDIX C – *Structure of the United Party**

(*Note :* Should be read from the bottom up)

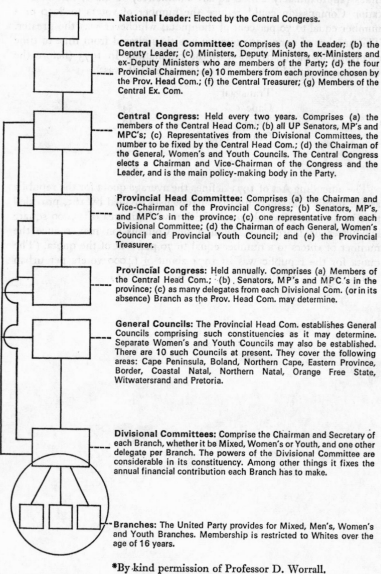

National Leader: Elected by the Central Congress.

Central Head Committee: Comprises (a) the Leader; (b) the Deputy Leader; (c) Ministers, Deputy Ministers, ex-Ministers and ex-Deputy Ministers who are members of the Party; (d) the four Provincial Chairmen; (e) 10 members from each province chosen by the Prov. Head Com.; (f) the Central Treasurer; (g) Members of the Central Ex. Com.

Central Congress: Held every two years. Comprises (a) the members of the Central Head Com.; (b) all UP Senators, MP's and MPC's; (c) Representatives from the Divisional Committees, the number to be fixed by the Central Head Com.; (d) the Chairman of the General, Women's and Youth Councils. The Central Congress elects a Chairman and Vice-Chairman of the Congress and the Leader, and is the main policy-making body in the Party.

Provincial Head Committee: Comprises (a) the Chairman and Vice-Chairman of the Provincial Congress; (b) Senators, MP's, and MPC's in the province; (c) one representative from each Divisional Committee; (d) the Chairman of each General, Women's Council and Provincial Youth Council; and (e) the Provincial Treasurer.

Provincial Congress: Held annually. Comprises (a) Members of the Central Head Com.; (b) Senators, MPC's and MPC's in the province; (c) as many delegates from each Divisional Com. (or in its absence) Branch as the Prov. Head Com. may determine.

General Councils: The Provincial Head Com. establishes General Councils comprising such constituencies as it may determine. Separate Women's and Youth Councils may also be established. There are 10 such Councils at present. They cover the following areas: Cape Peninsula, Boland, Northern Cape, Eastern Province, Border, Coastal Natal, Northern Natal, Orange Free State, Witwatersrand and Pretoria.

Divisional Committees: Comprise the Chairman and Secretary of each Branch, whether it be Mixed, Women's or Youth, and one other delegate per Branch. The powers of the Divisional Committee are considerable in its constituency. Among other things it fixes the annual financial contribution each Branch has to make.

Branches: The United Party provides for Mixed, Men's, Women's and Youth Branches. Membership is restricted to Whites over the age of 16 years.

**By kind permission of Professor D. Worrall.*

APPENDIX D – *Structure of the Progressive Party**

(*Note :* Should be read from the bottom up)

National Leader: Elected by the National Congress.

National Executive Committee: This is the supreme governing body of the Party save when the National Congress is in session. Comprises (a) the Leader; (b) the Chairman; (c) the Provincial Chairmen; (d) Representatives of the Regional Councils; and (e) 10 members elected by the National Congress.

National Congress: This is the supreme governing body of the Party. Meets every two years. Composed of (a) Leader of the Party; (b) Members of the National and Provincial Executives; (c) all Progressive MP's and MPC's; (d) one representative from each Regional Council; (e) Representatives from each constituency in a proportion determined by the National Executive Committee. Decisions are taken by majority vote, and all such decisions are binding on the Party and all its members.

Provincial Congress: Convened annually. Consists of (a) all MP's and MPC's in the province; (b) all members of the National Executive Committee and the Provincial Executive Committee concerned; (c) one representative from each Regional Council; (d) Representatives from each constituency in the province in a proportion determined by the Provincial Executive Committee.

Regional Council: There are 9 Regional Councils. They comprise (a) Members of the National Provincial Executive Committees resident in the area; (b) Progressive MP's and MPC's resident in the area; (c) Representatives from each constituency in the area on a basis determined from time to time by the Provincial Executive concerned. The Regional Councils supervise all Party activity in their areas of jurisdiction.

Constituency Executive Committee: Supervises all aspects of the Party's activity in its constituency. Membership and Branch representation set by the responsible Regional Council.

Branches: Any person over the age of 18 years and normally resident in South Africa who subscribe to the principles of the Party may apply for membership.

*By kind permission of Professor D. Worrall.

APPENDIX E – *The Franchise Qualifications of the Progressive Party (as at April 1974)*

The Party advocates an electoral system based on a qualified franchise. Full voting rights are granted to any South African citizen above the age of eighteen, provided he:

1 has passed Standard VIII* or its equivalent;
2 has reached Standard VI† and has the attainments of a semi-skilled worker;
3 is literate‡ and has the attainments of at least a skilled worker;
4 is literate and owns fixed property;§
   a married person is entitled to the economic but not the educational qualifications of the marriage partner.
5 has at any time been a voter for the House of Assembly.

Special Voters' Roll

There will be a special voters' roll for citizens who do not possess the qualifications required for registration on the ordinary voters' roll. Qualifications are:

1 citizenship;
2 age of eighteen, irrespective of sex;
3 literacy according to a prescribed test.

Special voters will be entitled to elect not more than 10 per cent of the members in the House of Assembly, in specially delimitated constituencies and in special elections held during the three months preceding each parliamentary general election. If at any time the number of voters registered on the special roll falls below 20 per cent

---

*Roughly equivalent to the standard supposedly reached the year before 'O' levels in the United Kingdom. There is no set examination but the school leaver must have attained the age of sixteen.

†Standard VI is usually attained between eleven and thirteen years.

‡Literacy will be adjudged according to an objective prescribed test set in one of South Africa's official languages.

§Income and property qualifications will be reviewed every five years by a committee headed by a judge and will be revised upwards or downwards as the purchasing power of money increases or decreases.

of the number registered on the ordinary voters' roll then the number
of special roll seats will be reduced *pro rata*.

Protection of Rights

The Progressive Party insists on a rigid (i.e. entrenched) constitution
intended to protect fully the rights of groups and of individuals.

1   Individuals will be protected by the proclamation of a detailed
    Bill of Rights.
2   Population groups will be protected by a radical reform of the
    present Senate, to be accorded co-ordinate powers with the House
    of Assembly and therefore able to exercise effective control over all
    legislation (other than financial).

In addition, the Senate will be constituted according to an electoral
method which will ensure that no candidate will succeed in being
elected (and that consequently no political party can gain control of
the Senate), if he does not enjoy the support of a meaningful percentage
of the members of each one of the various population groups. This
ensures that no population group or alliance of population groups will
be able to abuse the machinery of Parliament to subjugate or suppress
other groups.*

3   The rights of the Provinces which form an integral part of the
    Federal Republic will be entrenched.

*The majority report of the Molteno Commission suggested that 'a candidate
at a Senate election who receives the largest number of votes shall be declared
elected, provided that his votes include at least one-fifth of the total votes cast
by members of each community. If, however, the candidate with the largest
number of votes does not receive at least one-fifth of the votes cast by the
members of each community then the candidate would be elected who had
received the highest proportion of the votes of all the communities concerned,
i.e. the candidate whose ratio of votes of the community which favoured him
proportionately least is higher than any other candidates' ratio of the votes of
the community that favoured him proportionately least.

X gets:		Y gets:	
1200	white votes	4800	white votes
2500	African votes	500	African votes
800	coloured votes	200	coloured votes
4500		5500	

X would be returned because Y, although he heads the poll, has failed to get
one-fifth of the African votes and X's proportion of the White vote is higher
than Y's proportion of the African vote. In a minority report, A. Suzman, QC,
stated that he considered that these proposals gave undue emphasis to conflicting racial group interests [since some form of racially differentiated population register would have to be maintained].

Federation is defined by the Progressive Party as the existence of co-ordinate sovereignties, with powers that do not overlap, within the same state. The Party believes that wherever in South Africa there is an area with a peculiar predominant nature, it should be established as a separate and autonomous province. By 'autonomous' something less than complete independence was envisaged. However, should any of the 'Homelands' already be independent at the time of the introduction of a Progressive federation, its independence would be unaffected. Such homelands, together with any other states south of the Zambezi whether or not they had ever been part of the republic, could be invited to become provinces of a federal republic.

The provincial boundaries of South Africa should be substantially re-drawn to take into account demographic, economic and other factors.*

After the annual congress in Bloemfontein in November 1974, a commission was appointed to re-structure the Party's franchise proposals, basing them entirely on educational, and abolishing the economic qualifications.

*Speech made on federation by Zach de Beer at the Progressive Party National Congress in August 1972.

APPENDIX F – *Chronology – The Split, August 1959*

August 1959

TUESDAY II Eve of Congress Head Committee meeting. Douglas Mitchell announces his intention of forcing through his Land Act resolution.

WEDNESDAY 12 Heated Congress discussion over Graaff's Five Points – his compromise and alternatives to Verwoerd's Bantustan policy.

THURSDAY 13 Mitchell forces through his resolution. Graaff opposes it but says that he will not take a vote against him as a vote of no confidence in his leadership.

When Congress ends, eleven United Party members led by Jan Steytler, MP and S. F. Waterson, MP issue a statement from Bloemfontein protesting against the Congress's opposition to further purchase of land for African settlement by the Government.

They say they are 'deeply disturbed by the whole undertone of Congress', which in their opinion fails to face up to the increasingly urgent problems of South Africa as a multi-racial country.

FRIDAY 14 Douglas Mitchell, the Natal leader, flies to Cape Town and confers with Graaff.

SATURDAY 15 J. Hamilton-Russell, MP (who had associated himself with the dissidents but had not signed their statement) sees Graaff.

MONDAY 17 Various dissidents, including Helen Suzman, have interviews with Graaff in Cape Town.

TUESDAY 18 Hamilton-Russell, van Ryneveld and Waterson state that they wish to realign themselves with the United Party. Van Ryneveld and Waterson apologize publicly to Graaff. All the other dissidents, except Fourie, resign from the United Party.

WEDNESDAY 19 Professor I. S. Fourie resigns from the Party. Graaff declines to accept the resignation of Hamilton-Russell, Waterson and van Ryneveld. Accepting the other resignations, he expresses the hope that 'our differences will never deteriorate into rancour and bitterness'.

THURSDAY 20 In a Press statement the rebels say they wish to avoid 'fratricidal strife' within the United Party. They complain that most of the delegates at the Bloemfontein Congress 'showed a complete unwillingness to face up to the challenge of contemporary events here and in the rest of Africa'. Van Ryneveld withdraws his earlier statement and resigns from the United Party, becoming the eleventh member of Parliament to do so.

FRIDAY 21 The Progressive Group (as the rebels are now called) plan a meeting in Johannesburg for the following week.

During the week, the divisional committees of all but two of the dissenting MPs and MPCs pledge their support to the United Party.

The exceptions are Houghton and Musgrave (Durban).

BIBLIOGRAPHY

Books

ADAM, H., Ed., *South Africa: Sociological Perspectives*, Oxford University Press, 1971

BALLINGER, M., *From Union to Apartheid: A Trek to Isolation*, Juta and Co, 1969

BROOKES, E. H. and MACAULEY, J. B., *Civil Liberty in South Africa*, Oxford University Press, 1958

BROWN, D., *Against the World: A Study in White South African Attitudes*, Collins, 1966

CARTER, G. M., *The Politics of Inequality: South Africa since 1948*, Thames and Hudson, 1958

CARTER, G. M., KARIS, T. and STULTZ, N. M., *South Africa's Transkei: The Politics of Domestic Colonialism*, African Studies no. 19, Northwestern University Press, 1967

DOXEY, G. V., *The Industrial Colour Bar in South Africa*, Oxford University Press, 1961

HAHLO, H. R. and KAHN, E., *The Union of South Africa: The Development of its Laws and Constitution*, Juta and Co, 1960

HANCOCK, W. K., *Smuts: The Fields of Force 1919–1950*, Cambridge University Press, 1968

HEARD, K. A., *General Elections in South Africa, 1943–1970*, Oxford University Press, 1974

HEPPLE, A., *Verwoerd*, Pelican Books, 1967

HORRELL, M. (1), *Legislation and Race Relations*, SAIRR, revised edition, 1971

HORRELL, M. (2), *The African Homelands of South Africa*, SAIRR, 1973

KAHN, E. J., *The Separated People: A Look at Contemporary South Africa*, W. W. Norton and Co. Inc, New York, 1968

KRUGER, D. W., *The Making of a Nation*, Macmillan, 1969

LEVER, H., *The South African Voter: Some Aspects of Voting Behaviour with Special Reference to the General Elections of 1966 and 1970*, Juta and Co, 1971

MATHEWS, A. S., *Law, Order and Liberty in South Africa*, Juta and Co, 1971

MAY, H. J., *The South African Constitution*, 3rd edition, Juta and Co, 1955

MUNGER, E. S., *Afrikaner and African Nationalism: South African Parallels and Parameters*, Oxford University Press, 1967

PATON, A., *Hofmeyr*, Oxford University Press, 1964

POTHOLM, G. and DALE, R., Eds, *Southern Africa in Perspective*, The Free Press, 1972

ROBERTS, M. and TROLLIP, A. E. G., *The South African Opposition*, Longmans, Green, 1947.

ROBERTSON, J., *Liberalism in South Africa, 1948–1963*, Oxford University Press, 1971

SAMPSON, A., *The Treason Cage*, Heinemann, 1958

SCHOEMAN, B. M., *Van Malan tot Verwoerd*, Human and Rousseau, 1973

SOLOMON, BERTHA, *Time Remembered*, Howard Timmins, 1968

THOMPSON, L. M., *Politics in the Republic of South Africa*, Little, Brown and Co, Boston, 1966

TROUP, F., *South Africa: A Historical Introduction*, Eyre Methuen, 1972

VATCHER, W. H., Jnr, *White Laager: The Rise of Afrikaner Nationalism*, Pall Mall Press, 1965

WALKER, E. A., *A History of Southern Africa*, 3rd edition, Longmans Green and Co, 1957

WORRALL, D., ed., *South Africa: Government and Politics*, J. L. van Schaik Ltd, Pretoria, 1971

A Survey of Race Relations in South Africa, SAIRR, all editions, 1953–73

Government Publications

Union of South Africa: Debates of the House of Assembly (Hansard) All vols, 1953–61

Republic of South Africa: Debates of the House of Assembly (Hansard) All vols, 1961–73

Unpublished Thesis

An Analysis of the Extra-Parliamentary Political Decision Making Process in the Progressive Party of South Africa, A Meintjes (Submitted in fulfilment of the requirements for the degree of M.A. in the

Department of Political Science and Public Administration in the
University of South Africa), October 1973

Journals and Pamphlets

*The Policy of the Progressive Party of South Africa. A Summary and
Review*, issued for the Progressive Party of South Africa by M.
Osler, 1974

Spro-Cas Publication No. 6, *Towards Social Change*, Johannesburg,
1971

SAIRR, Condensation of Part II of the Original Memo submitted by
the SAIRR to the Native Laws Commission, vol. XIV, 1947

The *Forum*, all editions, 1953–63

Optima, 'Towards Racial Harmony', H. F. Oppenheimer, 6(3) Supple-
ment, September 1956

SAIRR, *A Digest of the Native Laws (Fagan) Commission*. Prepared by
Helen Suzman, Donaldson Blueprint Series no. 1, Johannesburg,
1948

Commonsense, 'How the Nation Voted', J. L. Grey, August 1943

Africa South, 'The White Opposition in South Africa', Stanley Uys,
African Political Movements, Jordan Ngubane, vol. 1, no. 1, October–
December 1956

Journal of Modern African Studies: 'Politics of Security. South Africa
under Verwoerd, 1961–66, Newell M. Stultz, vol. 7, 1969.

Journal of Commonwealth Studies, 'The South African Political System',
S. Trapido, vol. 4, 1965

American Political Science Review, 'Some Reflections on the Sociological Character of Political Parties', R. Michel, no. 21, November
1927, pp. 753–72.

Challenge, 'The Terrorism Act', Helen Suzman, January–February
1968

Molteno Report, vol. I, issued by the Progressive Party of South Africa,
November 1960

Molteno Report, vol. II, issued by the Progressive Party of South
Africa, August 1962

SAIRR, *The Tomlinson Report*, A Summary of the Findings and
Recommendations in the Tomlinson Commission Report, D.
Hobart Houghton, Johannesburg 1956

NOTES TO CHAPTERS

CHAPTER ONE

1. Led by Frederic Creswell, the Party stood for the protection of White labour against capitalism on the one hand and the encroachment by Black labour on the other.

2. *1915 election results:* SAP 54 seats; Unionists 40; Nationalists 27; Labour 3; Independents 6.

3. W. K. Hancock, p. 34.

4. E. A. Walker, p. 575.

5. W. K. Hancock, p. 33.

6. *1924 election results:* Nationalists 63; Labour 18; SAP 53; Independent 1.

7. M. Horrell (1), p. 8.

8. E. A. Walker, *op. cit.,* p. 618.

9. As both Acts affected the entrenched clauses in the South Africa Act, neither could be removed without a two-thirds majority of both Houses sitting together. See Appendix A for more detail.

10. See Appendix A.

11. W. K. Hancock, p. 218.

12. *1929 election results:* National Party 78; SAP 61; Creswell Labour 5; National Council Labour 3; Independent 1.

13. E. A. Walker, p. 628.

14. W. K. Hancock, p. 256.

15. Article 2(d).

16. Article 6(b).

17. Representation of Natives Act, 1936.

18. A. Paton, p. 219.

19. *Ibid.,* p. 303.

20. *1938 General Election* Malan secured only 24 per cent of the United Party seats but 58 per cent of their total number of votes. Results: United Party 111; Purified Nationalists 27; Dominion Party 8; Labour 6.

21. E. A. Walker, p. 693.

22. Professor H. Frankel. Letter dated 31 September 1973.

23. *Results of the 1943 election*

For Coalition		*Against Coalition (and Smuts)*
United Party	89	National Party 43
Labour Party	9	

Dominion Party   7
Independents   2
Natives' Representatives 3

Although elected separately they could be counted on to support Smuts.

24. Professor J. L. Grey, 'How the Nation Voted', *Commonsense*, August 1943.

25. Basis of Trusteeship. Speech to the SAIRR, Cape Town, 1944.

26. The *Star*, September 1949.

27. In 1946 it was estimated that there were 1 856 028 Africans in the urban centres.

28. Smuts, quoted by W. K. Hancock, p. 490.

29. Condensation of Part II of the original memorandum submitted by the SAIRR to the Native Laws Commission p. 63, vol XIV, no. 1, 1947.

30. SAIRR Memorandum, p. 77.

31. Professor W. Eiselen quoted by W. K. Hancock, p. 501.

32. The Native Laws Commission, para 63.

CHAPTER TWO

1. Paton, p. 228.

2. Special Report No. 39, Office of Census and Statistics. *The Indian Population of the Union, 1926.*

3. M. Horrell (1), p. 6.

4. G. M. Carter, p. 36.

5. By 1948 there were 228 000 Indians in Natal, 37 000 in the Transvaal, 16 900 in the Cape Province and 14 in the Orange Free State. Of these 113 400 lived in Durban, whose white population was 124 492.

6. Roberts and Trollip, pp. 174–5.

7. John Greene, *Commonsense*, March 1948, p. 107.

8. *Rand Daily Mail*, 14 November 1947.

9. *Rand Daily Mail*, 23 July 1948.

10. D. Molteno, 'Political Commentary', *Commonsense*, June 1948.

11. R. de Villiers, 'Good Luck is not Enough', *Commonsense*, February 1948.

12. In fact Malan had a majority of eight but the three Natives' Representatives could be counted on to vote with Smuts.

Election results	Seats	No. of votes
National Party	70 (43)	401 834
United Party	65 (89)	534 230
Labour Party	6 (9)	27 360
Afrikaner Party	9 (–)	41 885

The United and Labour Parties had an election pact, as did the National Party and the Afrikaner Party.

13. See Appendix B.

14. W. K. Hancock, p. 506.

15. Speech to the SAIRR, Cape Town, November 1944.

16. Act 23 of 1947.

17. W. K. Hancock, p. 516.

18. See Appendix C.

19. *Sunday Times*, June 1948.

20. See Appendix C.

21. WCM 2 October 1951.

22. *Ibid.*

23. Joyce Waring was a UP City Councillor. Her husband, Frank, was the UP member of Parliament for Orange Grove and her father, Arthur Barlow, the UP member of Parliament for Hospital. Both Waring and Barlow left the UP in 1953 and soon afterwards joined the National Party, in which Waring finally achieved Cabinet rank.

24. WCM 4 October 1949.

25. WCM 7 March 1950.

26. Act 21 of 1950. This measure extended to non-Whites generally the provisions of the original Hertzog Act of 1927 which prohibited sexual intercourse between Africans and Whites.

27. Act 30 of 1950. Basic to the rest of the apartheid legislation, it classified the population into racial categories. It aimed at a rigid system of race classification based on appearance and general acceptance and repute, and provided for the compilation of a register of the population and the issuing of identity cards. It defined White, Coloured and Native (later called Bantu) and empowered the Governor-General to make further sub-divisions. This was done by proclamation in 1959 (and amended in 1961) and divided Coloured into Cape Coloured, Cape Malay, Griqua, Indian, Chinese, 'other Asiatic' and 'other Coloured'. (From M. Horrell (1), pp. 13 and 10.)

28. Act 41 of 1950.

29. The *Forum*, 28 April 1950.

30. G. M. Carter, p. 89.

31. Act 44 of 1950. This Act widely defined the term 'Communism' to include not only Marxian socialism but also any doctrine or scheme which aimed at bringing about any political, industrial, social or economic change in South Africa by the promotion of disturbances or disorders . . . or which aimed at the encouragement of feelings of hostility between Black and White, the consequences of which were calculated to further the achievement of the doctrine or schemes such as those mentioned. The Communist Party was banned. The Minister of Justice was given powers to direct that a list be prepared of the members of any organization declared unlawful who would then be prohibited from attending gatherings, holding public office, belonging to any specified organizations or from leaving a defined area. To be banned under the Act forced a person into living death, isolated from society to become a non-person. The Minister could also ban organizations and publications, prohibit gatherings if he considered that these were likely to further or were furthering the aims of Communism. (*Vide* M. Horrell (1), p. 89.)

32. Act 23 of 1949. The representation given to South West Africa was out of all proportion to that given to South Africa itself since the territory had only 26000 voters. Its electoral quota was fixed at 4000 voters per constituency as opposed to the Union's quota of 9000.

33. Section 35 of the Act. See Appendix A.

34. Ndlwana v. Hofmeyr (NO) 1937. The Court declared that Parliament could adopt any procedure it thought fit and that the Courts could not question an Act of Parliament.

35. Harris and three others v. Donges. Cape Provincial Division of the Supreme Court.

36. M. Ballinger, p. 269.

37. Speech in Excelsior. OFS 6 October 1951.

38. WCM Annual General Meeting Report of the Chairwoman, 5 June 1951.

39. Act 35 of 1952.

40. WEC 23 June 1952.

41. G. M. Carter, p. 316.

42. WCM Speech by Louis Steenkamp, 6 May 1952.

43. WCM Annual General Meeting, 10 June 1952.

44. Interview with Ellen Hellmann.

45. *Rand Daily Mail*, 9 July 1952.

46. Speech taped by Dr M. M. Suzman, 10 December 1952.

47. Letter to S. Press, 23 December 1952.

CHAPTER THREE

1. Statement issued on 29 February 1952.

2. Act 3 of 1953.

3. Act 8 of 1953.

4. *Cape Times*, 9 May 1953.

5. *Cape Times*, 13 February 1953.

6. Taped Speech, Pridwin School, Rosebank, 2 March 1953.

7. WCM 3 March 1953.

8. *Die Burger*, 30 October 1952. Minister of Justice, Mr Swart.

9. *Election results*

Seats	NP	UP	Labour
Transvaal	43	22	2
OFS	13	—	—
Cape	30	24	—
Natal	2	11	2 (1 in a by-election)
SWA	6	—	—

There was an 87.8 per cent poll.

Total votes polled: NP 641000, UP 771000. Delimitation gave the NP 4 rural votes to 5 urban votes. Percentage votes: Nationalists 45.50 (previous election 39.96), United Front 54.40 (previous election 53.40).

10. Letter from Sir Albert Robinson to author. Robinson left South

Africa and went to live in Southern Rhodesia. He was a member of the Monckton Commission, became Federation High Commissioner in England in 1961 and was knighted in 1962.

11. The *Star*, 20 May 1953.

12. Letter to M. M. Suzman 24 July 1953.

13. *Ibid.*

14. *Ibid.*

15. Subsequently called the Matrimonial Affairs Bill, this piece of legislation did much to remove the harsh disabilities which Roman-Dutch law still inflicted on South African women.

16. Letter to M. M. Suzman, 24 July 1953.

17. The court's decision was based on an appeal by G. Lusu, an African who had, as an act of defiance, sat in the 'Whites Only' waiting room on Cape Town station and had been acquitted on a charge under the Railways Act of 1916.

18. The *Forum*, January 1954, vol. 2, no. 10. 'Reply to the Rebels', Helen Suzman.

19. After A. Hepple, pp. 106 ff.

20. Act 52 of 1951. Empowered magistrates to order the demolition of shanty dwellings and force the occupants to move elsewhere.

21. Act 54 of 1952. Allowed Africans born in South Africa to visit an urban area for a period of up to seventy-two hours without obtaining a special permit, extended the system of influx control to all urban areas, applied the law to women as well and extended the powers of local authorities to remove 'idle or undesirable' Africans.

22. Act 67 of 1952. Abolished the multitude of documents carried by Africans: made it compulsory for African women to carry passes for the first time; required all Africans over the age of sixteen to carry a reference book which included the holder's identity card, poll tax receipts, authorization to be within the specified area; and employer's monthly signature among other details.

23. Act 48 of 1953.

24. Hansard, 4 August 1953, col. 872.

25. *Ibid.*, cols. 869, 870.

26. *Ibid.*, cols. 1616, 1618.

27. This Bill was a re-enactment and amendment of the Act of 1924.

28. M. Horrell, (1) pp. 57–8.

29. Report-back meeting, Houghton, October 1953.

30. Act 47 of 1953.

31. After A. Hepple.

32. The *Forum*, August 1953.

33. Hansard, 17 September 1953, col. 3576.

34. Report-back meeting, Houghton, October 1953.

35. *Ibid.*

K

CHAPTER FOUR

1. *Pretoria News*, 21 October 1953.
2. Hansard, 15 February 1954, cols. 594, 596, 597.
3. Hansard, 17 February 1954, cols. 741 ff.
4. Hansard, 18 February 1954, cols. 783, 779.
5. Hansard, 5 February 1954, col. 194.
6. Hansard, 18 February 1954, col. 780.
7. Report-back, 1954.
8. Act 18 of 1954. Designed to amend Chapter IV of the Principal Act of 1936. It dealt with (a) labour tenants who worked for a farmer for a fixed number of weeks per year in return for the right to grow crops and run stock on a portion of the farm; (b) squatters who were maintained by certain farmers in order to provide labour pools or who rented land from one farmer but worked for another. The object of the Act was to discourage these systems and to encourage farmers to employ full-time labourers but the number would be restricted to five tenants per farm. The Act removed a previously binding obligation upon the Government to find alternative land for those Africans who were displaced. Within certain limits it enabled the authorities to offer them employment instead.
9. Act 19 of 1954. This Bill provided for the establishment of a government appointed Re-settlement Board to undertake the removal of more than 10000 African families from the western areas of Johannesburg and to re-settle them at Meadowlands or Diepkloof, further to the south.
10. Hansard, 25 March 1954, col. 2755.
11. Hansard, 24 February 1954, col. 1112.
12. Hansard, 27 April 1954, col. 4052.
13. Hansard, 31 March 1954, col. 3200.
14. Hansard, 10 February 1954, col. 368.
15. Hansard, 1 April 1954, col. 3206.
16. Hansard, 31 March 1954, col. 3202.
17. The Minister of Justice was empowered to prohibit listed people and those convicted under the Suppression of Communism Act from attending meetings or being members of specified organizations without giving them the opportunity of making representations in their defence and without furnishing his reasons. Act 15 of 1954.
18. Hansard, 1 June 1954, col. 5966.
19. Report-back, 1954.
20. *Provincial election results (previous figures in brackets)*

18 August 1954	*Transvaal*	*Cape*	*OFS*	*Natal*
National Party	45 (36)	30 (26)	25 (24)	4 (3)
United Party	23 (27)	24 (28)	0 (1)	21 (22)

21. *The Friend*, 16 November 1954.
22. The Native Policy of the United Party 1954, p. 26.
23. *Ibid.*, p. 18.
24. Translated in the *Forum*, January 1955, p. 42.

25. The United Party considered that the Select Committee heard its evidence and held its discussion on far too limited a basis. When on 18 May 1954 Malan asked leave to introduce the Separate Representation of Voters Act Validation and Amendment Bill, Strauss remarked that the measure would be defeated at the third reading and that it would be 'an empty gesture' to oppose it at so early a stage. Cf. G. M. Carter, p. 139.

26. Quoted in Hansard, 23 May 1955, col. 6050.

27. Hansard, 31 January 1955, col. 5.

28. Hansard, 9 February 1955, cols. 821, 824.

29. Hansard, 9 February 1955, cols. 860, 861.

30. Act 56 of 1955. A consolidating measure was passed later in the session and the Act became the Criminal Procedure Act no. 56 of 1955. Among other provisions the Act increased the Government's powers of control over activities deemed undesirable. The new laws increased the powers of judges, JPs and magistrates to issue search warrants authorizing the police to enter premises, to attend private as well as public meetings and to conduct searches, if there were grounds considered reasonable enough for believing that an offence was being committed on the premises, or that in consequence of the meeting security or the maintenance of law and order was likely to be endangered. Members of the police were empowered to proceed without a warrant if they considered that a delay in obtaining one would defeat the objects of the search. Penalties were laid down for wrongful, malicious or unreasonable search, cf. Horrell (1), p. 92.

31. Hansard, 21 March 1955, col. 2439.

32. Hansard, 21 March 1955, col. 3028.

33. Hansard, 21 March 1955, cols. 3032, 3034.

34. Act 27 of 1955. Increased the quorum in the Appellate Division from four to five with the proviso that in cases where the validity of any Act of Parliament was in question the quorum would be eleven, judgment to be the decision of at least six of the judges. Five further judges of appeal were appointed, bringing the total number to eleven.

35. Act 53 of 1955. The membership of the Senate was increased to eighty-nine. Nominated Senators were increased from eight to sixteen, elected Senators from South Africa were increased from thirty-two to sixty-five. South West Africa's four Senators and the four Senators elected by Africans were unaffected. Election (except of the Africans' Senators) was to be by majority vote on a 'ticket' system, instead of the previous system by which eight members from each of the four provinces were elected by the MPs and MPCs of each of the provinces concerned by proportional representation. This meant that the United Party elected all eight Natal Senators while the other fifty-seven Senators for the other three Provinces would be elected by the National Party. 'Thus the character and purpose of the Senate was to be changed. From having a composite character designed to reflect the relative strength of the forces in the country, it was to become simply a reflection of the lower

House, an echo of the majority party.' M. Ballinger, p. 305.

36. Hansard, 23 May 1955, col. 6003.

37. Hansard, 23 May 1955, col. 6025.

38. Hansard, 23 May 1955, cols. 6606, 6610.

39. This organization was originally called the Women's Defence of the Constitution League. It was a non-party political movement whose members, draped in black mourning sashes, were pledged (among other things) 'to dog the movements of Cabinet Ministers to remind the country continuously of the wrong and dishonour perpetrated'.

40. *Rand Daily Mail*, 15 June 1955.

41. Hansard, 16 June 1955, cols. 8044, 8045.

42. This speech to Helen's committee has been adapted from her report-back speech at the end of 1955. The author was informed by several committee members who were present at that time that the contents of both speeches were almost identical; unfortunately no record of the committee meeting is available.

43. The *Star*, 26 August 1955 and the *Forum*.

44. *Race Relations News*, 1955, p. 126.

45. Report-back meeting, 1955.

CHAPTER FIVE

1. *Forum*, January 1956.

2. Speech to a lunch hour forum. 15 June 1956. The Commission was headed by Professor F. R. Tomlinson. Its terms of reference were 'to conduct an exhaustive inquiry into and to report on a comprehensive scheme for the rehabilitation of the Native Areas with a view to developing within them a social structure in keeping with the culture of the Native and based on effective socio-economic planning'. Appointed in November 1950, the Commission presented its findings in October 1954 but its report was so lengthy that it had to be condensed and was finally presented in March 1956. In April 1956, the Government published a White Paper defining its attitude towards the Tomlinson Report.

For further details on the Tomlinson Report and the Government's White Paper see D. Hobart Houghton, *The Tomlinson Report: A Summary of the Findings and Recommendations*. Commission Report, pub. SAIRR, 1956.

3. Acts: 28/56; 36/56, 64/56, 69/56, 29/56, 71/56.

4. Helen was quoting Douglas Smit.

5. Joint Sitting, Hansard 15 February 1956, col. 40.

6. Act 9 of 1956.

7. Joint Sitting, Hansard, 23 February 1956, cols. 728, 724.

8. Act 30 of 1956.

9. Report-back 21 June 1956.

10. Act 28 of 1956. In terms of the Act, no further 'mixed' trade unions were allowed to be registered; machinery was created for splitting such unions along racial lines; it was laid down that any mixed unions

which continued to exist must create separate branches for White and non-White members and hold separate meetings. Clause 77 made provision for 'job reservation', that is for specified types of work to be reserved for persons of a specified racial group.

11. Hansard, 1 February 1956, cols. 791, 801.

12. Hansard, 2 February 1965, col. 847.

13. Hansard, 29 February 1956, col. 1636.

14. *Cape Argus*, October 1955.

15. Keynote address quoted in *Die Transvaler*, October 1956.

16. All resolutions quoted are taken from the Secret Agenda of the Congress.

17. The other MP was Mr R. A. P. Trollip, who subsequently left the United Party, joined the National Party and became Minister of Tourism, Immigration and Indian Affairs. The other seven delegates were unnamed.

18. The *Star*, 8 November 1956.

19. IRR Survey 1956/57, p. 44. The number of detainees later rose to 156. Only 30 persons were finally charged and all were acquitted in March 1961.

20. The bus boycott began on 7 January 1957 when the Public Utility Transport Corporation which transported approximately 45 000 Africans daily from the townships into Johannesburg raised its fare by 1d. After an *ad hoc* committee formed by the commuters had had its appeal rejected by the Transportation Board, it launched a boycott campaign against PUTCO. There was a 100 per cent response and over 15 000 Africans began walking daily the nine miles from Alexandra Township to Johannesburg. By 20 January, a sympathetic boycott had broken out throughout the entire Johannesburg–Pretoria area. While even the UP appreciated that the boycott was motivated less by politics than by sheer economic necessity, the Minister of Transport claimed that it had been launched by the ANC in order to test its strength and to find out how much support and discipline it could exact from the Africans. The police harassed the boycotters, often arresting them and those sympathetic Whites who gave them lifts. On 1 March 1957 PUTCO withdrew its buses throughout the Witwatersrand and for some weeks there were no buses to boycott in Johannesburg. Finally, with the passing of the Native Transportation Amendment Act (53 of 1957) which was rushed through all its stages in one day and provided that a portion of the Native Service Levy could be used for subsidizing transport services, PUTCO reintroduced the old lower fare. The boycott ended on 1 July 1957.

21. Report-back, 1957.

22. Report-back, 1956 and report-back 1957.

23. *Ibid.*

24. J. R. Neame, The *Forum*, July 1957.

25. Hansard, 6 May 1957, col. 5407.

26. Act 36 of 1957. This Bill dealt mostly with influx control and the

powers of local authorities. It placed further limitations on the categories of Africans qualified to remain in urban areas; it extended the definition of an 'undesirable' and increased restrictions on the entry of Whites into African townships. Its most controversial clause was the 'Church clause' which stated that if the local authority concerned concurred, if the church concerned had been afforded reasonable time to make representations, and if the Minister had considered the availability or otherwise of alternative facilities, he could direct that the attendance of Africans at any church or religious service in the White part of a town must cease from a specified date. He could do so if in his opinion the African congregation was causing a nuisance or if he considered its numbers to be undesirably large. The Act also restricted 'mixed' gatherings in schools, hospitals, clubs and 'similar institutions' as well as at places of entertainment. (Horrell (1), p. 78.)

27. Act 69 of 1957. This Act stipulated that the Nursing Council could only consist of white persons. Provision was made for advisory boards to be elected by black nurses. The Nursing Association was also required to set up separate branches for members of each racial group and arrange separate meetings. The controlling board consisted of Whites, elected by white nurses, although Blacks could elect advisory committees. The Act also made it an offence to employ a white nurse or student nurse under the supervision of a black nurse (except in cases of emergency).

28. Report-back speech, 1957.

29. Hansard, 3 April 1957, col. 4033.

30. Hansard, 8 April 1957, col. 4292.

31. Ibid., cols. 4314,4315.

32. Rand Daily Mail, 10 August 1957.

33. Rand Daily Mail, 1 August 1957.

34. The enlarged Senate would be replaced by a more compact body of much the same size as the previous Senate. Forty-one members, ten nominated by the Governor-General-in-Council with half the nominated members being selected on the grounds mainly of their thorough acquaintance with the reasonable wants and wishes of the black races. Specified educational and property qualifications would once again be required. Four to five white Senators would be elected directly by suitably qualified Coloureds in all Provinces. African representation would be increased to six Whites. The 'more reasonable' class of African was to have a direct vote, while the remainder would continue to vote through an electoral college: but the author has been unable to discover any definition of what constituted a 'more reasonable' class of African.

35. Quoted in the Sunday Express.

36. A. Hepple and L. Lovell – statement issued before April 1958.

37. Die Transvaler, 15 February 1958. Quoted in K. A. Heard, pp. 72 and 73.

38. Rand Daily Mail, 25 March 1958.

39. 1958 Election results: National Party 103; United Party 53;

Natives' Representatives 3; Coloured Representatives 4 (elected separately). If voting had been based on the 1953 delimitation, the National Party would only have gained three seats. There was a 5 per cent voting swing to the Nationalists who gained six seats from the United Party. The United Party gained three seats from Labour and three from Independents.

40. He was re-elected to the Cape Town seat of Rondebosch which its sitting member, Colonel R. D. P. Jordan, had resigned in his favour. Leo Kowarsky, a liberal, similarly resigned the Yeoville (Johannesburg) seat to S. J. Marais Steyn, who had been defeated in Vereeniging. Jan Steytler held Queenstown by thirteen votes.

41. MPs for Pinelands, Cape, East London (North) and Hospital (Johannesburg) all of whom were to break away with the Progressives.

42. Press digest no. 16, *Sunday Times*, 26 April 1958.

43. Act 31 of 1958.

44. Hansard, 13 August 1958, cols. 1988,1999.

45. Act 47 of 1958. This Act provided that as from 1 January 1959 every male African aged eighteen and over must pay basic general tax at the rate of R3.50 a year, instead of R2.00 as previously. As from 1 January 1960 men earning more than R360 a year became liable to pay further amounts on a sliding scale, and for the first time African women became liable to taxation; they, too, were required to pay this additional general tax on a sliding scale. (M. Horrell (1), p. 73.)

The minimum taxable income for Whites, Coloureds and Indians is R732 per annum, and is even higher for married men, while no differentiation is made between married and unmarried Africans in this respect.

46. Hansard, 16 September 1958, col. 3945.

47. Report-back, 1958.

48. A. Hepple, p. 133.

49. Report-back, 1958.

50. The *Star*, 29 October 1958.

51. Press digest no. 44, 6 November 1958, quoting The *Star*, 3 November 1958.

CHAPTER SIX

1. The portfolio of Native Affairs was now called Bantu Administration and Development, the Government having dropped the word 'Native' in favour of 'Bantu'. For brevity's sake, the author has abbreviated it into Bantu Administration.

2. Hansard, 16 February 1959, col. 919. The Minister later denied having said this. He claimed to have said: 'If the English Press gives me two years, leaves me alone, leaves the Bantu alone, then I guarantee a new South Africa.' (Hansard, 16 February 1959, col. 920.)

3. Hansard, 7 February 1959, col. 1096.

4. Interview with Boris Wilson, Zach de Beer, Colin Eglin.

5. Hansard, 27 January 1959, cols. 63, 64, 65.

6. In the progressive group were Helen, Ray Swart, Zach de Beer, Colin Eglin, Jan Steytler, 'Sakkies' Fourie, Ronnie Butcher, Townley Owen-Williams, Harry Lawrence backed up by Douglas Smit, J. Hamilton-Russell and Sydney Waterson. The middle group comprised Graaff, Marais Steyn, Jack Higgerty, T. Gray Hughes, J. L. Horak, Piet van der Byl and Jack Basson, while the conservatives were Douglas Mitchell, Col. O. Shearer, Vause Raw, Miles Warren, Louis Steenkamp, R. Badenhorst-Durrant, Sannie van Niekerk, G. N. Oldfield, Captain B. Henwood, M. Streicher and Frans Cronje.

7. Act 46 of 1959. The Act abolished the Parliamentary representation of Africans. It recognized eight African national units – North Sotho, South Sotho, Tswana, Zulu, Swazi, Xhosa, Tsonga and Venda. Initially it provided for five Commissioners-General to represent the Government in these areas. The constitution and powers of Bantu territorial, regional and tribal authorities were more clearly defined; and it was laid down that representatives of territorial authorities would be appointed in urban areas.

In the White Paper accompanying the Bill, the Government declared its intention of returning to the basic aims, pursued between 1913 and 1936 of identifying each of the various African communities with its own land in the Reserves; and secondly, of ensuring that Africans who entered the 'white' areas (i.e. the remainder of South Africa) came only as migrant labourers (cf. M. Horrell (1), p. 23).

8. Hansard, 18 May 1959, cols. 6001, 6002.

9. *Die Burger*, quoted in the *Forum*, September 1959.

10. Raw was referring to the Battle of Blood River on 16 December 1838 when a commando of Boers set out to avenge the massacre of Piet Retief and his comrades by the Zulu king, Dingaan. In a three-hour battle fought on the banks of the Tugela river over 3000 Zulus were slain and three Boers slightly wounded. Although it did not break the Zulu power, it was a significant moral victory for the Boers.

11. Hansard, 2 June 1959, col. 7182. *Sunday Express*, 14 June 1959.

12. Harry Lawrence, memorandum to Graaff, 3 May 1959.

13. Hansard, 18 May 1959, cols. 6036, 6039.

14. Harry Lawrence, letter to Graaff, 3 June 1959.

15. Letter from H. F. Oppenheimer to H. Lawrence, 12 June 1959.

16. Act 45 of 1959. Provided for the establishment of separate university colleges for African, Coloured and Indian students. From dates determined by the Government, no new black students were allowed to enrol at the 'open' universities with the exception of the Natal Medical School.

17. Hansard, 9 April 1959, col. 3259 ff.

18. Hansard, 10 April 1959, col. 3424.

19. Act 41 of 1959. The amending Bill greatly extended Ministerial powers in respect of the control of trade unions and virtually freed the Minister from any legal curbs previously contained in the Act as far as job reservation was concerned.

20. Hansard, 15 June 1959, cols. 8237 ff.

21. Due to the South African obsession with a 'fair deal for the farmer', the *platteland* constituencies often had many more delegates than did their urban counterparts. After the Congress was over Badenhorst Durrant boasted to Ray Swart whom he met at Johannesburg airport, 'I did a good job at Congress.' 'What job did you do?' asked Swart. 'Well, I organized to get you people out of the party.' Swart: 'How did this happen?' Durrant: 'Don't you remember? I was away from Parliament a great deal of last session . . . this is what I was doing.' (Conversation reported to the author by Ray Swart, 1974.)

22. *Eastern Province Herald*, 31 July 1959. The paper listed the conservatives as: Douglas Mitchell, Vause Raw, Louis Steenkamp, Henry Tucker, R. B. Badenhorst-Durrant, Miles Warren, Sannie van Niekerk as well as several MPCs and junior members of the Party. With prophetic accuracy, it listed the progressives as Zach de Beer, Colin Eglin, Clive van Ryneveld, Ronald Butcher, Townley Owen-Williams, Ray Swart, Helen Suzman, Boris Wilson, John Cope and 'Sakkies' Fourie.

23. Durban Point Division rejected any proposals for a Common Roll system as direction for Native political development in South Africa while Christiana/Harrismith rejected 'the concept of a common voters' roll as a possible direction for the political development of the Native in South Africa'.

24. The Head Committee was given a précis of points affecting the Native and Colour Policy to be dealt with by Union Congress at the insistence of the Central Executive Committee:

1 Re-affirmation of the 1954 policy save for proposed amendments.
2 Rejection of Bantustan policy.
3 Extension of political rights to the North.
4 White leadership position.
5 Common Roll.
6 Direct representation (black men in Parliament).
7 Future of Reserves: a) Development, b) Acquisition of further land.
8 Effects of Bantustan policy in relation to a) the protectorates, b) South West Africa.
9 Qualification of Coloured voters.
10 Coloureds in the Northern Provinces.
11 Senate reform.
12 Geographical and racial federation.
13 Immigration.
14 Party discipline.

25. *Rand Daily Mail*, 12 August 1959.
26. Letter from Graaff to H. Lawrence, 9 September 1959.
27. *Ibid.*, p. 2.
28. *Ibid.*
29. P. 6 of the minority report signed by Graaff, Gray Hughes, Senator D. Jackson, Lawrence and Douglas Mitchell.
30. Letter from Walter Stanford to H. Lawrence, 21 August 1959.

31. Letter from Graaff to H. Lawrence, 9 September 1959.
32. Leo Boyd, Memorandum to author entitled 'Events Prior to the Formation of the Progressive Party'.
33. Graaff's Letter to H. Lawrence, 9 September 1959, *op. cit.*, p. 3.
34. As set out by Graaff to Lawrence, p. 4.
35. *Ibid.*, pp. 3–4.
36. Quoted by Walter Stanford to H. Lawrence, 21 August 1959.
37. Graaff to Lawrence, *op. cit.*, 9 September 1959, p. 5.
38. *Ibid.*
39. *Ibid.*
40. Leo Boyd, *op. cit.*, p. 2. The original signatories were Helen, Zach de Beer, Jacqueline Beck (Cape Town), Townley Owen-Williams, Leo Boyd, J. van Z. Steytler, R. A. F. Swart, C. W. Eglin, C. B. van Ryneveld, Sidney Waterson, W. Steytler (Jan Steytler's brother). Kathleen Mitchell although present did not sign the original statement.
41. Letter from Helen to J. Wright, 15 September 1961.
42. Author's interview with Sir de Villiers Graaff.
43. Letter from Sidney Waterson to Harry Lawrence, 10 September 1959.
44. *Cape Times*, 19 August 1959.
45. He said: 'Under the strain of the ensuing few days I was persuaded to stay within the United Party on the grounds that by doing so I would be in a position more effectively to further the views which I hold and have always held . . . Accordingly I issued a statement that I endorsed Sir de Villiers Graaff's statement of Native Policy.

'On further consideration I have come to the conclusion that I can better advance the aims for which I stand outside the UP. I therefore withdraw the statement I made on Tuesday.' (*Cape Times*, 19 August 1959.)
46. Letter from W. Stanford to H. Lawrence.
47. Letter from Zach de Beer to H. Lawrence.
48. *Cape Times*, 19 August 1959.
49. J. Steytler – statement issued to SAPA, 20 August 1959.
50. Minutes of the meeting, Johannesburg, 23–4 August 1959.
51. Helen Suzman to J. Wright, *op. cit.*, 15 September 1959.

CHAPTER SEVEN

1. Speech entitled 'Splitting the Vote' written in 1960.
2. Minutes, meeting held 23–4 August 1959.
3. Initially there were eleven sub-committees: Consultation with non-Europeans (Steytler, Swart, Cope, Eglin, Suzman); Group Areas, Urban Africans and Pass Laws (Wilson, van Ryneveld, Cope, Mitchell); Labour and Economic Affairs (Suzman, Williams, Butcher); Education (Boyd, Eglin, Kowarsky); Agriculture and Marketing (Steytler, Fourie, Swart); Health and Social Welfare (De Beer, Hall, Mitchell, Beck);

Transport (Butcher); Finance and Taxation (Butcher, Borkum, Boyd); Local Government (Hall, Einstein, Wilson); Constitutional Matters and Franchise (De Beer, de Kock); Republic Issue (Swart, Hall, Cope, Butcher and Fourie); Party constitution (De Beer, Eglin, de Kock, van Ryneveld); Consultation with Afrikaner Intellectuals (De Beer, Hofmeyr) (Minutes 23 August 1959).

4. *Ibid.*

5. It was also decided that up to three Johannesburg seats could be fought by independent Progressive candidates but no seats were fought in that city.

6. *Cape Times*, 16 October 1959.

7. H. Lawrence, resignation statement, *Cape Argus*, 16 September 1959.

8. Minutes, meeting 21 September 1959.

9. *Rand Daily Mail*, 5 December 1959.

10. The *Star*, 21 December, 1959.

11. Molteno was an outstanding advocate and an expert on constitutional law. He was the Natives' Representative for Cape Western from 1937–48.

12. The *Star*, 13 November 1959.

13. Charles S. Whitehouse to author, 10 April 1973.

14. Author's interview with E. Hellmann, 1973.

15. Z. de Beer to J. Steytler, 24 October 1959.

16. 1. The maintenance and extension of the values of Western civilization, the protection of fundamental human rights and the safeguarding of the dignity and worth of the human person, irrespective of race, colour or creed.

2. The assurance that no citizen of . . . South Africa shall be debarred on grounds of race, religion, language or sex, from making the contribution to our national life of which he or she may be capable.

3. The recognition that in . . . South Africa there is one nation which embraces various groups differing in race, religion, language and traditions, that each group is entitled to the protection of these things and of its right of participation in the government of the nation; and that understanding, tolerance and good-will between the differing groups must be fostered.

4. The maintenance inviolate of the Rule of Law.

5. The promotion of social progress and the improvement of living standards through the energetic development of a modern economy based on free enterprise, whereby the national resources of men and materials can be fully utilized.

6. The promotion of friendly relations with other nations, more particularly those who share with us the heritage of Western civilization.

17. The Congress resolved: 'Only when internal peace is guaranteed through a constitution which protects the tradition, language, culture,

way of life and share in government, of all sections of our population, and only when external security is protected through ensured membership of the Commonwealth, in which South Africa should play a positive and responsible part, can a change to republicanism be considered without real danger.

'When these conditions are fulfilled and if the matter is then still an issue in South Africa, it will have become one of preference rather than principle and at that stage the people of South Africa should choose the form of government they prefer.'

18. *Cape Argus*, 8 December 1959.
19. G. M. Carter, T. Karis, N. Stultz, pp. 23 and 25.
20. Hansard, 20 January 1960, cols. 86, 97.
21. Hansard, 20 January 1960, col. 109.
22. Speech to both Houses of Parliament, 3 February 1960.
23. *Die Transvaler*, February 1960.
24. Report-back, 1960.
25. Hansard, 21 March 1960, col. 3732.
26. *Ibid.*, cols. 3759, 3760.
27. *Ibid.*, col. 3790.
28. The final figures for Sharpeville and Langa were: 71 dead, 217 wounded and 17 policemen injured.
29. Quoted by M. Ballinger, p. 429.
30. Act 34 of 1960. If the Governor-General was satisfied that the safety of the public or the maintenance of public order was seriously threatened or likely to be threatened in consequence of the activities of the PAC or ANC, he could declare these bodies and their subsidiary branches and committees to be unlawful organizations. Immediately after the Act was promulgated the ANC and PAC were declared to be unlawful. (M. Horrell (1), p. 95.)
31. Hansard, 29 March 1960, col. 4302.
32. *Ibid.*, col. 4324.
33. Report-back, 1960 and speech entitled 'Splitting the Vote', 1960.
34. Hansard, 30–1 March 1960, cols. 4526, 4527.
35. Pratt was later tried, found to be insane and sent to a State Mental Hospital from which he first tried to escape and then committed suicide.
36. M. Ballinger, pp. 435–6.
37. Hansard, 20 May 1960, cols. 8337 ff.
38. Report-back, 1960.
39. *Ibid.*
40. *Die Vaderland*, quoted by A. Hepple, *op. cit.*, p. 177.
41. Undated hand-written speech by Z. de Beer.
42. Memorandum to Dr Steytler from the National Organizing Secretary of the PP, 11 November 1960.
43. The arrangements for the referendum were simple and were conducted on virtually the same lines as a general election, the vote

being counted for each parliamentary constituency using the boundaries
operative at the 1958 election. The question on the ballot paper was
'Are you in favour of a republic for the Union?'

Results	For	Against	Total For	Total Against
Cape	271418	269784	850458	774878
Transvaal	406632	325041 (– 1000 error)		
Natal	43299	135598		
OFS	110171	33438		
SWA	19938	12017		

percentage poll 90.75
percentage in favour 52.3

44. Act 32 of 1961.

45. Their number diminished during the 1961 session to ten. As a
Natives' Representative, Walter Stanford had left Parliament at the
end of 1960 and Boris Wilson resigned for 'business reasons' early in
1961.

46. The Factories and Building Bill and the Separate Amenities
Bill.

47. The members of the Commission, announced by Steytler in
Parliament on 5 February 1960, were: D. Molteno QC (convenor),
ex-Chief Justice A. Centlivres, ex-Justice L. Blackwell, Professor L. M.
Thompson, professor of History, UCT, Professor S. Marais, professor
of History at the University of the Witwatersrand, Dr E. Broakes,
former Natives' Representative in the Senate and at that time a staff
member at the University of Natal, K. A. Heard, staff member at the
University of Natal, H. F. Oppenheimer, the hon. J. G. N. Strauss,
Advocate A. Suzman, QC, Selby Ncobo, a former lecturer in Economics
at Fort Hare, Dr D. E. van der Ross, principal of the Bettiswood Training
College, and Dr Z. J. de Beer.

48. *Rand Daily Mail*, 17 November 1960.

49. *Die Burger*, 17 November 1960.

50. Hansard, 14 February 1961, col. 1309, 1310.

51. *Rand Daily Mail*, 16 September 1961.
Die Vaderland, 7 September 1961, Press digest nos. 34 and 35.

52. *Rand Daily Mail*, Press digest no. 30.

53. Voting statistics from K. A. Heard, ch. 7.

54. The National Union was formed by Basson on his expulsion from
the National Party in 1959 as a result of his opposition to the Bantu
Self-Government Act. Its programme overlapped on several issues with
the United Party's plan of 'Ordered Advance' (1960) and 'Racial Federation' (1961). The National Union was soon dissolved and its founder
joined the United Party.

55. *Sunday Times*, 15 October 1961.

56. Letter to Houghton voters, 7 September 1961.

57. Report-back, 1961.

58. H. Lever, p. 17.

59. The *Star*, 27 September 1961. Press digest no. 37.

60. *Final Results* (*Seats*) (*Previous results in brackets*)

		percentage votes
NP	105 (102)	46.26
UP	49 (42)	37.54
PP	1 (9)	8.62
NU and others		
−	(−)	7.58

61. H. Suzman (PP)   5405
    H. Miller (UP)   4841
                      ―――
                       564

CHAPTER EIGHT

1. Reported in an interview with Lin Menge, *Rand Daily Mail*, 20 January 1960.

2. Author of the book *Parliamentary Procedure in South Africa: A Short Guide to the Rules and Practice of the Union House of Assembly*.

3. See also Hansard, 10 May 1962, cols. 5345, 5346.

4. Hansard, 23 January 1962, col. 78.

5. Hansard, 25 January 1962, cols. 198, 199.

6. Report-back, 2 August 1962.

7. Act 48 of 1963. In terms of the Act, African parts of the Transkei became a separate territory (certain towns and certain white farming areas were excluded). The Act (still in force in 1974) provided for a legislative Assembly composed of sixty-four chiefs and forty-five elected members. All adult citizens qualified for the franchise. The Assembly elected a Cabinet, consisting of a Chief Minister, who was also the Minister of Finance, and five other Ministers holding the portfolios of Justice, the Interior, Education, Agriculture and Forestry, Roads and Works. The Republican Parliament retained control over defence, external affairs, internal security, postal and related services, railways, immigration, currency, banking, customs and excise and the Transkeian constitution itself. (M. Horrell (1), p. 74).

8. Report-back, 8 August 1963.

9. *Die Volksblad*, January 1962.

10. *Parktown*   *Johannesburg North*
    UP   4847   UP   4968
    PP   4382   PP   4191

    Majority   465   Majority   777

11. *Rand Daily Mail*, 19 February 1962.

12. Hansard, 23 February 1962, cols. 1539, 1540.

13. *Ibid.*, cols. 1554, 1555.

14. Act 39 of 1961.

15. *Votes cast per Party in contested seats 1961*

Votes cast	*Rejected*	*UP*	*NU*	*NP*	*PP*	*Others*
785 156	4378	295 489	38 773	360 468	66 433	19 625

(*vide* K. A. Heard, pp. 142–3)

16. Section 21 of the Act created the offence of sabotage, providing that penalties on conviction would be those laid down for treason and could include the death penalty. Among other clauses the Act introduced the system of house arrest, empowering the Minister to order persons not to leave specified premises or areas at all or during the week, at weekends and public holidays, prohibiting them (in some cases) from receiving any visitors except a lawyer or a doctor unless these persons had also been banned. (M. Horrell (1), p. 99.)

17. *Sunday Times* and *Sondagblad*, 13 May 1962.

18. Hansard, 21 May 1962, col. 6066.

19. *Rand Daily Mail*, 23 November 1962.

20. A. Hepple, pp. 239–41.

21. *Rand Daily Mail*, 19 February 1962.

22. Hansard, 23 January 1963, col. 108.

23. Report-back, 8 August 1963.

24. Hansard, 23 January 1963, col. 108.

25. Act 37 of 1962.

26. The retrospective date on which the ANC and PAC had been declared unlawful under the Unlawful Organizations Act (34 of 1960).

27. The other sections opposed by the United Party were 1, 2, 4 and 8, but 17 was the most far-reaching, giving as it did powers to the police of indefinite re-arrest of released ninety-day detainees.

28. Hansard, 24 April 1963, col. 4670.

29. Report-back, 8 August 1963.

30. *Ibid.*, cols. 4672, 4680.

31. One of the results of Helen's forcing a division was for the Committee on Standing Rules and Orders to amend its regulations to clip Helen's wings. Although she could still record her vote independently and the need for a seconder to an amendment made by her was removed, any call for a division had to be supported by three members. This spared the United Party the embarrassment of having to cross the floor and crowd on to the Nationalist benches. After the 1974 election the official Opposition was again subjected to this embarrassment.

32. Report-back, 8 August 1963.

33. *Dagbreek*, 23 June 1963.

34. *Die Burger*, 7 March 1964.

35. Hansard, 25 February 1964, cols. 1953, 1954.

36. Undated speech 1964.

37. *Vide* Janet Robertson, p. 224.

38. Act 96 of 1965.

39. Hansard, 11 June 1965, cols. 7928, 7930.

40. *Ibid.*, col. 7949.

41.

South Cape Constituency		*North Cape Constituency*	
O. Wollheim (PP)	7375	W. J. van Heerden (PP)	4825
UP candidate	3746	UP candidate	4541
	3629		284

42. *White Provincial Elections*

| | Final Seats | | | |
	NP	UP	PP	Ind.
Cape	32	22	–	–
Cape Coloured	–	–	2	–
Natal	8	16	–	1
OFS	25	–	–	–
Transvaal	51	17	–	–
	116	55	2	1

The United Party lost nine seats to the National Party (three in the Transvaal, four in Natal, two in the Cape) and one to an Independent.

43. *Die Transvaler*, 26 March 1965.

44. *Cape Times*, 11 November 1965.

45. Act 72 of 1965. Previously the election of coloured representatives took place not less than eight days before the polling day fixed for white voters. (Act 46 of 1951) (M. Horrell (1), p. 17.)

46. Report-back, 1 November 1966.

47. Act 51 of 1968. The Separate Representation of Voters Amendment Act (50 of 1968), passed at the same time, provided that Coloured representatives in the House of Assembly and the Cape Provincial Council would cease when these bodies were dissolved before the 1970 elections.

48. The *Star*, 22 April 1968.

49. The *Star*, 15 November 1965.

50. *Sunday Times*, 27 March 1966.

51. *Post*, March 1966.

52. H. Lever, p. 86.

53. *Ibid.*, p. 101.

54. The United Party retained the provincial seat in Houghton until 1974 by a clear majority, showing that thousands of voters were voting for Helen as a personality while their true loyalty did not in fact lie with the Progressives. Even in 1974 (when the parliamentary and provincial elections were held simultaneously) Helen's majority was significantly larger than that of her Progressive running mate.

55. Helen Suzman   5796
     A. D. Bensusan   5085
     ──────
     711   percentage poll 80.2

Election Results (seats)	NP	UP	PP
Transvaal	62	10	1
Cape	38	16	–
OFS	15	–	–
Natal	5	13	–
SWA	6	–	–
	126	39	1

(plus the four Coloured representatives).

The Progressive Party lost heavily in those seats which in 1961 had provided only marginal victories for the United Party, viz. Parktown 2949 (1961 = 85), Orange Grove 5339 (1961 = 517). In East London North, Steytler polled only 1080 votes to his United Party opponent's 6820.

56. Report-back, 1966.

57. Tsafendas, a Greek–Portuguese of Coloured extraction from Mozambique, was found insane. He blamed his attack on Verwoerd on a giant tapeworm with serrated edges which tormented his intestines.

58. Report-back, 1966.

59. *Ibid.*

60. Letter to Canada, 2 May 1969.

61. Hansard, 14 October 1966, col. 4246.

62. Act 24 of 1967.

63. Act 83 of 1967.

64. Very wide definitions are applied to the type of action for which a person may be found guilty of participation in terrorist activities. The jurisdiction of the Court is completely excluded for any person detained under Section 6 of the Act. Unlike the 90-day and the 180-day detention without-trial provisions, there is no attempt even at dissimulating a limit to the period of detention. It is made quite clear since nobody other than the Minister and the police have access to the person detained, that he can be held in solitary confinement. The Section does stipulate '*if circumstances so permit*, a detainee shall be visited in private by a Magistrate at least once a fortnight', but there is no provision in the law nor would the Minister give any assurance, that the next-of-kin would be given any information whatsoever about a person who had been detained.

65. Act 86 of 1969.

66. Act 101 of 1969.

67. *Dagbreek*, 29 January 1967.

68. *Sunday Express*, 5 February 1967.

69. *Dagbreek*, 12 February 1967.

70. Hansard, 14 April 1969, cols. 3880, 3881, 3882, 3883.

71. *Die Transvaler*, 17 September 1969.

72. *Rand Daily Mail*, 28 November 1969.

73. *Die Vaderland*, 28 November 1969.

74. The National Party nominated 144 candidates, the UP 138, the HNP 77 and 'others' 14.

75. *Natal Mercury*, 11 April 1970.

76. The countrywide percentage poll was lower than the 1966 figure. (74.7 per cent as opposed to 75.9 per cent in 1966.)

Final Results – no. of seats. (*1966 results in brackets*)

NP	117* (126)	percentage votes	54.3
UP	47 (39)		37.4
PP	1 (1)		3.5
HNP	– (3)		3.6

*In the Langlaagte by-election held shortly afterwards the NP gained another seat, bringing its total to 118. (This figure includes the six South African seats.)

77. H. Suzman   7087
    L. Steyn   5038

    $\overline{}$
    2049 percentage poll 80.5

78. Dr W. Nkomo, President of the SAIRR at that time.

CHAPTER NINE

1. *Provincial election results (previous figures in brackets)*

Seats	UP	NP	PP
Transvaal	19 (18)	54 (50)	–
OFS	–	25	–
Cape	18 (22)	36 (32)	2 (Cape coloured representatives)
Natal	19 (13)	3 (8)	–

2. *Natal Daily News*, 21 October 1961.
3. *Rand Daily Mail*, 20 February 1971.
4. *Die Vaderland*, 22 February 1971.
5. New territorial authorities, with wider powers than they had previously possessed, were constituted during 1968 and 1969 for the Ciskei, Tswana area (named BophutaTswana), South Sotho area (Basotho Qwaqwa), Shangaan area (Gazankulu), North Sotho area (Lebowa) and Venda. After some years of negotiations between the Government and representatives of the Zulu people, the latter agreed to accept the Bantustan scheme. Chief Gatsha Buthelezi, a former opponent of the Government, was unanimously elected Chief Executive Officer for the scattered enclaves of Natal to be known as KwaZulu (cf. M. Horrell (2), p. 53).
6. Act 41 of 1971.
7. Hansard, 6 May 1971, col. 5950.
8. Quoted in the *Rand Daily Mail*, 12 October 1971.
9. Letter to G. Ralfe, 24 October 1971.
10. *Die Vaderland*, 14 October 1971.
11. *Rapport*, 17 October 1971.
12. Protest meeting, Witwatersrand University, 4 November 1971.
13. The National Union of South African Students (NUSAS) was founded in 1924 to promote and represent the interests of students of all races and colours in South African universities and colleges. The Afrikaans universities broke away from NUSAS and formed their own Union when, in 1936, the question of admitting the black University College of Fort Hare arose. NUSAS has always taken a strong line against apartheid legislation.

The University Christian Movement was formed in 1967 under the aegis of the Methodist, Roman Catholic, Anglican, Presbyterian and Congregational Churches. It disbanded in 1972 following continual police harassment of its leaders, withdrawal of support by four of the five sponsoring churches and unwillingness on the part of its black members, as their 'black consciousness' grew, to work within a multi-racial framework.

The Christian Institute was founded in 1963. Its aims are 'to serve the Church of Christ in every possible way' through multi-racial and inter-denominational methods. It is headed by a controversial Afrikaner clergyman, the Reverend C. T. B. Naudé.

14. The Select Committee initially had six National Party and three United Party members appointed to serve on it. Unable to complete its work when the session ended, it was converted into a Commission of Inquiry whose terms of reference were wider than those of the Select Committee. In August its first chairman, Mr J. Kruger, resigned on being appointed a Deputy Minister and Mr A. L. Schlebusch was nominated chairman. Its sittings were held *in camera* and full evidence was not published. If a witness so requested, his identity was not disclosed. No information about the proceedings was allowed to be divulged by witnesses and other persons present during the inquiry.

The effect was that representatives and members of the organizations under investigation were unaware of the evidence given by others relating to them or their organizations. They were unable to cross-examine witnesses or to refute any allegations that might have been made without their knowledge, nor could they lead their own evidence or call their own witnesses. The participation of counsel was limited to advising clients as to their legal right. Its terms of reference allowed the Commission to inquire into the personal beliefs and conduct of anyone under investigation (cf. *Institute of Race Relations Handbook* 1972, pp. 53 and 54).

15. *Institute of Race Relations Handbook* 1973, pp. 24 and 25.

16. Act 52 of 1973.

17. Hansard, 11 May 1973, col. 6321.

18. Hansard, 15 May 1973, col. 6572.

19. *Sunday Times*, 20 August 1972.

20. *By-election results*

Johannesburg West		Vereeniging	
NP	5345	NP	5271
UP	3903	UP	3193
PP	559	PP	192
		LLP	31
60.8 per cent poll		62.3 per cent poll	

(Land and Labour Party – a short-lived splinter group)

21. Act 70 of 1973. The Bill conferred limited rights upon certain categories of African workers to strike after certain conciliation procedures had been observed. The scarcely-used works committees were extended into a highly complicated system consisting of liaison committees, works committees and co-ordinating works committees, which the Minister hoped would provide adequate negotiating machinery between African workers and their employers.

22. The first interim report recommended that a permanent bipartisan statutory Parliamentary Commission be established on internal security, to continue the work begun by the existing Commission in respect of 'organizations which exist already and which may from time to time come to light'. The second report concerned NUSAS, while the third, tabled in April 1973, dealt with the Wilgespruit Fellowship Centre, where experimental psychology and what was termed 'sensitivity training' were carried on under the aegis of the South African Council of Churches. The Commission considered the activities of the Centre to be morally subversive.

23. The eight people were the president of NUSAS, P. J. Pretorius, a former president, N. Curtis, two vice-presidents, Paula Ensor and P. le Roux, the general secretary, Miss S. Lapinsky, C. Keegan, R. Turner and C. Wood. Curtis fled the country in 1974.

24. Hansard, 28 February 1973, col. 1592.

25. *Rand Daily Mail*, 28 February 1973.

26. *Institute of Race Relations Handbook* 1973, pp. 4 and 5.

27. Progressive Party Fact Paper No. 117, April 1973.

28. Four of the banned Blacks were members of the South African Students' Organization (SASO) which had broken away from NUSAS in 1970, and whose aims were to build Blacks into a position of nondependence on Whites. SASO accepted the premise that before the black people joined 'the open society' they should first close their ranks to form themselves into a solid group to oppose the definitive racism that was meted out by the white society; to work out their direction clearly and to bargain from a position of strength. They should work together towards a self-sufficient political, social and economic unit and in this manner they would help themselves towards a deeper realization of their potential worth as self-respecting people.

Two others were full-time field workers of the Black Community Programme of Spro-cas (a special project for Christian action in society and jointly run by the Christian Institute and the SACC) and the remaining two were officials of the Black Peoples Convention, a recently formed organization whose object was to provide a political home for all black people who could not reconcile themselves to working within the framework of separate development and to promote black solidarity.

29. Hansard, 8 March 1973, col. 2265.

30. For the first time in South African electoral history, parliamentary and provincial council elections were held on the same day. Since the UP member of Parliament for Pinelands (Cape) had been killed in an air crash after the election had been announced, the parliamentary seat remained vacant and was won by Dr Alex Boraine for the Progressives by thirty-four votes at a subsequent by-election.

31. The Progressives won Orange Grove and Rondebosch as well as Parktown on a 'split ticket' with only their parliamentary candidates being elected. Johannesburg North, Sea Point and Houghton saw the election of Progressive provincial as well as parliamentary candidates.

Graaff had discreetly moved from Rondebosch to another constituency when the 1973 delimitation increased the Progressive element among the voters.

Helen Suzman	7618	Selma Browde	6395
J. Senekal	3655	I. Schlapobersky	4859
Majority	3963	Majority	1536

Final results (previous results in brackets)

NP   123 (118)
UP   41 (47)
PP   6 (1)*

*7 after Pinelands by-election.

32. Speech in Johannesburg City Hall, 3 March 1975.

INDEX

Compiled by Gordon Robinson

Turner, R., 308
Turvey, Mrs I., 54

Umkonto We Sizwe (Spear of the
Nation), 201, 213
Union Federal Party, 66
Union Jubilee celebrations, 176, 177 fn,
185
United Nations pressure, 216
Union Native Council Bill (1926), 21
United Democratic Front
formation, 55; 1953 election spells
death, 66
United Party
formation, 28; principles, 28;
disenfranchisement of Cape Africans,
28–9, 40; neutrality question divides
party, 29–31; forms coalition
government (1939), 31; coalition wins
1943 election, 35; migratory workers
policy, 37–9; amalgam of varying
political views, 40–1, attitude to
Indians, 41–2; government post-war
reconstruction problems, 42–3; enters
into darkness with loss of 1948
election, 44–5; administrative reform,
46–7; Strauss becomes leader on
death of Hofmeyr, 49; schismatic
attitude to Group Areas Bill, 50, 65;
fights Suppression of Communism Act,
50–1; opposes Coloured
disenfranchisement, 52–5; joins
United Democratic Front, 55;
dichotomy between liberals and
conservatives, 56, 64–70, 73–5, 80, 82,
91–2, 95–6, 99–103, 105, 106–7,
112–15, 123–5, 130–4, 136–65;
refusal to oppose Public Safety Act,
64; middle of the road policy to
apartheid, 65; defeat at 1953 election
causes rifts, 66; overtures to
conservatives from Malan, 67, 70;
compromise over Coloured vote, 68,
70, 73–4, 79; acceptance of Native
Labour Bill, 78; opposes Bantu
Education Bill, 79; economic
integration policy, 82–5, 90, 91;
committed to removals scheme, 87;
pledged to white leadership, 90; attack
on Criminal Procedure and Evidence
Amendment Bill, 95–7; opposition to
Senate Bill, 98, 110; about face on
franchise issue, 98–100; resignations
on franchise issue, 100; four-year
campaign to oust liberals, 107, 147;
fights the South Africa Act
Amendment Bill, 109–10; condemns
Verwoerd's 'Native Bills', 111–12;
leadership questioned and changed,
113–15; constitutional policy, 116;
exposes education and immigration
policies, 118–19; attack on Verwoerd,
119–21; fights religious restrictions,
121; Senate plan, 123–4; severe defeat
in 1958 elections, 127; fights taxation
Bill, 129; split on Nationalist plans
for removing Natives' Representatives

and promoting Bantu self-government,
136–65, 279–80, 297, 298; resigning
members form Progressive Party,
158–64; change of course on Unlawful
Organizations Bill, 179–80, 189;
anti-republican policy, 187; electoral
pact with National Union Party
(1964), 194; disagree with General
Laws Amendment Bills, 206;
capitulates on third Bill, 214;
disagreement Criminal Procedures
Amendment Bill, 219–20; onset of
optimism, 234; dubious civil liberties
record, 235–6; some gains in 1970
election, 236; 'Young Turks' revolt,
250–2; two-faced attitude to student
banning, 255–6, 257; internal disarray,
258; reformist breakaway, 263–4;
structure of, 274
United South African National Party
formed as a result of merger between
South African Party and National
Party, 27; becomes known as 'United
Party', 28; see also United Party
University Christian Movement, 244,
306–7
University College of Fort Hare, 306
University of the North, 247
Unlawful Organization Bill, 179, 182,
189; Act (1960), 300, 303
uprising of miners (1922), 20

Vanderbijlpark riots, 178
Verligte Action, 249
Verwoerd, Dr Hendrik, 11, 95 fn, 108
111, 129, 132, 143, 153, 174, 178–9,
191–3, 196, 201, 202, 209, 215, 219,
220
controls lives of Blacks as Minister
of Native Affairs, 75–9, 119;
personality, 76; philosophy of
'separate development', 76–7;
abolishes Natives' Representative
Council, 77; measures against urban
Africans, 77–8; educational brain-
washing of Africans, 78–9; savage
attack by Helen Suzman, 83;
enunciation of policy, 84; infamous
epigram, 86–7; second most powerful
man in Cabinet, 94; employment of
migratory labour, 94; United Party's
Public Enemy Number One, 119;
rules almost independent of
Parliament, 119; prohibits freedom of
worship, 120; argumentative logic,
121; elected leader, 130; promoting
African self-government, 135–40, 145,
148, 154, 155, 201; announces
Republic referendum, 175–6, 177,
186; attempt on his life, 183;
proclamation announcement, 187;
application rejected at Commonwealth
Conference, 188; attempt to eliminate
Progressives, 190; champion of white
nationalism, 210–11; master planner
217; 1966 manifesto, 223;